T0178556

Lecture Notes in Computer Science   13358

More information about this series at https://link.springer.com/bookseries/558

Lorenzo Cavallaro · Daniel Gruss ·
Giancarlo Pellegrino · Giorgio Giacinto (Eds.)

Detection of Intrusions and Malware, and Vulnerability Assessment

19th International Conference, DIMVA 2022
Cagliari, Italy, June 29 – July 1, 2022
Proceedings

Springer

Editors
Lorenzo Cavallaro
University College London
London, UK

Giancarlo Pellegrino
CISPA Helmholtz Center for Information
Security
Saarbrücken, Germany

Daniel Gruss
Graz University of Technology
Graz, Austria

Giorgio Giacinto 🆔
University of Cagliari
Cagliari, Italy

ISSN 0302-9743   ISSN 1611-3349 (electronic)
Lecture Notes in Computer Science
ISBN 978-3-031-09483-5   ISBN 978-3-031-09484-2 (eBook)
https://doi.org/10.1007/978-3-031-09484-2

This Springer imprint is published by the registered company Springer Nature Switzerland AG
The registered company address is: Gewerbestrasse 11, 6330 Cham, Switzerland

Preface

We would like to welcome you all to the proceedings of the 19th Conference on Detection of Intrusions and Malware & Vulnerability Assessment (DIMVA 2022). It's been almost two decades since the inception of DIMVA and it is a privilege to have witnessed over the years the high-quality research that the conference has always been able to attract.

We would like to thank the Program Committee for putting a high-quality program together; reviewing is part of what most of us call "professional service" and we know that for many, if not all of us, it is actually an opportunity to nurture the next-generation of scientists and, in a way, contribute indirectly to the advancement of our research field while building a strong, diverse, and inclusive community.

This year we received 39 valid submissions and accepted 11 papers (10 full papers and one short paper), keeping DIMVA's acceptance rate competitive at 28.2%. Given the short timeframe, we built a larger PC than prior years to ensure a more manageable load. On average, each paper received three reviews and each PC member (sometimes with the help of external reviewers) received up to three papers to review.

PC members and external reviewers engaged in online discussions, exchanging more than 200 messages. Given the ongoing COVID-19 pandemic, we opted to keep discussions online, with no physical nor virtual PC meeting as the thorough discussions (and reviews) helped us to converge on a final decision quite easily in most cases.

We would like to express our gratitude to the Program Committee members and external reviewers for the time spent reviewing papers, participating in the online discussions, and shepherding some of the papers to ensure the highest quality possible. We also deeply thank the members of the Organizing Committee and the Steering Committee for their hard work. Of course, we are wholeheartedly thankful to the German Informatics Society and the University of Cagliari for supporting and hosting an in-person (fingers crossed!) DIMVA 2022.

Our final thanks go to all participants, authors, and attendees, who are at the core of our conference and community – thank you so much for always making DIMVA and its 19th edition such an interesting conference.

We hope that science, education, and love and respect for everyone may help us to work out differences peacefully and bring us closer than ever before. Enjoy DIMVA 2022!

June 2022

Lorenzo Cavallaro
Daniel Gruss
Giancarlo Pellegrino
Giorgio Giacinto

Organization

Steering Committee Chairs

Flegel, Ulrich   Infineon Technologies, Germany
Meier, Michael   University of Bonn and Fraunhofer FKIE,
         Germany

Steering Committee

Almgren, Magnus   Chalmers University of Technology, Sweden
Bardin, Sébastien   CEA, France
Bilge, Leyla   NortonLifeLock Research Group, France
Blanc, Gregory   Télécom SudParis, France
Bos, Herbert   Vrije Universiteit Amsterdam, The Netherlands
Bruschi, Danilo M.   Università degli Studi di Milano, Italy
Bueschkes, Roland   BearingPoint, Germany
Caballero, Juan   IMDEA Software Institute, Spain
Cavallaro, Lorenzo   University College London, UK
Debar, Hervé   Télécom SudParis, France
Dietrich, Sven   City University of New York, USA
Giuffrida, Cristiano   Vrije Universiteit Amsterdam, The Netherlands
Haemmerli, Bernhard   Acris GmbH and HSLU Lucerne, Switzerland
Holz, Thorsten   Ruhr-University Bochum, Germany
Jahnke, Marko   CSIRT, Germany
Julisch, Klaus   Deloitte, Switzerland
Kreibich, Christian   ICSI, USA
Kruegel, Christopher   University of California, Santa Barbara, USA
Laskov, Pavel   University of Liechtenstein, Liechtenstein
Maggi, Federico   Huawei Technologies, Italy
Maurice, Clémentine   CNRS, CRIStAL, France
Neves, Nuno   University of Lisbon, Portugal
Perdisci, Roberto   University of Georgia and Georgia Institute of
         Technology, USA

Polychronakis, Michalis   Stony Brook University, USA
Rieck, Konrad   TU Braunschweig, Germany
Seifert, Jean-Pierre   TU Berlin, Germany
Sommer, Robin   ICSI, USA
Zurutuza, Urko   Mondragon University, Spain

General Chair

Giorgio Giacinto   University of Cagliari, Italy

Program Co-chairs

Lorenzo Cavallaro   University College London, UK
Daniel Gruss   TU Graz, Austria

Publication Chair

Giancarlo Pellegrino   CISPA, Germany

Program Committee

Alis, Jorge Blasco   Royal Holloway University of London, UK
Almgren, Magnus   Chalmers University of Technology, Sweden
Arp, Daniel   TU Berlin, Germany
Bardin, Sébastien   CEA List, France
Bianchi, Antonio   Purdue University, USA
Blanc, Gregory   Télécom SudParis, France
Cono D'Elia, Daniele   Sapienza University of Rome, Italy
Dacier, Marc   KAUST, Saudi Arabia
Daniel, Lesly-Ann   KU Leuven, Belgium
Dietrich, Sven   City University of New York, USA
Dolan-Gavitt, Brendan   New York University, USA
Fratantonio, Yanick   Cisco Talos, USA
Graziano, Mariano   Cisco Talos, USA
Guarnieri, Marco   IMDEA Software Institute, Spain
Hauser, Christophe   University of Southern California, USA
Kapravelos, Alexandros   North Carolina State University, USA
Kemerlis, Vasileios   Brown University, USA
Kinder, Johannes   Bundeswehr University Munich, Germany
Kotzias, Platon   Norton Research Labs, USA
Kruegel, Christopher   University of California, Santa Barbara, USA
Lanzi, Andrea   University of Milan, Italy
Laperdrix, Pierre   CNRS, France
Lee, Wenke   Georgia Institute of Technology, USA
Leita, Corrado   VMware, USA
Lin, Zhiqiang   Ohio State University, USA
Lipp, Moritz   Amazon Web Services, USA
Maggi, Federico   Huawei Technologies, Germany
Matic, Srdjan   IMDEA Software Institute, Spain

Meier, Michael	University of Bonn and Fraunhofer FKIE, Germany
Muench, Marius	Vrije Universiteit Amsterdam, The Netherlands
Nikiforakis, Nick	Stony Brook University, USA
Nikolich, Anita	University of Illinois at Urbana-Champaign, USA
Pagani, Fabio	University of California, Santa Barbara, USA
Palit, Tapti	Purdue University, USA
Pellegrino, Giancarlo	CISPA Helmholtz Center for Information Security, Germany
Pendlebury, Feargus	Meta, USA
Pierazzi, Fabio	King's College London, UK
Razavi, Kaveh	ETH Zurich, Switzerland
Rieck, Konrad	TU Braunschweig, Germany
Schwarz, Michael	CISPA Helmholtz Center for Information Security, Germany
Sekar, R.	Stony Brook University, USA
Sgandurra, Daniele	Huawei Technologies, Germany
Shin, Seungwon	KAIST, South Korea
Stringhini, Gianluca	Boston University, USA
Suarez-Tangil, Guillermo	IMDEA Networks Institute, Spain
Tapiador, Juan	Universidad Carlos III de Madrid, Spain
Thomas, Sam L.	BINARLY, Inc., UK
Toffalini, Flavio	EPFL, Switzerland
Van Bulck, Jo	KU Leuven, Belgium
Wang, Gang	University of Illinois at Urbana-Champaign, USA
Wressnegger, Christian	Karlsruhe Institute of Technology, Germany
Yap, Roland	National University of Singapore, Singapore
Zanero, Stefano	Politecnico di Milano, Italy
Šrndić, Nedim	Huawei Munich Research Center, Germany

Additional Reviewers

Dannehl, Moritz	Bundeswehr University Munich, Germany
Menguy, Grégoire	CEA LIST, Université Paris-Saclay, France
Recoules, Frédéric	CEA LIST, Université Paris-SAclay, France

Contents

Hybrid Pruning: Towards Precise Pointer and Taint Analysis

Dipanjan Das[1]([✉]), Priyanka Bose[1], Aravind Machiry[2], Sebastiano Mariani[3],
Yan Shoshitaishvili[4], Giovanni Vigna[1], and Christopher Kruegel[1]

[1] University of California, Santa Barbara, CA, USA
{dipanjan,priyanka,vigna,chris}@cs.ucsb.edu
[2] Purdue University, West Lafayette, IN, USA
amachiry@purdue.edu
[3] VMware, Inc., Palo Alto, CA, USA
smariani@vmware.com
[4] Arizona State University, Tempe, AZ, USA
yans@asu.edu

Abstract. Pointer and taint analyses are the building blocks for several other static analysis techniques. Unfortunately, these techniques frequently sacrifice *precision* in favor of *scalability* by over-approximating program behaviors. Scaling these analyses to real-world codebases written in memory-unsafe languages while retaining precision under the constraint of practical time and resource budgets is an open problem.

In this paper, we present a novel technique called *hybrid pruning*, where we inject the information collected from a program's dynamic trace, which is accurate by its very nature, into a static pointer or taint analysis system to enhance its precision. We also tackle the challenge of combining static and dynamic analyses, which operate in two different analysis domains, in order to make the interleaving possible. Finally, we show the usefulness of our approach by reducing the false positives emitted by a static vulnerability detector that consumes the improved points-to and taint information. On our dataset of 12 CGC and 8 real-world applications, our hybrid approach cuts down the warnings up to 21% over vanilla static analysis, while reporting 19 out of 20 bugs in total.

Keywords: Pointer analysis · Taint analysis · Static vulnerability detection

1 Introduction

Pointer analysis is a fundamental static program analysis technique that computes the set of abstract program objects that a pointer variable may or must point to. Pointer information is an indispensable pre-requisite for various techniques operating across a spectrum of domains, ranging from programming languages, to software engineering, to system security. One such notable client is

L. Cavallaro et al. (Eds.): DIMVA 2022, LNCS 13358, pp. 1–22, 2022.
https://doi.org/10.1007/978-3-031-09484-2_1

taint analysis, which determines the set of objects in a program that are affected by external inputs. The analysis is bootstrapped by marking an initial set of objects that can directly be influenced by an external source (*e.g.*, an attacker) as *tainted*. During taint propagation, the taint engine consults the points-to set of the destination operand of a program instruction, and propagates taint labels according to the taint policy, and the taint labels of the source operands. Therefore, an over-approximated points-to set quickly leads to taint explosion, resulting in most of the program objects getting incorrectly tainted. Many static vulnerability detection techniques employ either pointer, or taint analysis, or a combination of both [29]. In order to not miss bugs, these techniques strive to be *sound*, rather than *complete*. Consequently, such vulnerability detection clients generate numerous false positives. A precise pointer or taint analysis improves the false positive rate of a static vulnerability detector, thereby making the overall result more amenable to manual triaging.

As the size of the target program grows, precise, whole program pointer and taint analyses become prohibitively expensive. Though field, context, or flow sensitivity increases the analysis precision, such an analysis pays the price in terms of the overhead associated with the metadata management, and enumeration of individual field, context, or flow. Oftentimes, the analyses make unsound choices in order to remain scalable, *e.g.*, restricting the exploration within a specific sub-system, or making certain *soundy* assumptions [29] .

In this paper, we propose *hybrid pruning* – a novel program analysis paradigm that augments the state-of-the-art static analysis techniques with dynamic trace information. Our algorithm improves both the pointer and taint analyses at those program points where static reasoning is imprecise, and precise dynamic information is available. With the recent tide of research in fuzzing, it has become easier to generate high-quality dynamic traces with deeper program penetration. If the dynamic trace is available along a certain program path, our algorithm injects guaranteed, precise yet partial ground truth to aid the static analysis component. Although inherently *unsound* in principle, our strategy transitively improves the analysis at all those program points which were previously using the imprecise static information, thus multiplicating the advantage. However, leveraging a dynamic trace for static analysis is non-trivial, as they operate in two different analysis domains, *e.g.*, concrete instructions and run-time memory allocations *vs.* SSA-based IR and abstract memory objects. Our approach lifts the dynamic trace to the static domain to make the interleaving possible. Of course, dynamic analysis tools, such as fuzzers, will likely not succeed in exercising all possible program paths. To compensate for the lack of dynamic coverage, we fall back to the conservative static analysis for all other program paths for which a dynamic trace is absent. We demonstrate two different modes of *hybrid pruning* – *opportunistic* (H_o) and *propagation-only* (H_P), and show when one is better than the other depending on the quality of the dynamic trace collected. These two modes operate along a spectrum of *soundness* and *usability*. The improvement in points-to and taint analyses is positively correlated with the dynamic coverage. If the dynamic coverage is moderate, the H_o mode is preferred. This mode is designed to be more robust against the lack of dynamic information, because it conservatively switches to pure static mode where dynamic information is unavailable. On the other hand, the H_P mode shows promise when we have high confidence in the quality of dynamic information, as just the dynamic facts are propagated using the static analysis algorithms in this mode.

Our work is motivated by the observation that the static bug detectors are oftentimes notorious in emitting warnings in a volume which far surpasses the triaging ability of the human experts. For example, as on May 7, 2022, Coverity [3], a popular static bug detector, has emitted $47,038$ warnings in the Linux kernel version 5.18.0-rc4, of which $9,137$ are still outstanding. We envision *hybrid pruning* as a technique to improve the state-of-the-art in the static bug detection. Therefore, to evaluate the applicability of our technique in the real world, we extended DR.CHECKER [29], a purely static bug finder, to make use of *hybrid pruning*. As we anticipated, the precise points-to and taint information indeed reduced the number of false positives, while maintaining a comparable true positive rate. On our evaluation of 12 CGC [13] applications, the bug detectors relying on the H_o mode emit up to 36% less warnings, while the H_P mode reduces warnings up to 56%. We additionally show that, in spite of reducing significant fraction of warnings, the vulnerability detectors are still able to detect 15 (H_P) and 19 (H_o) out of 20 bugs in the CGC [13] and the real-world datasets combined.

Contributions. This paper makes the following contributions:

1. **Technique.** We propose *hybrid pruning*, a new hybrid program analysis technique that combines dynamic information with the vanilla static analysis to develop precise pointer and taint analyses.
2. **Applicability.** To demonstrate the effectiveness of our hybrid technique, we have further developed a vulnerability detection system as a client of our improved pointer and taint analyses. It exhibits significantly lower false positive rate as compared to its static counterpart.
3. **Evaluation.** We implement our approach in a practical prototype, and show its efficacy in an experimental evaluation on two different datasets, *i.e.*, CGC [13], and a collection of popular real-world programs.

2   Background

In this section, we equip the reader with the background information required to understand our approach.

2.1   Flow-Sensitive, Static Points-To Analysis

We provide a brief overview of an Andersen-style, flow-sensitive, static points-to (SPT) analysis technique, which we will use later on to demonstrate our hybrid approach. The goal of any static points-to analysis is to determine the set of objects that a given pointer can point to, at any point in the program. Specifically, a points-to analysis answers a membership query *IsPtsTo (p, x)*, which indicates whether a memory object x is in the points-to set of the pointer p. A flow-sensitive points-to analysis computes the points-to set of the pointers according to the control-flow of the program. Given a program, the analysis starts by generating constraints for every pointer according to their usage in the program. The solution to the generated constraints gives the points-to results for all the pointers. A points-to analysis either categorizes, or transforms any program statement into one or more of the statements in Fig. 1.

$$\frac{\boxed{p = \&x}}{l_x \in PtsTo(p)} \text{ ADDRESS-OF} \qquad \frac{\boxed{p = q}}{PtsTo(p) \supseteq PtsTo(q)} \text{ COPY} \qquad \frac{\boxed{p = {}^*q}}{PtsTo(p) \supseteq PtsTo(*q)} \text{ DEREFERENCE}$$

$$\frac{\boxed{{}^*p = q}}{PtsTo(*p) \supseteq PtsTo(q)} \text{ ASSIGN}$$

Fig. 1. The premise (highlighted) of an inference rule represents the type of the statement encountered in a program, and the conclusion corresponds to the constraints in SPT.

$$\frac{PtsTo(p) \supseteq PtsTo(q) \quad l_x \in PtsTo(q)}{l_x \in PtsTo(p)} \text{ COPY} \qquad \frac{PtsTo(p) \supseteq PtsTo(*q) \quad l_r \in PtsTo(q) \quad l_x \in PtsTo(r)}{l_x \in PtsTo(p)} \text{ DEREFERENCE}$$

$$\frac{PtsTo(*p) \supseteq PtsTo(q) \quad l_r \in PtsTo(p) \quad l_x \in PtsTo(q)}{l_x \in PtsTo(r)} \text{ ASSIGN}$$

Fig. 2. Rules to solve the SPT constraint graph.

Constraint Generation. The analysis iterates over the statements in a program, and collects the constraints according to the rules in Fig. 1, where l_x and *PtsTo(p)* denote the location of the variable x, and the points-to set of the pointer p respectively. The constraints are usually managed by creating a *constraint graph*, where the nodes represent pointers or memory objects, and edges represent the constraints.

Constraint Solving. Once the constraints are generated, each of the constraints will be solved until a fixed point is reached, *i.e.*, no changes occur to the points-to set of all the pointers. The rules in Fig. 2 are used to solve the generated constraints.

2.2 Static Taint Tracking

Static Taint Tracking (STT) [36] is a data-flow tracking technique used to track the flow of the tainted data within a program. STT is most commonly used in vulnerability detection, where the program input is tainted, and vulnerabilities are modeled as an usage of unsanitized data in the sensitive operations. For example, a usage of tainted data in an arithmetic operation can cause an integer overflow or an underflow bug. Similarly, an out-of-bounds access bug can occur when tainted data is used as the index in an array. STT consists of the following components:

Taint Source. Functions that read an input from the user, or the environment, *e.g.*, `read`, `scanf` are considered as taint sources. The variables into which the data is read are labeled as *tainted*.

Taint Propagation. Typically, the result (destination) of an operation is labeled *tainted* if any one of its operands (source) is already tainted, *e.g.*, for a binary operation $r \leftarrow f(a, b)$, taint propagates to r if either a or b is tainted.

An STT requires points-to information to track the flow of tainted data through pointers. To inject taint, the STT must know to which objects the source pointer can point, so that it can taint all those objects. Note that an imprecise pointer analysis could result in over-tainting, resulting in many data elements being incorrectly considered as tainted [41]. In this paper, we use the taint propagation rules similar to the ones proposed in DR. CHECKER [29].

3   Motivation

3.1   Running Example

We use the code in Listing 1.1 to explain various aspects of our technique. To generate execution traces, we exercise the program with a test suite. However, the part of the code highlighted in *red* is ***not*** executed in any of the dynamic runs.

Points-to. The `process_buf()` function returns either of its `char` pointer arguments (`res` at Line 10, or `req` at Line 13) depending on the value of `r` (Lines 8 and 11). `c_buff` gets assigned the pointer returned by the `process_buf()` call once at Line 28 (`res_buff`), then again at Line 35 (`greq`), and lastly at Line 47 (`q`).

Taint. At Line 32, the program reads user data into the buffer pointed to by `c_buff`, which, in turn, points to `res_buff`.

Bugs. There are five array indexing operations (Lines 37–41, 50). However, the operation at the Line 39 could lead to an out-of-bounds write of `buff`, because `res_buff` gets *tainted* at Line 32 (via `c_buff`). In turn, the index `res_buff[0]` can contain a value greater than the size of `buff` (*i.e.*, 16). Likewise, the `write` at Line 50 can lead to an out-of-bounds write of the buffer pointed by `c_buff` (*i.e.*, q from Line 47). The remaining three indexing operations are safe.

3.2   Imprecision in Vanilla Static Analysis

Consider an STT technique based on the SPT analysis that we presented in Sect. 2 on our example in Listing 1.1. The call to read_user_data taints object ids {3, 1, 4, 2} because of the points-to set of c_buff@28. At Lines 37, 39, 40, 41, and 50, we are using data from the tainted objects (*i.e.*, {3, 1, 4, 2}) as indices to write to arrays. Consequently, any static vulnerability detection technique that relies only on the STT information, and checks for the use of tainted data as an array index (unsafe operation) will raise a potential out-of-bounds alert. However, as described in Sect. 3.1, only the buffer pointed to by res_buff contains tainted data. Therefore, only the warnings raised at Lines 39 and 50 are true positives. Next, we show how we use dynamic information to improve the precision of static analysis techniques to eliminate these false positives.

```
1  #define BSIZE 512
2  // global object, ID: 1
3  char greq[BSIZE];
4  // global object, ID: 2
5  char gres[BSIZE];
6  char *process_buf(IOLevel r, char *res, char *req) {
7    switch(r) {
8      case IORECV:
9        ...
10       return res;
11     case IOSEND:
12       ...
13       return req;
14   }
15   return NULL;
16 }
17
18 int main(...) {
19   // stack object, ID: 3
20   char req_buff[BSIZE];
21   // stack object, ID: 4
22   char res_buff[BSIZE];
23   // stack object, ID: 5
24   char buff[16];
25   char *c_buff, *t_buff;
26   ...
27   // The return value will be res_buff
28   c_buff = process_buf(IORECV, res_buff, req_buff);
29   ...
30   // Read user (tainted) data into the buffer
31   // pointed to by c_buff, i.e., res_buff
32   read_user_data(c_buff, BSIZE);
33   ...
34   // The return value will be greq
35   c_buff = process_buf(IOSEND, gres, greq);
36   ...
37   buff[req_buff[0]] = 'R';
38   // BUG: Potential out of bounds write
39   buff[res_buff[0]] = 'S';
40   buff[greq[0]] = 'r';
41   buff[gres[0]] = 's';
42   ...
43   if (...) {
44     // heap object, ID: 6
45     char *q = getenv(...);
46     t_buff = c_buff;    // c_buff points to greq here
47     c_buff = q;
48     ...
49     // BUG: Potential out of bounds write
```

```
50      c_buff[res_buff[0]] = '1';
51      ...
52   }
53   ...
54   return 0;
55 }
```

Listing 1.1. Example program to demonstrate the effectiveness of *hybrid pruning*. The region highlighted in red is ***never*** executed in any of the dynamic runs.

3.3   Precision Gain Due to *Hybrid Pruning*

First, we exercise the program either using tests, or by fuzzing, to collect dynamic points-to and taint facts. Then, we augment the static pointer and taint analysis techniques with the recorded dynamic facts in either of the following two ways – *propagation-only* (H_P), or *opportunistic* (H_o).

Table 1. Tainted objects (✓: Tainted, ✗: not Tainted) when different points-to analysis techniques are used. The colors green and red represent true positives, and false positives respectively.

Objects		Tainted data?	Static taint tracking (STT)		
ID	Name	(Ground truth)	Flow-Sens PT	H_P-PT	H_o-PT
1	greq	✗	✓	✗	✗
2	gres	✗	✓	✗	✗
3	req_buff	✗	✓	✗	✗
4	res_buff	✓	✓	✓	✓
5	buff	✗	✗	✗	✗
6	q	✗	✗	✗	✗

Table 2. Vulnerability warnings of static taint tracking when different points-to analysis techniques are used. The color green represents true positives, and red represents false positives and false negatives respectively.

Vulnerability warnings	Static taint tracking (STT)		
(Ground truth)	Flow-Sens PT	H_P-PT	H_o-PT
Out-of-bounds write on Line 39	1	1	1
Out-of-bounds write on Line 50	1	0	1
False positives	3	0	0
Total warnings	5	1	2

Table 3. Dynamic points-to information collected for the example in List-ing 1.1. N/A indicates that the code corresponding to the pointer is not executed in any of the dynamic runs.

Pointer	Dynamic points-to
q	N/A
buff	{5}
req_buff	{3}
greq	{1}
res_buff	{4}
gres	{2}
req	{1, 3}
res	{2, 4}
return	{3, 1, 4, 2}
c_buff@28	{4}
c_buff@35	{2}
c_buff@47	N/A

Propagation-only (H_P). In this mode, the static analysis is first initialized with the recorded dynamic facts. Then, the static pointer and taint analysis algorithms propagate those dynamic facts even to those program points that are not executed dynamically. In other words, the information generated at any program point is derived ***only*** from the dynamic information, but propagated by the static analysis rules. The benefit of the H_P over dynamic-only analysis is that the former compensates for the lack of dynamic information by static propagation of dynamic facts, at the program points where the dynamic information is absent. Greater the dynamic coverage is, more effective the H_P mode will be in eliminating the spurious points-to and taint sets. The H_P *hybrid pruning* strategy, when applied to static points-to (SPT) and static taint-tracking (STT) analyses, yields H_P-PT (propagation-only points-to) and H_P-TT (propagation-only taint-tracking) analyses, respectively.

In Listing 1.1, H_P-PT prunes the over-approximated SPT set of c_buff@28 from $\{3, 1, 4, 2\}$ to $\{4\}$. Consequently, an STT that relies on H_P-PT correctly taints only the object with id 4 (res_buff), thus improving the precision of the taint analysis, as shown in Table 1 (Column H_P-PT). Furthermore, as shown in Table 2 (Column H_P-PT), a static vulnerability detection technique that uses this hybrid taint-tracking emits no false warnings. However, for cases where dynamic information is inadequate, *e.g.*, the points-to information of c_buff@47 is absent, the H_P mode might fail to compute certain information. The missing information might introduce false negatives, as shown in Table 2 (Column H_P-PT), where using H_P-PT resulted in missing the vulnerability in Line 50 of Listing 1.1.

▶ *Difference between* H_P *and classic dynamic analysis.* Since H_P mode propagates dynamic facts using static algorithms, it essentially compensates for the 'lost' information at certain program points. In Listing 1.1, a purely dynamic approach would compute an empty points-to set for t_buff@46, because Line 46 was never executed in any of the dynamic runs. However, Line 35 was dynamically executed, which made c_buff@35 point to greq. That information will be propagated in H_P mode, resulting in t_buff@46 correctly pointing to the greq buffer.

Opportunistic (H_o). As explained above, the points-to and taint information that the H_P mode propagates might be incomplete due to lack of dynamic coverage at certain program points – resulting in false negatives. To alleviate this issue, we use the dynamic information in the H_o mode only at those program points that are executed dynamically. For all other program points, we use the static information. Opportunistic use of the dynamic facts conservatively preserves the static points-to and taint sets at those program points where the dynamic information is not available. The only difference between the H_o and the H_P modes is that the H_o allows static information to be generated, while the H_P does not. The H_o *hybrid pruning* strategy, when applied to static points-to (SPT) and static taint-tracking (STT) analyses, yields H_o-PT (opportunistic points-to) and H_o-TT (opportunistic taint-tracking) analyses, respectively.

In Listing 1.1, though the code highlighted in red is not dynamically executed, H_o-PT infers the points-to relation between c_buff@47 and object with id 6. Consequently, an STT that relies on H_o-PT correctly taints the relevant buffer, as shown in Table 1 (Column H_o-PT). Furthermore, as shown in Table 2 (Column H_o-PT), a static vulnerability detection technique that uses this hybrid taint-tracking emits no false warnings, yet discovers both the vulnerabilities.

4   Hybrid Pruning

Our technique works in three steps. First, we generate the dynamic facts (Sect. 4.1), *e.g.*, points-to and taint sets, by exercising the program with a test suite, or using fuzzing. In the next phase, which we call *domain re-mapping* (Sect. 4.2), we lift the dynamic facts to the same domain as that of the static ones, so that a unified analysis becomes possible. Finally, we run the static analysis, and inject (Sect. 4.3) the dynamic facts, wherever available, thus eliminating potentially spurious points-to and taint sets at those program points. Note that the precision improvement is **not only** local to the point of injection, but also carried forward to the downstream analysis sites by the static algorithms. For example, "fixing" an over-approximated points-to set progressively taints fewer objects further down the analysis. Finally, we run a number of vulnerability detectors (Sect. 4.4), which uses the hybrid facts to eliminate spurious warnings.

4.1   Generation of Dynamic Facts

During a program's execution, we record **(i)** the allocation and deallocation of program objects, **(ii)** the read and write accesses on those objects, **(iii)** the callsite-based program context of the instructions involved in (i) and (ii), and **(iv)** the arguments of the input API, *e.g.*, read. Once this information is collected, we compute the dynamic points-to and taint information corresponding to those memory objects from the recorded trace. Next, we describe how we recover the dynamic facts from the collected trace in detail.

Dynamic Context. We keep track of a function's call-stack c at run-time, by emulating a parallel stack updated at every call and ret instruction. For every instruction I, we compute its dynamic context $\Delta(I) = (c, \tau)$, where c is the call-stack with which I is executed, and τ is an unique identifier for each I.

Memory Objects. We maintain the tuple $(sz, rt, \Delta(I))$ for each memory object o allocated, or deallocated by an instruction I, where sz is the size of the object (in bytes), rt is its run-time address, and $\Delta(I)$ being its dynamic context. We extract the size sz of the local and global memory objects from their types. The size of the heap object is extracted from the *size* argument passed to the allocation routines, *e.g.*, malloc. Note that, different instances of an object o with the same context $\Delta(I)$ might get created at different points in time in an execution, or even across different executions. We merge the dynamic facts associated with all those instances of an object o, by its context $\Delta(I)$, at the end of trace collection. For each object o created by the same instruction I with the same context $\Delta(I)$, we compute its id $\pi(o) = \{hash(\Delta(I), \tau(I))\}$, which uniquely identifies the object for a given context.

Points-to Facts. To compute the points-to sets, we track all the write operations to the program objects. Assume, a memory write instruction writes to the address w_d of a memory object $o_d = (sz_d, rt_d, \_)$. If the value being written to is a memory address w_s of an object $o_s = (sz_s, rt_s, \_)$, then we make the offset $(w_d - rt_d)$ of the object o_d point to the offset $(w_s - rt_s)$ of the object o_s. Formally, the updated points-to set $\rho(o_d, w_d - rt_d) = \rho(o_d, w_d - rt_d) \cup (\pi(o_s), w_s - rt_s)$.

Taint Facts. We use the same taint sources as that of static taint analysis. However, different from the static case, dynamically we taint the exact number of bytes read by an input API, *e.g.*, a read(fd, buf, count) call taints count bytes of the buffer buf.

4.2 Domain Re-mapping

Hybrid pruning seeds static analysis algorithms with the dynamic information. Static analysis operates on an intermediate representation (IR), and models program memory in terms of abstract objects. However, dynamic analysis executes native CPU instructions, and objects are created at run-time on the program stack, or heap. We use the following two-fold approach to bridge this gap. First, we assign a unique instruction id τ to each IR instruction. Additionally, to represent a memory object, we use a unique object id π as discussed earlier. We include both the τ and π in the dynamic events, and the generated dynamic facts. During the static analysis, we re-use the same τ as that of the dynamic analysis, and use identical definition of static context as that of dynamic context $\Delta(I)$. Hence, the static and dynamic object id π evaluates to be the same, for the same object, created in the same context. The *hybrid pruning* leverages this fact to establish the equivalence between a dynamic memory object, and its static counterpart.

4.3 Injection of Dynamic Facts

We augment both the static pointer and taint analyses with the dynamic information to achieve *hybrid pruning*. For the pointer analysis, we leverage the flow-sensitive analysis from SVF [45]. Our static taint analysis engine is flow-, context-, and field-sensitive. In addition to the family of input APIs, *e.g.*, scanf, gets, *etc.*., we consider the command-line arguments of the program as the taint sources. The taint analysis is parameterized by the underlying pointer analysis, *i.e.*, while propagating the taint labels, it queries the pointer analysis for the points-to sets of the destination operand of an instruction. Taint sinks are determined by the taint policies of the respective vulnerability detectors. Depending on how we inject dynamic facts during static analysis, we develop two modes of *hybrid pruning* – *propagation-only* and *opportunistic*.

$$\frac{PtsTo(p) \supseteq PtsTo(q) \quad dynV(q) \quad l_x \in DynPtsTo(q)}{l_x \in PtsTo(p)} \text{DynCopy} \qquad \frac{PtsTo(p) \supseteq PtsTo(q) \quad \neg dynV(q) \quad l_x \in PtsTo(q)}{l_x \in PtsTo(p)} \text{ICopy}$$

$$\frac{PtsTo(p) \supseteq PtsTo(*q) \quad l_r \in PtsTo(q) \quad dynV(r) \quad l_x \in DynPtsTo(r)}{l_x \in PtsTo(p)} \text{DynDereference}$$

$$\frac{PtsTo(p) \supseteq PtsTo(*q) \quad l_r \in PtsTo(q) \quad \neg dynV(r) \quad l_x \in PtsTo(r)}{l_x \in PtsTo(p)} \text{IDereference}$$

Fig. 3. Rules to solve the hybrid constraint graph.

Propagation-only (H_P). In this case, we propagate just the dynamic facts using static analysis rules. For the SPT we presented in Sect. 2, we can achieve H_P *hybrid pruning* by (i) *not* generating any ADDRESS-OF constraints, and (ii) modifying the COPY and DEREFERENCE constraints to consider only the dynamic information. While (i) prevents generation of any new static fact, (ii) ensures propagation of dynamic facts following the SPT rules. We split the constraint-solving rules in Fig. 2 depending on the availability of the dynamic information. Specifically, we follow the DYNCOPY and DYNDEREFERENCE rules as shown in Fig. 3, to process the COPY and DEREFERENCE instructions in the H_P mode. The $dynV(p)$ predicate checks whether the program point corresponding to the pointer p has been dynamically executed. If so, we consider the dynamic points-to set returned by the $DynPtsTo(p)$ predicate. In the H_P mode of STT, we ignore all the static taint sources. We use just the dynamic taint information for all the dynamically executed instructions. In effect, we consider only those instructions that have been both dynamically executed, and found to be tainted. Due to the space constraint, we refrain from presenting the modified transfer functions for the taint propagation.

Opportunistic (H_o). In this case, we generate new static facts, if dynamic information is unavailable. If the later is available at a program point, it is given priority over its static counterpart. For the SPT we presented in Sect. 2, we can achieve the H_o *hybrid pruning* by (i) generating the ADDRESS-OF constraints, and (ii) modifying the COPY and DEREFERENCE constraints to give preference to dynamic information, if available. Otherwise, the constraint solving rules are made to use static information. Policy (i) ensures the generation of new static facts, which compensates for the lack of dynamic coverage. In fact, if the dynamic information is available, we use the same constraint-solving rules as in the case of the H_P mode, while processing the COPY and DEREFERENCE instructions. However, we also introduce two new rules, *viz.*, ICOPY and IDEREFERENCE as shown in Fig. 3, to deal with those cases when dynamic information is absent. The H_o strategy falls back to SPT in that case. In the H_o mode of STT, we enable the static taint sources. Also, we propagate the static taint except when the dynamic information is available at an instruction, it is given priority. In other words, the taint engine never taints an instruction that has been dynamically executed, yet was never tainted.

4.4 Vulnerability Detection

The vulnerability detectors use the taint information to detect potentially buggy program points. Since, the taint analysis itself is a client of the pointer analysis, the checkers run when both the pointer and taint analyses are over. In our research prototype, we only use detectors capable of finding spatial vulnerabilities, *e.g.*, buffer overflow, out of bounds, *etc.*. Temporal bugs, *e.g.*, use after free, double free, *etc.*, are considered out of scope. Specifically, we use the taint-based bug detectors, *i.e.*, *Improper Tainted-Data Use Detector* (ITDUD), and *Tainted Loop Bound Detector* (TLBD) from the DR. CHECKER [29] project. ITDUD monitors whether tainted data is used in risky functions *e.g.*, `strcpy`, `memcpy`, *etc.*. Where as, `TLBD` checks if the loop bound can possibly be tainted.

4.5   Implementation

To generate the dynamic facts, we instrument the program using LLVM 7.0 [5]. The static and hybrid analysis engines are based on SVF 7.0 [45]. We extended SVF to add support for taint analysis, while using its pointer analysis (`fspta`) out-of-the-box. We use the `DataFlowSanitizer` [6] (`DFSan`), a generic dynamic data flow analysis LLVM pass, which instruments the program to perform dynamic taint tracking. The `DFSan` also handles memory taint by maintaining a *shadow* memory [37]. Our analysis injects and propagates taint automatically, and collects all the tainted instructions and memory objects. The vulnerability checkers are adapted from the DR. CHECKER [29].

5   Evaluation

We evaluate the effectiveness of our approach in a downstream security application, *e.g.*, vulnerability detection. We show that using our hybrid points-to and taint analysis we generate fewer false-positives (warnings that are *not* real bugs), while still detecting *real* bugs.

5.1   Evaluation Setup

Dataset. Our approach was evaluated on the following two datasets.

CGC. The corpus of 246 programs [13] used by DARPA in the Cyber Grand Challenge (CGC) [4]. We chose to use `cb-multios` [33], a port of the CGC challenge set to Linux x86 by TRAIL OF BITS. `cb-multios` project failed to port five programs to Linux. Moreover, the programs are meant to be compiled in 32-bit, while our `DFSan` based implementation generates only 64-bit binaries owing to the limitation imposed by the shadow memory mechanism. Due to unsupported architecture, 89 programs aborted with an early memory corruption inside the custom heap allocator. From the remaining ones, we randomly sampled 12 programs containing spatial vulnerabilities to include in our dataset.

Real-World. Though CGC programs mimic real-world applications both in terms of complexity and functionality, we collected 8 vulnerable versions (Table 4) of 4 distinct real-world GNU applications containing only *spatial* vulnerabilities from the CVE database [2]. We used the test suites available with the respective versions of those utilities to exercise those programs.

Instrumentation. This step was carried out on an Ubuntu 18.04.3 LTS, 64-bit system equipped with an Intel Core i7-4770 (3.40 GHz) CPU, and 32 GB of memory, under moderate workload.

Trace Collection. We re-used the same setup from the previous phase. The programs were exercised by their respective test suite. Real-world applications were let to run until they gracefully exit. However, many CGC programs being interactive, and menu-driven in nature, they run in a waiting loop until a specific program option is chosen, *e.g.*, sending a QUIT command. It is not guaranteed that the test cases will drive the programs to completion. To ensure the convergence of the experiment, we imposed a hard time-limit of 15 s per program execution by sending a SIGTERM signal, and installed signal handlers to record traces at termination.

Hybrid Analysis. We deployed this analysis to a Celery [1] cluster consisting of 8 servers with an analysis time-limit of 6 h per program, per configuration. Each server was equipped with an Intel Xeon E5645 2.40 GHz CPU, and 96 GB of memory, running Ubuntu 16.04.6 LTS, 64-bit. Despite the time-limit in place, *none* of the analyses was observed to hit the limit.

5.2 Vulnerability Detection

We measured the effectiveness of our pruning strategy in terms of the reduction of warnings due to the following two reasons—**(i)** We were interested to understand if our technique is able to significantly bring down the number of warnings emitted by a static bug detector such that those alarms can be verified by the analysts manually. **(ii)** We had the partial knowledge of the vulnerabilities (ground truth) present in our dataset. In other words, we did not have the knowledge of all the bugs contained in our subjects. Both the sources of building the ground truth— the bugs documented with the CGC dataset, and the CVE database records for the vulnerable real-world programs—were incomplete. Therefore, we could only confidently determine the true positives for bugs by associating the warnings to our known bugs. However, a similar strategy would incorrectly flag a warning, which is indeed a bug, as a false positive just because the associated bug report is not present in our (incomplete) ground truth. Establishing a complete ground truth would not only require the involvement of human experts, but also would be hard to scale to all the programs included in our dataset.

Warning Reduction Factor (WRF). To measure the effectiveness of *hybrid pruning*, we introduce the notion of *warning reduction factor* (WRF), a metric that captures the effect of *hybrid pruning* on emitted warnings, *w.r.t.* the baseline static vulnerability detection technique. An WRF = 0%, the worst-case scenario for our technique, corresponds to no improvement due to *hybrid pruning* over the static analysis. A non-zero WRF quantifies the improvement in performance induced by *hybrid pruning*. We define WRF as the fraction of warnings that are **not** raised by our hybrid (H_o/H_P) analysis. Formally, WRF $= (|\omega_\mathcal{B}| - |\omega_\mathcal{H}|)/|\omega_\mathcal{B}|$, where $|\omega_\mathcal{B}|$ and $|\omega_\mathcal{H}|$ denote the number of warnings reported by the baseline and the hybrid analyses respectively.

Table 4. Warnings emitted, and corresponding bugs (true positives) discovered by bug finders based on pure static, H_o, and H_p modes of points-to and taint analyses. ✓ and ✗ denote if the bug has been found or missed by an analysis.

Subject	Static	Warnings			
		H_o	Bug found?	H_p	Bug Found?
CROMU_00026	249	199	✓	158	✗
CROMU_00027	141	99	✓	98	✓
CROMU_00029	261	223	✓	177	✗
CROMU_00030	305	210	✓	148	✓
CROMU_00076	321	233	✓	141	✗
CROMU_00084	700	459	✓	389	✓
CROMU_00088	528	357	✓	320	✓
KPRCA_00001	209	163	✓	105	✓
NRFIN_00033	93	77	✓	51	✓
NRFIN_00041	268	196	✓	196	✓
TNETS_00002	33	26	✓	25	✓
YAN01_00011	32	29	✓	29	✓
readelf-2.28 (CVE-2017-6969)	2255	1872	✓	999	✗
readelf-2.28 (CVE-2017-8398)	2255	1872	✓	999	✓
readelf-2.30 (CVE-2018-10372)	3038	2582	✓	1231	✓
readelf-2.32 (CVE-2019-14444)	3061	2663	✓	1176	✓
readelf-c0e331c (CVE-2017-15996)	2369	2037	✗	996	✗
date-15fca2a (CVE-2014-9471)	581	238	✓	192	✓
locate-4.2.30 (CVE-2007-2452)	1038	571	✓	343	✓
grep-235aad7 (CVE-2012-5667)	539	426	✓	270	✓

Results and Analysis. In this experiment, we ran the bug detectors (Sect. 4.4) in three different configurations: **(A) static-*only*:** flow-sensitive static points-to + static taint **(B)** H_o- *only*: flow-sensitive H_o points-to + H_o taint, and **(C)** H_p-*only*: flow-sensitive H_p points-to + H_p taint. To demonstrate the reduction in the warnings, we evaluated our approach on the CGC [13] dataset. The static-*only* configuration, which emits the *most* number of warnings, serves as the baseline

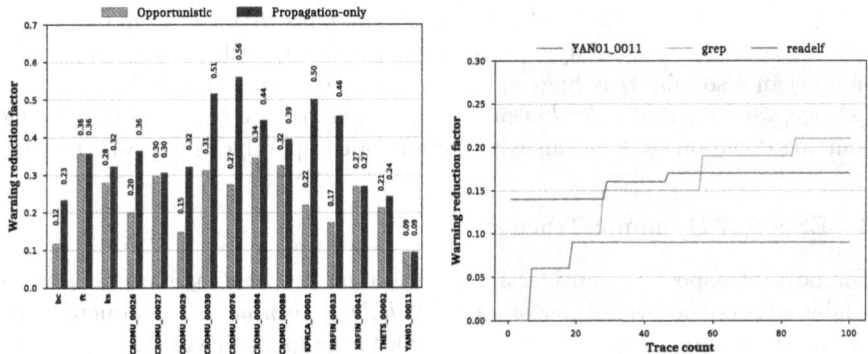

(a) Warning reduction by *hybrid pruning* (b) Warning reduction with dynamic trace compared to baseline analysis

Fig. 4. Analysis of warning reductions

for this experiment. Figure 4 shows the reduction in the number of warnings when H_o-*only* and H_P-*only* analyses are used. Further we observe that the WRF increases as the size (lines of code), and the complexity (*e.g.*, pointer-heavy programs), the number of taint sources, or the dynamic coverage increases. Intuitively, the first three factors make the analysis harder for a static bug detector, thus generating larger number of spurious warnings. The fourth factor, *i.e.*, the dynamic coverage, indeed benefits the hybrid analysis, as we show in Sect. 5.3. The H_o-*only* configuration reduces the warnings up to 36% (WRF=0.36), while the reduction in the H_P-*only* configuration is higher, up to 56% (WRF=0.56). We argue that this is no worse than any dynamic-*only* analysis system (*e.g.*, fuzzing) which suffers from insufficient coverage. H_P-*only* mode is helpful only when we have high confidence in the completeness of the dynamic information, *e.g.*, the test suite is exhaustive, providing good coverage. If the dynamic coverage is lacking, H_o-*only* mode is preferred.

This study reinforces the trade-off [51] between *usability* and *soundness*. We envision our bug detection system to be used in practice in either of these two modes: **(a) Conservative:** When an analyst chooses to minimize the likelihood of missing bugs, but is ready to tolerate a reduced reduction in the warnings; H_o-*only* mode is helpful. **(b) Priority:** When an analyst prioritizes finding the *most* number of bugs in a small time window, thus requiring a significant reduction in spurious warnings; H_P-*only* mode is a perfect fit.

While cutting down the number of warnings is desirable, it is not sufficient because of the potential risk of missing the true bugs. To evaluate the impact of *hybrid pruning* on the bug detection capability of the static bug detectors, we ran the same on both the CGC [13] and the real-world datasets. Table 4 summarizes the bugs discovered by the bug detectors while running in the H_P-*only* and H_o-*only* configurations. While the former is found to miss five bugs, the later misses just one bug. Intuitively, though insufficient dynamic coverage exhibits greater warning reduction in the H_P-mode, it misses more bugs than the H_o-mode, which compensates for the lack of dynamic coverage, by design. Please note that, even H_o-mode can also miss true bugs in some cases. We discuss that in Sect. 6.

Hence, we show that *hybrid pruning* enable scalable and efficient bug triaging by cutting down on false alarms while retaining comparable true-positive rate.

5.3 Effect of Dynamic Trace

An important aspect to consider is how the quantity of dynamic information available affects the overall performance of *hybrid pruning*. We conducted this experiment on three subjects, *i.e.*, YANO1_00011, grep and readelf in $H_o$mode; where we gradually inject more dynamic traces into our analysis system. We use fuzzing as an inexpensive way of trace generation, and randomly pick 100 traces. Every time a new trace is introduced, we continuously monitor the performance of our analysis system in terms of warning (WRF) reductions. With more traces being made available, pointer analysis improves, as additional dynamic information yields new points-to sets not discovered before. Moreover, taint analysis improves due to the combined improvement in the points-to sets, as well as the reduction in the spurious static taint sets. Since the bug detectors consume both the pointer and the taint information, the number of warnings reduces over time. Initially, the WRF increases, and then becomes stable at the point when the dynamic coverage saturates. We observe that the performance of *hybrid pruning* is positively correlated with the amount and the quality (coverage) of the dynamic trace. We present in Fig. 4b. Specifically, for every subject, the corresponding line gradient in Fig. 4b represents the correlation of WRF with the trace count, *e.g.*, gradient increases mean WRF increases as we add more traces.

Gradient Increases. Points-to result improves when additional dynamic information yields new points-to sets that has dynamically never been seen before by the analysis. Also, taint can improve either due to more precise points-to sets, or additional dynamic taint information overriding its static counterpart at newer program points. Warning improves as it is positively correlated to the improvement of either or both the factors.

Gradient Unchanged. Neither points-to, nor taint improves. Typically, it is the case when multiple traces exercise the same program path.

Gradient Decreases. Increased dynamic information can discover more target objects pointed to by the same pointer; thereby increasing the size of its points-to set. Similarly, extensive dynamic information available at the same program point can newly *taint* an object which was found not to be *tainted* in prior runs.

6   Limitations and Discussion

Potential False Negatives. Our pruning strategy is context-insensitive, meaning that the different call contexts of the same callee method are indistinguishable from each other.

```
 1  void square(int* p) {
 2      *p = (*p) * (*p);    // Unsafe binary operation
 3  }
 4
 5  int main() {
 6      int n, c = 50, i;
 7      scanf("%d", &i);
 8      if (i < 100) {
 9          scanf("%d", &n);     // Tainted input
10          square(&n);
11      } else
12          square(&c);
13      return 0;
14  }
```

Listing 1.2. False negative of *hybrid pruning*. Instructions in green are dynamically executed while the red ones are not.

In Listing 1.2, `square` is being called from two different contexts at Line 10 and Line 12, making p point to $\{n, c\}$. The tainted input n can flow to the multiplication operation at Line 2, if and only if i is less than 100. However, assume that the program is exercised *only* with test cases having i greater than 100. Therefore, in all the dynamic runs, the constant c is passed to the `square` call at Line 12, which establishes the dynamic points-to relation $p \rightarrow c$. During *hybrid pruning*, when the algorithm evaluates the points-to set of p due to the call at Line 10, it will find that the instructions of `square` have already been dynamically visited, albeit from a different context (Line 12). The context-insensitive pruning strategy disregards the difference in call-sites. At this point, the dynamic points-to set will be given preference, and consequently the static points-to relation $p \rightarrow n$ gets killed. Due to the missing points-to relation, the taint engine will no longer propagate the taint to the multiplication operation at Line 2. In turn, the `ITDUD` vulnerability detector will fail to detect the potentially unsafe binary operation. To summarize, the context-insensitive pruning strategy can lead to false negatives in both the pointer and taint analyses, as well the vulnerability detection. As we show in Sect. 5, the performance of *hybrid pruning* is positively correlated with the quantity, and the quality (coverage) of the available dynamic trace.

Theoretical Limitation. To detect temporal bugs, *e.g.*, use-after-free (UAF), double free, *etc.*, a bug detector needs to have both the *reachability* (if the attacker can trigger the events), and the *timing* (if the attacker can control the sequence of events) information. Therefore, the taint information alone is not enough in order to detect this kind of bugs. However, such a bug detector could still benefit from the precise pointer information to infer if different events, *e.g.*, *use*, *free*, *etc..*, are operating on the same program objects. Hence, how the hybrid points-to information improves the discovery of the temporal bugs could be an interesting research direction to explore.

Applicability to Other Analyses. Since *hybrid pruning* is inherently unsound, it is the best fit for applications where *soundness* is not a strict necessity, for example, in static vulnerability detection, limited cases of call-graph and control-flow graph construction, dynamic symbolic execution, *etc..*. Indirect call resolution is a challenging problem—a purely static pointer analysis is likely to miss potential targets unless it is configured to be 'overly' conservative, in which case, it may become unusable. Hybrid pruning can indeed be effective, because it can restrict such a pointer to a smaller set of interesting targets.

7   Related Work

In this section we will discuss state-of-the-art techniques related to our work.

Pointer Analysis: Pointer analysis is a fundamental program analysis technique with a very rich literature [42,20,44,43], and wide applications [23,27]. Steensgaard *et. al.* [44] provides a linear time algorithm based on type inference techniques for pointer analysis. Anderson inclusion-based pointer analysis is another important milestone for pointer analysis which provides good precision compared to Steensgaard *et. al.* with an acceptable performance overhead [43]. Yulei *et. al.*perform value-flow, and pointer analysis in an iterative manner to improve the precision of both [45]. Pointer analysis techniques are designed to be sound as they are mostly used in compiler optimization. However, there are other clients of pointer analysis that does not have this requirement. Vulnerability detection is one such client where less false positives [8], and more precision is required. There are few unsound pointer analysis techniques tailored for bug detection [11,9,12]. Similarly, speculative execution is one such client where the occasional lost of soundness is acceptable [24]. In order to achieve precision, one can also use dynamic analysis which is precise, but can never be sound. Marcus *et. al.*proposes a technique to compute pointer analysis results dynamically, which are called dynamic points-to results [19,32]. They also show that the static pointer analysis results are an order of magnitude imprecise than dynamic points-to results. Another work shows how the dynamic points-to results can be used for program slicing [31]. Additionally, David *et. al.*integrates pointer analysis with Dynamic symbolic execution to increase the precision of pointer analysis [46]. However, dynamic information heavily relies on the tests, and can never be sound. In this work, we explore the possibility of augmenting the static pointer analysis—which is imprecise but sound with dynamic points-to—which are precise but unsound. We then show how this can be used to increase the precision of vulnerability detection techniques.

Taint Analysis: Taint tracking is a data flow tracking technique to track the effect of user data at various program points [36]. Static taint tracking [28] requires a precise pointer analysis, else it usually ends up with Taint explosion [41], tainting all program data. Consequently, almost all the static taint tracking techniques are developed for Java [28] and other strongly typed languages where the pointer analysis results are relatively precise. Dynamic taint tracking(DTT) [36,25] is usually performed by instrumenting program instructions [25], resulting in memory and run-time overhead. Though several techniques have been developed to improve the run-time overhead; it still suffers from the lack of dynamic coverage [22,30,21,47].

Vulnerability Detection. Nevertheless imprecise, the importance of static analysis in vulnerability detection is undeniable. A large body of work on the static detection of vulnerabilities in C/C++ programs has evolved over the last two decades. Engler et al.first explored this domain using various static analysis techniques [50,17,52]. Other techniques target only specific classes of vulnerabilities, such as, buffer overflows [16,18,53], memory leaks [49], integer anomalies [35,48], and format string errors [38]. However, as the complexity of software grows, these techniques either do not scale, or incur a large number of false positives.

The key motivation behind this work is to bring the best of both the worlds together,*i.e.*, the *scalability* offered by the static analysis, and the *precision* guaranteed by the dynamic analysis. We attempt to combine both in a novel way, such that, we can draw on the strengths of each. There exists previous attempts that combine static and dynamic analysis for various applications [26,39,40,14,15,7,10]. Tapti *et. al.*combines static analysis with dynamic data flow tracking (DFT) to increase the the precision of pointer analysis [34]. They used this precise pointer analysis to protect memory disclosure, and transient execution attacks. Other techniques have aimed to improve vulnerability detection as a downstream client, *e.g.*, using dynamic analysis to verify the results of static analysis, guiding fuzzing through static program analysis, using static analysis to localize program faults in untested code from fuzzer generated crash, *etc.*. [26,39,40,14]. However, none of them combine the static and dynamic analysis in an interleaved way to improve the points-to, and taint analysis— which is further used in vulnerability detection to reduce the false warnings. To our knowledge, we are the first to explore this direction.

8   Conclusion

In this paper, we introduce *hybrid pruning* where we improve the precision of static points-to and taint analyses by combining dynamic information collected from program's run-time trace in a novel way. We propose two different modes of operation, *viz.*, H_o and H_P, whose applicability is decided by the amount of dynamic information available. Our in-depth evaluation demonstrates both significant improvement in the precision of the points-to sets, and the reduction of the taint sets. When static vulnerability detection is used as a client of the improved pointer and taint analyses, the former is able to find 19 out 20 bugs in

CGC and real-world software, where as cutting down 21% of the false warnings – making the analysis outcome more amenable to manual triaging.

Acknowledgements. We thank our shepherd Daniele Cono D'Elia and anonymous reviewers for their valuable feedback. This material is based upon work supported by ONR under Award No. N00014-17-1-2897.

References

1. Celery: Distributed task queue. http://www.celeryproject.org
2. Common vulnerabilities and exposures. https://cve.mitre.org
3. Coverity linux scan. https://scan.coverity.com/projects/linux
4. Darpa cyber grand challenge. https://www.darpa.mil/program/cyber-grand-challenge
5. The llvm compiler infrastructure. https://llvm.org
6. Llvm dataflowsanitizer pass. https://clang.llvm.org/docs/DataFlowSanitizer.html
7. Banerjee, S., Devecsery, D., Chen, P., Narayanasamy, S.: Iodine: fast dynamic taint tracking using rollback-free optimistic hybrid analysis (2019)
8. Bessey, A., et al.: A few billion lines of code later: using static analysis to find bugs in the real world. Commun. ACM **53**, 66–75 (2010)
9. Biallas, S., Olesen, M.C., Cassez, F., Huuck, R.: Ptrtracker: pragmatic pointer analysis. In: 2013 IEEE 13th International Working Conference on Source Code Analysis and Manipulation (SCAM), pp. 69–73. IEEE (2013)
10. Borrello, P., D'Elia, D.C., Querzoni, L., Giuffrida, C.: Constantine: automatic side-channel resistance using efficient control and data flow linearization. In: CCS 2021 (2021)
11. Buss, M., Brand, D., Sreedhar, V., Edwards, S.A.: A novel analysis space for pointer analysis and its application for bug finding. Sci. Comput. Program. **75**(11), 921–942 (2010)
12. Buss, M., Edwards, S.A., Yao, B., Waddington, D.: Pointer analysis for C programs through AST traversal (2005)
13. Caswell, B.: Cyber grand challenge corpus (2017)
14. Csallner, C., Smaragdakis, Y., Xie, T.: DSD-crasher: a hybrid analysis tool for bug finding. ACM Trans. Softw. Eng. Methodol. (TOSEM) **17**(2), 8 (2008)
15. Devecsery, D., Chen, P.M., Flinn, J., Narayanasamy, S.: Optimistic hybrid analysis: accelerating dynamic analysis through predicated static analysis (2018)
16. Dor, N., Rodeh, M., Sagiv, M.: CSSV: towards a realistic tool for statically detecting all buffer overflows in C. In: Proceedings of the ACM SIGPLAN 2003 Conference on Programming Language Design and Implementation, PLDI 2003, pp. 155–167. ACM, New York (2003)
17. Engler, D., Chen, D.Y., Hallem, S., Chou, A., Chelf, B.: Bugs as deviant behavior: a general approach to inferring errors in systems code. In: Proceedings of the Eighteenth ACM Symposium on Operating Systems Principles (2001)
18. Ganapathy, V., Jha, S., Chandler, D., Melski, D., Vitek, D.: Buffer overrun detection using linear programming and static analysis. In: Proceedings of the 10th ACM Conference on Computer and Communications Security, CCS 2003, pp. 345–354. ACM, New York (2003)
19. Gross, A.: Evaluation of dynamic points-to analysis (2004)

20. Hardekopf, B., Wiedermann, B., Cook, W.R., Lin, C.: A formal specification of pointer analysis approximations. In: submission to Programming Language Design and Implementation (PLDI) (2009)
21. Ho, A., Fetterman, M., Clark, C., Warfield, A., Hand, S.: Practical taint-based protection using demand emulation. In: ACM SIGOPS Operating Systems Review, vol. 40, pp. 29–41. ACM (2006)
22. Jee, K., Kemerlis, V.P., Keromytis, A.D., Portokalidis, G.: Shadowreplica: efficient parallelization of dynamic data flow tracking. In: Proceedings of the 2013 ACM SIGSAC Conference on Computer & Communications Security, pp. 235–246. ACM (2013)
23. Kahlon, V.: Bootstrapping: a technique for scalable flow and context-sensitive pointer alias analysis. In: Proceedings of the 29th ACM SIGPLAN Conference on Programming Language Design and Implementation, pp. 249–259 (2008)
24. Kelsey, K., Bai, T., Ding, C., Zhang, C.: Fast track: a software system for speculative program optimization. In: International Symposium on Code Generation and Optimization, CGO 2009 (2009)
25. Kemerlis, V.P., Portokalidis, G., Jee, K., Keromytis, A.D.: libdft: practical dynamic data flow tracking for commodity systems. In: ACM Sigplan Notices, vol. 47, pp. 121–132. ACM (2012)
26. Kim, S., Kim, R., Park, Y.B.: Software vulnerability detection methodology combined with static and dynamic analysis. Wirel. Pers. Commun. **89**(3), 777–793 (2016)
27. Lhoták, O., Chung, K.C.A.: Points-to analysis with efficient strong updates. In: Proceedings of the 38th Annual ACM SIGPLAN-SIGACT Symposium on Principles of Programming Languages, pp. 3–16 (2011)
28. Machiry, A.: The need for extensible and configurable static taint tracking for c/c++ (2017). https://machiry.github.io/blog/2017/05/31/static-taint-tracking
29. Machiry, A., Spensky, C., Corina, J., Stephens, N., Kruegel, C., Vigna, G.: DR. CHECKER: a soundy analysis for linux kernel drivers. In: 26th USENIX Security Symposium (USENIX Security 2017), Vancouver, BC, pp. 1007–1024. USENIX Association (2017)
30. Ming, J., Wu, D., Xiao, G., Wang, J., Liu, P.: Taintpipe: pipelined symbolic taint analysis. In: USENIX Security Symposium (2015)
31. Mock, M., Atkinson, D.C., Chambers, C., Eggers, S.J.: Improving program slicing with dynamic points-to data. In: Proceedings of the 10th ACM SIGSOFT Symposium on Foundations of Software Engineering, SIGSOFT 2002/FSE-10, pp. 71–80 (2002)
32. Mock, M., Das, M., Chambers, C., Eggers, S.J.: Dynamic points-to sets: a comparison with static analyses and potential applications in program understanding and optimization. In: Proceedings of the 2001 ACM SIGPLAN-SIGSOFT Workshop on Program Analysis for Software Tools and Engineering, PASTE 2001, pp. 66–72 (2001)
33. Trail of Bits. Darpa challenge binaries on linux, osx, and windows (2016). https://github.com/trailofbits/cb-multios
34. Palit, T., Moon, J.F., Monrose, F., Polychronakis, M.: Dynpta: combining static and dynamic analysis for practical selective data protection. In: 2021 IEEE Symposium on Security and Privacy (SP) (2021)
35. Sarkar, D., Jagannathan, M., Thiagarajan, J., Venkatapathy, R.: Flow-insensitive static analysis for detecting integer anomalies in programs. In: Proceedings of the 25th Conference on IASTED International Multi-Conference: Software Engineering, pp. 334–340. ACTA Press (2007)

36. Schwartz, E.J., Avgerinos, T., Brumley, D.: All you ever wanted to know about dynamic taint analysis and forward symbolic execution (but might have been afraid to ask). In: Proceedings of the 2010 IEEE Symposium on Security and Privacy (2010)
37. Serebryany, K., Bruening, D., Potapenko, A., Vyukov, D.: Addresssanitizer: a fast address sanity checker. In: USENIX ATC (2012)
38. Shankar, U., Talwar, K., Foster, J.S., Wagner, D.: Detecting format string vulnerabilities with type qualifiers. In: Proceedings of the 10th Conference on USENIX Security Symposium, SSYM 2001, Berkeley, CA, USA, vol. 10. USENIX Association (2001)
39. Shastry, B., et al.: Static program analysis as a fuzzing aid. In: Dacier, M., Bailey, M., Polychronakis, M., Antonakakis, M. (eds.) RAID 2017. LNCS, vol. 10453, pp. 26–47. Springer, Cham (2017). https://doi.org/10.1007/978-3-319-66332-6_2
40. Shastry, B., Maggi, F., Yamaguchi, F., Rieck, K., Seifert, J.P.: Static exploration of taint-style vulnerabilities found by fuzzing. In: 11th USENIX Workshop on Offensive Technologies. USENIX Association (2017)
41. Slowinska, A., Bos, H.: Pointless tainting?: evaluating the practicality of pointer tainting. In: Proceedings of the 4th ACM European Conference on Computer systems, pp. 61–74. ACM (2009)
42. Smaragdakis, Y., Balatsouras, G., et al.: Pointer analysis. Found. Trends Program. Lang. $\mathbf{2}(1)$, 1–69 (2015)
43. Sridharan, M., Fink, S.J.: The complexity of Andersen's analysis in practice. In: Proceedings of the 16th International Symposium on Static Analysis (2009)
44. Steensgaard, B.: Points-to analysis in almost linear time. In: Proceedings of the 23rd ACM SIGPLAN-SIGACT Symposium on Principles of Programming Languages (1996)
45. Sui, Y., Xue, J.: SVF: interprocedural static value-flow analysis in LLVM. In: Proceedings of the 25th International Conference on Compiler Construction (2016)
46. Trabish, D., Kapus, T., Rinetzky, N., Cadar, C.: Past-sensitive pointer analysis for symbolic execution. In: Proceedings of the 28th ACM Joint Meeting on European Software Engineering Conference and Symposium on the Foundations of Software Engineering, pp. 197–208 (2020)
47. Venkataramani, G., Doudalis, I., Solihin, Y., Prvulovic, M.: Flexitaint: a programmable accelerator for dynamic taint propagation. In: High Performance Computer Architecture (2008)
48. Wang, X., Chen, H., Jia, Z., Zeldovich, N., Kaashoek, M.F.: Improving integer security for systems with kint. In: OSDI (2012)
49. Xie, Y., Aiken, A.: Context-and path-sensitive memory leak detection. In: ACM SIGSOFT Software Engineering Notes. ACM (2005)
50. Xie, Y., Chou, A., Engler, D.: Archer: using symbolic, path-sensitive analysis to detect memory access errors. In: Proceedings of the 9th European Software Engineering Conference Held Jointly with 11th ACM SIGSOFT International Symposium on Foundations of Software Engineering, ESEC/FSE-11 (2003)
51. Xie, Y., Naik, M., Hackett, B., Aiken, A.: Soundness and its role in bug detection systems. In: Workshop on the Evaluation of Software Defect Detection Tools (2005)
52. Yang, J., Twohey, P., Engler, D., Musuvathi, M.: Using model checking to find serious file system errors. ACM Trans. Comput. Syst. (TOCS) $\mathbf{24}(4)$, 393–423 (2006)
53. Zitser, M., Lippmann, R., Leek, T.: Testing static analysis tools using exploitable buffer overflows from open source code. In: ACM SIGSOFT Software Engineering Notes, vol. 29, pp. 97–106. ACM (2004)

Establishing the Contaminating Effect of Metadata Feature Inclusion in Machine-Learned Network Intrusion Detection Models

Laurens D'hooge[✉][iD], Miel Verkerken[iD], Bruno Volckaert[iD], Tim Wauters[iD], and Filip De Turck[iD]

IDLab, Department of Information Technology, Ghent University - imec,
Technologiepark-Zwijnaarde 126, Gent, Belgium
laurens.dhooge@ugent.be

Abstract. Modern datasets in intrusion detection are designed to be evaluated by machine learning techniques and often contain metadata features which ought to be removed prior to training. Unfortunately many published articles include (at least) one such metadata feature in their models, namely destination port. In this article, it is shown experimentally that this feature acts as a prime target for shortcut learning. When used as the only predictor, destination port can separate ten state of the art intrusion detection datasets (CIC collection, UNSW-NB15, CIDDS collection, CTU-13, NSL-KDD and ISCX-IDS2012) with 70 to 100% accuracy on class-balanced test sets. Any model that includes this feature will learn this strong relationship during training which is only meaningful within the dataset. Dataset authors can take countermeasures against this influence, but when applied properly, the feature becomes non-informative and could just as easily not have been part of the dataset in the first place. Consequently, this is the central recommendation in this article. Dataset users should not include destination port (or any other metadata feature) in their models and dataset authors should avoid giving their users the opportunity to use them.

Keywords: Intrusion detection · Machine learning · Shortcut learning · Dataset issues

1 Introduction

Intrusion detection systems (IDS) are part of multi-layered network defenses. They are tasked with identifying unusual patterns that are a consequence of malicious use of the network. In the academic literature, modern intrusion detection methods rely on machine learning (ML) to accomplish this goal. They are evaluated on a set of specialty datasets. Method recognition as an improvement over the current state-of-the-art is conditioned on its ability to outperform previous methods on standard classification metrics. Intentional manipulation notwithstanding, it is still possible that choices in dataset (pre)processing lead to overly optimistic results.

The goal of this article is to demonstrate that one common choice in the preprocessing stage unintentionally overstates the results in a major way. That choice is to keep destination port in the feature set. Destination port is part of the network flow metadata quadfecta: source and destination IP addresses and ports. While most researchers do realize that IP addresses would bias the model and that source port should never be informative because it is randomly assigned by the operating system, destination port gets to stay in the training data much more frequently. It is kept in the training data often without a stated motivation or analysis. If a motivation is given, then it tends to align with the statement that the feature contains relevant information to identify attacks that are bound to specific services. From a theoretical perspective there is some merit to this statement, although it too introduces unnecessary bias in the model. Most importantly, the datasets are not generated in a way that counterbalances the potential bias of destination port. Depending on the attack type in the dataset, the distribution of destination port can exhibit significant scatter for attacks and concentrated values for the selection of (emulated) benign services. This pattern is quickly picked up by learning methods and then acts as a shortcut, leading to inflation of the results.

We demonstrate that the shortcut learning effect of destination port in ML-IDS is real and that proposed methods which include it are not screened out during peer review. In order to demonstrate the effectiveness of destination port, it is used as the single predictor to classify ten state-of-the-art IDS datasets (and their different subsets, i.e. attack classes). Destination port can separate the datasets with accuracies between 70 and 100% (overview results in Tables 2, 3 and 4). When using the other metadata features as single predictors, their models reach similar heights of undeserved classification performance (summarized results in Subsect. 4.7).

Accuracy can be used as a metric because the dataset is balanced by class label prior to sampling train and test portions. Without this balancing, using accuracy as a metric would be very misleading due to the inherent class imbalance in many of the IDS datasets. Even though this balancing reduces the amount of samples to train and test on, the accuracy on a second test set (the remainder of the samples, always one class) stays in-line with the results on the balanced test set. Furthermore, the results on a 20–80 train-test split, rather than the typical 80–20 split, are just marginally worse, indicating that even fewer samples are enough to learn the relation between destination port and the class label.

The recommendation that follows from this analysis is simple. The destination port should be viewed as part of the metadata features to be omitted during preprocessing. Proposed methods that keep it (or any other metadata feature) should be sent back during review to re-evaluate the method without its (or their) inclusion. This issue can be addressed at the source by dataset authors if they would stop providing the metadata features altogether when they publish new datasets.

The remainder of this article is laid out in six other sections. The related work introduces the datasets and demonstrates that the problem of metadata inclusion is widespread in the literature. The methodology provides the details regarding algorithm choice, dataset preprocessing and the ML pipeline. In the interest of full transparency, all datasets and preprocessing code (original, clean, and dirty with metadata as used in this analysis) are openly available at https://gitlab. ilabt.imec.be/lpdhooge/ids-dataset-collection. The code for this analysis is also openly stored on the same platform at https://gitlab.ilabt.imec.be/lpdhooge/ ids-metadata-contamination. Section 4 (results) is primarily conveyed through Tables 2, 3 and 4 with additional explanation in textual format in the subsections. The results also cover the other metadata features (source and destination IP addresses, source port and metadata time features) in a summarized format. The common patterns are discussed in Sect. 5 after which the article concludes and proposes future work into uncovering non-metadata contaminant features in IDS datasets.

2   Related Work

This section briefly introduces the concept of shortcut learning, followed by introductions for each of the ten datasets that are part of the analysis (Subsect. 2.2). Subsequently a non-exhaustive list (Table 1) of published methods is presented in which the authors included one or more metadata features from the aforementioned datasets. It is not difficult to find published articles, even with high citation counts (recorded through Google Scholar in March 2022) which included features prone to shortcut learning in their models.

2.1   Shortcut Learning

The issue of shortcut learning refers to the ability of learning algorithms to find and exploit spurious correlations in the data. This commonly happens when the dataset has an insufficient sampling of the problem and/or the data generation process left artifacts in the data. The algorithms learn to recognize the artifacts and seemingly perform well on the original dataset's test set(s). However, when exposed to a broader test set, the models fail to maintain their performance. Good ML practitioners use methods from the domains of interpretable ML and explainable artificial intelligence (XAI) to check whether their models have learnt shortcuts. Especially in the context of deep neural networks, the issue has gotten much attention [9]. More pertinent to this application domain, the issue of spurious correlations in cybersecurity-related ML research has been raised by Arp et al. [4].

2.2   State of the Art Datasets

For clarity's sake, when metadata features are mentioned, they include source and destination IPs, source and destination ports, timestamps and NetFlow IDs. As the objective of this article is to definitively place destination port among the metadata features which ought not to be used in models, we will always refer to it as a metadata feature.

NSL-KDD, ISCX-IDS2012 and the CIC Collection. The university of New Brunswick has the longest-standing history within the field of generating (network) intrusion datasets. It is the leading university in the Canadian Institute for Cybersecurity (CIC), a partnership between government, academia and industry. In 2009 they published an updated version of KDD99, dubbing it NSL-KDD [34], to address KDD99's shortcomings. NSL-KDD subsequently dominated as the dataset of choice, indirectly expanding the lifespan of KDD99 well beyond a decade of use. Interestingly, NSL-KDD (and KDD99) did not include destination port explicitly, instead opting to include a service field which contains the same information, abstracted away from any specific port. The ability of this destination port proxy to contaminate will be evaluated (Sect. 4.1).

In 2012, the first dataset from their own testbed was published. The paper which introduced the methodology behind ISCX-IDS2012 [32] laid out a framework of attack execution and user simulation at various levels of automation. The research group chose to develop their own feature extractor (ISCXFlowmeter) which operates on reconstructed network flows. The flow feature set of ISCX-IDS2012 was limited and also included reconstructed packet payloads (20 features: 9 flow, 4 payload, 1 label, 6 metadata). All targets (labels) were pre-encoded by the dataset authors in a binary *attack/normal*. A higher level of resolution for the labeling is not available.

The foundational parts had been put in place to build upon and refine the dataset generation. In 2017, this resulted in CIC-IDS2017 [30], which uses a new flow-level feature extractor CICFlowmeter, which outputs 80 features. The variety of attacks was increased and the labeling much more granular (individual attacks within 6 broad attack classes). The same attack class divisions were kept in next year's CSE-CIC-IDS2018 [30]. The CIC collection also includes the specialized CIC-DoS2017 [12] and CIC-DDoS2019 [31] datasets with even more attacks in their respective classes.

Thanks in part to the quality, ease of access and ease of use of the CIC collection, adoption has grown rapidly. For the foreseeable future, these datasets will see further adoption until they displace NSL-KDD.

CTU-13. The technical university of Prague published a specialized intrusion detection dataset in 2014 [8], centered around 13 captures of botnets, intermixed with normal and background traffic. The traffic is intricately labeled at flow-aggregation level. The flow extraction was done by the open source tool Argus. 9 flow-based features were captured and 1 label (plus 4 metadata features).

UNSW-NB15. The university of New South Wales has arguably published the second most widely adopted intrusion detection dataset [21]. The authors specifically set out to modernize the IDS data landscape, in response to the obsolescence of the attacks in the KDD collection. The dataset is geared towards machine learning, with 49 features (4 metadata, 2 labels and 43 content). Like NSL-KDD, the dataset authors published designated train and test sets to encourage researchers to publish results at least starting from the same data selection. These pre-selections no longer include destination port as a feature (though its presence is still reflected in the service feature).

CIDDS Collection. The CIDDS dataset collection (CIDDS-001 [25] & CIDDS-002 [26]), published by the university of Coburg in 2017 is less well-known, but is quite similar to CIC-IDS2017 in terms of experimental aim and methodology. A potential reason for its lack of adoption may lie in the amount of features it includes. Out of 16 total features, 5 are explicitly metadata and 4 are related to labeling, leaving only 7 features to learn from.

2.3   Proposed ML-IDS Systems

All datasets in Subsect. 2.2 contain destination port or equivalent information. The metadata inclusion does allow researchers more flexibility, but also places the burden of selecting the a priori features to remove with them. Invariably, this leads to proposals which keep certain metadata features, while others do not. In Table 1, we outline recent, (often well-cited) IDS proposals validated on any of the aforementioned datasets which included (at least) destination port (or service, its equivalent).

Some of the proposed methods tried to eliminate the metadata features, but failed to accomplish this because they added newly engineered features based on the original metadata. For newly engineered features, computed from the flow features after grouping by IP addresses in the dataset [5,23], it should not be surprising that the results are excellent. The experimental setups for data generation typically have no overlap in the roles for their nodes. A node's role is either attacker or victim (or in some datasets: other infrastructure) and maintains this role throughout the data generation process.

3   Evaluation Methodology

The methodology is straightforward, all datasets (as downloaded straight from their sources) underwent preprocessing including: ensuring data integrity with regard to expected feature types (as described by the dataset authors) and removing invalid and duplicate samples. During this preprocessing stage, maximal attention was given to clean up dataset quirks while retaining as many samples as possible. During this stage, the entire feature set (i.e. including metadata features) was taken into account when evaluating sample uniqueness. To

Table 1. Published articles on the included datasets which included metadata features in their models

Ref	Year	Citations	Metadata inclusion
NSL-KDD			
[13]	2017	8	Service (numerical encoding)
[33]	2020	75	Service (OHE encoding)
[7]	2020	7	Feature-selected service
[41]	2020	169	Feature selection method found service as a top feature
[38]	2021	6	Service (OHE encoding), kept after feature selection
[20]	2021	7	Service
ISCX-IDS2012			
[39]	2013	102	All metadata features
[3]	2015	28	Only metadata features
[6]	2017	32	Leaky new features (time-aggregation) metadata features included
[5]	2018	7	Leaky new features, derived from IP metadata
[19]	2021	6	All metadata features
CTU-13			
[6]	2017	32	All metadata features
[27]	2018	15	Categorical metadata features (IPs, service/port)
[29]	2019	14	All metadata features
[23]	2019	21	Leaky new features, aggregated from IP metadata
UNSW-NB15			
[11]	2017	106	Service
[14]	2019	29	Service
[40]	2019	21	All metadata features
[16]	2020	37	Service
[20]	2021	7	Service
[24]	2021	0	Service
CIDDS-001/CIDDS-002			
[2]	2018	59	All metadata features
[36]	2018	87	All metadata features
[1]	2019	94	All metadata features
[10]	2019	3	All metadata (except 'date first seen')
[35]	2020	23	Source and destination port
CIC-IDS2017			
[18]	2020	57	Destination port
[41]	2020	169	Feature selection method found destination port as a top feature
[20]	2021	7	Several metadata features
CSE-CIC-IDS2018			
[15]	2020	63	At least destination port
[17]	2020	73	Destination port
CIC-DDoS2019			
[28]	2020	3	Destination port
[24]	2021	0	Timestamp and source port
[37]	2021	1	Destination port

be as transparent as possible, the preprocessing code and datasets are publicly available at https://gitlab.ilabt.imec.be/lpdhooge/ids-metadata-contamination.

The actual experiments use the preprocessed datasets and add three specific preprocessing steps. After the data is loaded, only the destination port and the target (label) are kept. The label is binarized which collapses all attacks into one label. Subsequently, the dataset is balanced with regard to the label before splitting into train and test sets.

The remainder (remaining samples of the majority class) is kept as a secondary verification for the trained model. The balancing is done so that the standard classification metrics remain informative. For the remainder, accuracy $\frac{TP+TN}{TP+TN+FP+FN}$ is reported. However, if the majority of the samples in the subset was malicious (positive class), then the remainder only contains malicious samples and the evaluation metric simplifies to the true positive rate (i.e. recall $\frac{TP}{TP+FN}$). Conversely, if the majority of the samples in the subset was benign, then the metric for the remainder simplifies to the true negative rate ($\frac{TN}{TN+FP}$).

Representation of attack classes was considered sufficient if at least 200 samples exist in the dataset. This does lead to some missing results in the tables. No feature scaling is applied, because the selected ML algorithm does not require uniform ranges for the features. If scaling were to be applied, then the choice to balance the datasets before scaling would bias the scaling parameters towards the minority class. Two train-test split options have been tested (80–20 and 20–80). The 80-train, 20-test split typically outperforms the 20–80 split, but the difference is often marginal.

The selected algorithm was a random forest with fixed hyperparameters (most importantly, maximally 16 levels deep, 10 individual estimators, each given access to a different 50% of the training set). One could optimize these parameters further (especially the depth can be reduced even below 8 without significant performance loss). The splitting mechanism of decision trees is ideal to clearly separate a categorical feature such as destination port. Regression models (linear or otherwise) with 1 feature (i.e. coefficient) are underparametrized to capture the distribution. That shortcoming could be alleviated by one-hot-encoding the destination port to create a separate binary feature for every unique value. Modern, overparametrized models such as the various flavors of neural networks would be able to model the distribution, even if not one-hot-encoded, but at a significantly higher computational cost.

For every dataset, 10 independent iterations have been completed and the reported classification metrics are averages with standard deviations.

3.1   Two Notes on Methodological Design Choices

Time-Aware Train and Test Sets. Most datasets include a timestamp or another time-related feature that could be used to create time-aware data splits. The importance of such time-aware splits to combat concept drift and to reach greater real-world generalization has been well-established in malware classification [22]. However, in the authors' view, current intrusion detection datasets have issues in this regard when compared to malware detection datasets. Malware datasets have multi-year histories which do give rise to actual concept drift in the form of malware (family) mutations as well as fully novel samples and families. Intrusion detection datasets are typically gathered from one-off experiments where the variety of attacks is much lower (a handful of representatives per attack class), where there are no variations of the included attacks and where the time span is at most a couple of weeks. Due to a lack of interoperability between the academic IDS datasets, expanding variety and time frames through combination is impossible. The authors do concede that using time-aware dataset splits would partially eliminate the contaminating influence of destination port, especially in the combined datasets with multiple attack classes all squeezed into one label *malicious*.

The Drawbacks of Balancing. Two issues raised in the "Dos and Don'ts of Machine Learning in Computer Security" by Arp et al. [4] are linked to our choice to balance the datasets to keep standard classification metrics informative. Creating class-balanced train and test sets does avoid accuracy from becoming an inappropriate measure of performance, but the balancing leads the evaluation further away from the real-world and potentially under-estimates the false positive rate by ignoring the base rate of benign traffic. The same issue of bias in the evaluation due to imbalanced testing (away from a real-world estimate of the true class balance) was also identified in [22].

4   Results

The results are presented, grouped per dataset or per collection of datasets when appropriate. The textual summaries and explanations with regard to the expectedness of the results accompany the tabular formats for the same data. The results conclude with a Subsect. 4.7 dedicated to the contaminating influence of other metadata features in the IDS datasets.

4.1   NSL-KDD

When adhering to the author-provided train-test split for NSL-KDD (Table 2), the performance of the service (i.e. destination port) model is 75% accurate on the test set. It is held back by its recall (65.6%), not by its precision (89.8%) indicating that the authors added attacks in the test set which targeted different services. Still, the single feature metadata model managed to score 50% better than random. Dataset users who do not adhere to the designated train-test split, can expect the destination port model to rise to 90% accuracy with recall and precision now equally at 89–90% (regardless of 80–20 or 20–80 train-test split). Researchers who still use NSL-KDD should therefore stick to the author-provided train-test split, since that split is not merely the result of sampling the entire dataset.

4.2   ISCX-IDS2012

For ISCX-IDS2012, the individual subsets have been tested, as well as the concatenated total dataset. The subsets represent different classes of attacks

(Table 2 HTTP-DoS, DDoS by botnet, SSH brute forcing and infiltration from within the network).

There are huge differences in the discriminative power of destination port between the subsets of ISCX-IDS2012. For the brute force and infiltration subsets, accuracy varies between 95 and 100%. One of the subsets for which the authors state that it contains no attacks, does contain more than 2000 attack samples and it too can be classified with an accuracy well above 99%.

This contrasts sharply with the results on the HTTP-DoS and DDoS (by botnet) subsets for which classification accuracy is no more than 66%. This is easily explainable when grouping the data by class and listing their distributions. The HTTP-DoS attacks predictably target port 80 and port 443. The DDoS attacks also overwhelmingly targeted port 80 (32034/32183 positive samples).

The generated benign traffic always includes *browsing* by simulated users, which means that ports 80 and 443 have significant representation. This highlights the futility of using destination port. If the benign and attack traffic are kept proportional for common ports, then the feature is useless. However, if this is not guaranteed, then the feature reveals itself to be an ideal shortcut by which the classification performance gets overstated.

4.3 CTU-13

The CTU-13 (Table 3) dataset captured 7 distinct botnets in various configurations for a total of 13 scenarios. Some results are missing, but this is due to the authors' decision that subsets with less than 200 samples of the minority class are not evaluated further. Destination port by itself yields 4 models with 70–80% accuracy, 3 with 80–90% accuracy and 2 with 90–100% accuracy. The dataset authors provide a table with details about which botnet behaviors and targets were activated in each scenario. Linking these with the results for destination port as a single predictor, it is revealed that the best classification scores, obtained on scenarios 3, 5, 8, 9 (arguably) and 13, all used the botnet for port scanning. The inherent scatter of port scanning compared to the focused user simulation, yields an easily separable distribution.

4.4 UNSW-NB15

UNSW-NB15, like NSL-KDD, has designated train and test sets. The authors realized the potential for destination port to serve as a shortcut and omitted it as a feature from the designated sets. The dataset is also published in full format which plenty of researchers have used instead of the preselected train and test sets. That rawer version does contain destination port as a feature and when kept, can single-handedly perform 50% better than random (Table 3).

Although the preselected sets no longer have destination port, they (again like NSL-KDD) do still include a feature named service. The labeling for this feature is less granular when compared to its labeling in NSL-KDD, many flows have an empty service label. Solely relying on service to classify the designated test set yields a meager 56.7% accuracy. The drop in performance is not attributable to the sparse labeling of the service field. When the samples with empty service values are removed a new model is trained on the preselected training set and tested on the preselected test set, it is still just 55% accurate.

The difference is attributable to the different distributions for the same feature (for both targets), between the designated train and test selections. This will lead to poor generalization, which is painfully obvious when using a metadata feature as the only predictor. However, if these distributional shifts are present enough for the other features, then performance will always be weakened. A random forest suffers hard from these distributional shifts, but the loss of performance would be observable in any model. If dataset authors provide preselected train and test splits, they should be wary of this distributional issue.

4.5   CIDDS Collection

CIDDS-001. The creation methodology of CIDDS-001 included a completely controlled internal network with multiple segments and a publicly available external server. The internal network is attacked by machines connected on the same internal infrastructure. The external server is also attacked by author-controlled attackers outside of the internal network. The external server exposes services on the internet (on ports 80 and 443) and as such may have been probed and or attacked during the dataset collection period. The authors made this choice consciously, but also acknowledge that this has implications for the labeling of the dataset. Only the attacks executed by the dataset authors were explicitly labeled as such.

The vast majority of the samples is collected on the internal network (99+%, ~5.5 million samples). A destination port model is more than 70% accurate on the internal network and at least 85% accurate on the external network (Table 3). The added *confusion* on the internal network is again due to the mixture of benign and malicious traffic on port 80. Even though the authors (probably without direct intention) balanced somewhat on port 80, they did not for port 443. Port 443 is the most common port for benign traffic in the internal dataset (600000+ samples), but the attack frequency against the same service is vanishingly small (< 2500) samples.

CIDDS-002. The CIDDS-002 documentation and publication explicitly mention that the dataset is a port scanning dataset. Compared to CIDDS-001, there is no external network anymore. All attacks are executed within the internal network architecture set up in earlier work. All port scanning was done with the nmap tool and the dataset authors list the scanning type (protocol) and timing controls as the primary sources of variance between the attacks. Predictably, destination port is a serious contaminant in CIDDS-002, yielding models with accuracies in excess of 96% (Table 3).

4.6   CIC Collection

The CIC data collection is displacing the older datasets as the new data of choice to model and compare ML-based network intrusion detection systems. Samples from a range of attack classes and normal user behavior are included in the main IDS datasets (2017 & 2018) and the pure network attacks DoS (2017) and DDoS (2019) have special, augmented representations in the form of specialty datasets. Yet, despite the advances made by the CIC research team to improve the state-of-the-art in dataset generation, the datasets are extremely vulnerable to shortcut learning through the destination port metadata feature (Table 4).

CIC-IDS2017. Starting with CIC-IDS2017 and its seven attack classes (of which six are included because infiltration only has 36 positive samples in CIC-IDS2017), classification of a destination port model on the whole dataset is 91.8% accurate. At the individual attack class resolution level, the accuracy of destination port models is exaggerated further beyond 95–99%.

CIC-DoS2017. The CIC-DoS2017 dataset is impacted to a lesser degree, because its attacks directly target web servers on port 80 and a tiny fraction targeted at port 443, both of which also had been included in the user simulation. Still the destination port model can 100% reliably predict benign on all other ports, ultimately leading to an accuracy of 71.6%.

CSE-CIC-IDS2018. The follow-up CIC-IDS dataset, was released one year after CIC-IDS2017 and includes the same attack categories with better representation and execution on Amazon Web Services (AWS) infrastructure. Unfortunately, all attack classes except infiltration are very vulnerable to shortcut learning if the destination port is part of the model. By itself, it can predict the entire dataset with 90% accuracy and within the subsets, the accuracy of the feature regularly jumps to 99.9+%. Only for infiltration is the accuracy far below 90%, reaching just 55–65%. Upon inspection of the data broken down by label, the five most common ports for both subsets of infiltration attacks (53, 443, 3389, 445 and 80) are shared at about equal frequency by the samples for both targets. Those samples represent 75% of the samples of infiltration subset 1 and 66% of the samples of infiltration subset 2.

CIC-DDoS2019. The variance in CIC-DDoS2019 is captured with 91.5% accuracy by a destination port model. The individual attack sets of CIC-DDoS2019 are captured even better, often reaching 95–99% accuracy. Any proposed models that included the feature should be dismissed out-of-hand because this feature by itself can generate a near-perfect model.

Table 2. Results of the pure destination port (service) models on NSL-KDD and ISCX-IDS2012.

Subset	Accuracy	Precision	Recall	Remainder acc
NSL-KDD				
Designated-train-test-split	75.4 ± 0.9%	89.8 ± 0.1%	65.6 ± 1.6%	–
Straight-sampling	90.0 ± 0.2%	89.9 ± 1.2%	90.1 ± 1.5%	–
ISCX-IDS2012				
HTTP-DoS	67.9 ± 1.3%	94.5 ± 0.9%	37.5 ± 2.2%	97.8 ± 0.3%
Unspecified	99.7 ± 0.2%	99.5 ± 0.3%	100 ± 0.0%	99.3 ± 0.0%
Infiltration	95.3 ± 0.3%	98.4 ± 0.2%	92.2 ± 0.5%	98.4 ± 0.1%
Brute force	100 ± 0.0%	100 ± 0.0%	100 ± 0.0%	100 ± 0.0%
DDoS	57.9 ± 0.3%	54.4 ± 0.3%	100 ± 0.0%	15.9 ± 0.0%
Combined	66.3 ± 0.2%	96.4 ± 0.4%	34.0 ± 0.4%	98.7 ± 0.1%

4.7   Other Metadata Features

Although they are much more frequently stripped from evaluation, as they should be, other metadata features are present in the IDS datasets. This subsection summarizes their effectiveness as shortcut features across the included datasets. Full numerical results for these other metadata features are stored in the online repository for this experiment.

Source IP. Source IP addresses are easily recognized as a source of contamination. IDS datasets typically have defined, disjoint sets of nodes that will function either as attacker or as target. Unsurprisingly, ML methods quickly pick up on this pattern, often leading to perfect models for the included data sets. Deriving new features after grouping by source IP (blocks) should also be discouraged, because the composition of those groups will be heavily skewed and leak into the derived features.

Source Port. Source port should not be considered as a genuine feature, because the choice is determined by the operating system (OS). Furthermore, the range of available ports for use as source port OS-specific. On the author's personal Linux system, this range encompasses 32768 to 60999 by default. Conversely, on the author's Windows system, this range starts at 1025 and ends at 65535. At worst, if the data generation design used only Linux systems as attackers and only Windows systems as targets, the non-overlapping portions of these ranges would immediately identify a node's role. In the included datasets, using just the source port as a predictor leads to models with 60 to 90+% accuracy.

Table 3. Results of the pure destination port (service) models on CTU-13, UNSW-NB15 and the CIDDS collection. Po = Portscan, Br = Bruteforce, Pi = Pingscan

Scenario	Accuracy	Precision	Recall	Remainder acc
CTU-13				
1. Neris	79.3 ± 0.4%	72.1 ± 0.7%	95.4 ± 0.3%	63.2 ± 0.0%
2. Neris	88.1 ± 0.6%	86.8 ± 1.0%	89.7 ± 0.7%	86.5 ± 0.1%
3. Rbot	99.2 ± 0.2%	98.9 ± 0.4%	99.5 ± 0.3%	98.4 ± 0.0%
5. Virut	84.5 ± 1.3%	89.0 ± 0.4%	80.8 ± 11.3%	89.2 ± 8.9%
8. Murlo	96.6 ± 0.8%	99.4 ± 0.5%	93.7 ± 1.4%	99.4 ± 0.1%
9. Neris	71.1 ± 0.2%	65.1 ± 0.3%	91.3 ± 0.1%	51.1 ± 0.0%
12 .NSIS.ay	74.9 ± 1.5%	72.7 ± 1.8%	79.4 ± 2.5%	71.0 ± 0.3%
13. Virut	83.7 ± 0.2%	96.0 ± 0.3%	70.2 ± 0.5%	97.0 ± 0.0%
Combined	70.6 ± 0.2%	64.9 ± 0.2%	90.0 ± 0.2%	51.1 ± 0.0%
UNSW-NB15				
Raw UNSW-NB15	75.7 ± 0.2%	73.3 ± 4.0%	82.3 ± 9.9%	69.2 ± 10.0%
CIDDS-001				
External-2 (Po,Br)	89.7 ± 0.7%	92.6 ± 0.%	86.0 ± 1.3%	93.3 ± 0.3%
External-3 (Po,Br)	85.9 ± 0.4%	85.1 ± 0.7%	87.2 ± 0.7%	84.7 ± 0.2%
External-4 (Po,Br)	86.1 ± 1.8%	90.7 ± 1.9%	80.4 ± 0.%	91.6 ± 1.1%
Internal-1 (Po,Pi,DoS,Br)	71.0 ± 0.0%	68.0 ± 0.1%	79.3 ± 0.3%	62.6 ± 0.3%
Internal-2 (Po,Pi,DoS,Br)	70.7 ± 0.1%	66.4 ± 0.1%	84.0 ± 0.2%	57.3 ± 0.2%
Internal-combined	71.2 ± 0.1%	67.6 ± 0.1%	81.6 ± 0.1%	60.9 ± 0.1%
External-combined	86.4 ± 0.4%	85.9 ± 0.5%	87.1 ± 0.4%	85.7 ± 0.1%
Combined	71.2 ± 0.0%	67.6 ± 0.1%	81.4 ± 0.1%	61.1 ± 0.0%
CIDDS-002				
Internal-1 (Po)	97.3 ± 0.0%	98.8 ± 0.0%	95.9 ± 0.1%	98.8 ± 0.0%
Internal-2 (Po)	96.6 ± 0.1%	98.3 ± 0.1%	94.8 ± 0.2%	98.3 ± 0.0%
Combined	96.3 ± 0.5%	98.9 ± 0.1%	93.7 ± 0.9%	98.9 ± 0.1%

Table 4. Results of the pure destination port (service) models on the CIC collection.

Subset	Accuracy	Precision	Recall	Remainder acc
CIC-IDS2017				
Botnet	97.4 ± 0.6%	95.9 ± 1.4%	99.1 ± 0.4%	96.1 ± 0.3%
Bruteforce	99.6 ± 0.0%	99.3 ± 0.1%	100 ± 0.0%	99.3 ± 0.0%
DDoS	95.5 ± 0.1%	91.7 ± 0.2%	100 ± 0.0%	100 ± 0.0%
DoS	94.5 ± 0.0%	90.0 ± 0.1%	100 ± 0.0%	88.9 ± 0.0%
Portscan	98.4 ± 0.1%	98.2 ± 0.2%	98.6 ± 0.1%	98.4 ± 0.1%
Webattacks	95.0 ± 0.9%	90.9 ± 1.7%	100 ± 0.0%	88.9 ± 0.0%
Combined	91.8 ± 0.0%	86.6 ± 0.1%	99.1 ± 0.0%	84.6 ± 0.0%

(continued)

Table 4. (*continued*)

Subset	Accuracy	Precision	Recall	Remainder acc
CIC-DoS2017				
DoS	71.6 ± 0.3%	63.8 ± 0.3%	100 ± 0.0%	42.9 ± 0.0%
CSE-CIC-IDS2018				
Botnet	98.3 ± 0.0%	98.6 ± 0.2%	98.1 ± 0.1%	98.6 ± 0.1%
Bruteforce	100 ± 0.0%	99.9 ± 0.0%	100 ± 0.0%	99.9 ± 0.0%
DDoS-1	91.0 ± 0.1%	84.7 ± 0.1%	100 ± 0.0%	100 ± 0.0%
DDos-2	99.8 ± 0.0%	99.6 ± 0.0%	100 ± 0.0%	99.6 ± 0.0%
DoS-1	91.4 ± 0.2%	85.4 ± 0.4%	100 ± 0.0%	82.7 ± 0.0%
DoS-2	100 ± 0.0%	100 ± 0.0%	100 ± 0.0%	100 ± 0.0%
Infiltration-1	55.2 ± 0.3%	53.7 ± 0.5%	79.1 ± 1.1%	30.9 ± 1.2%
Infiltration-2	63.7 ± 0.3%	80.8 ± 0.6%	36.2 ± 0.6%	91.5 ± 0.4%
Webattacks-1	94.3 ± 2.7%	90.0 ± 4.2%	100 ± 0.0%	84.2 ± 0.0%
Webattacks-2	90.7 ± 1.6%	84.3 ± 2.3%	99.6 ± 0.5%	82.8 ± 0.2%
Combined	89.7 ± 0.0%	87.0 ± 0.1%	93.3 ± 0.0%	86.1 ± 0.0%
CIC-DDoS2019				
DNS	99.0 ± 0.2%	99.3 ± 0.2%	98.7 ± 0.5%	97.6 ± 0.0%
LDAP-1	99.3 ± 0.4%	99.7 ± 0.4%	98.8 ± 0.8%	98.9 ± 0.4%
MSSQL-1	99.1 ± 0.3%	99.5 ± 0.4%	98.6 ± 0.6%	100 ± 0.0%
NETBIOS-1	99.1 ± 0.3%	99.5 ± 0.5%	98.7 ± 0.5%	100 ± 0.0%
NTP	97.3 ± 0.2%	99.1 ± 0.2%	95.5 ± 0.4%	94.8 ± 0.6%
SNMP	98.5 ± 0.7%	98.9 ± 0.8%	98.1 ± 0.9%	97.7 ± 0.4%
SSDP	99.2 ± 0.5%	99.2 ± 0.7%	99.1 ± 0.6%	100 ± 0.0%
UDP-1	99.2 ± 0.2%	99.5 ± 0.2%	98.8 ± 0.3%	100 ± 0.0%
SYN-1	98.1 ± 1.1%	99.3 ± 0.7%	97.0 ± 1.9%	100 ± 0.0%
TFTP	96.3 ± 0.2%	98.8 ± 0.1%	93.7 ± 0.4%	99.0 ± 0.4%
UDPLAG-1	99.0 ± 0.2%	99.6 ± 0.2%	98.2 ± 0.4%	99.4 ± 0.1%
LDAP-2	94.3 ± 0.4%	92.8 ± 0.6%	96.0 ± 0.7%	93.9 ± 1.3%
MSSQL-2	96.1 ± 0.4%	95.0 ± 0.8%	97.5 ± 0.7%	92.3 ± 0.0%
NETBIOS-2	94.9 ± 0.9%	94.5 ± 1.4%	95.2 ± 1.7%	98.6 ± 2.2%
PORTMAP	97.6 ± 0.3%	97.1 ± 0.4%	98.0 ± 0.5%	97.1 ± 0.7%
SYN-2	92.6 ± 0.2%	91.7 ± 0.5%	93.6 ± 0.3%	93.6 ± 0.3%
UDPLAG-2	96.2 ± 0.3%	95.9 ± 0.5%	96.5 ± 0.7%	97.7 ± 0.4%
UDP-2	96.6 ± 0.8%	96.0 ± 1.2%	97.2 ± 0.6%	95.6 ± 5.7%
Combined	91.7 ± 0.1%	91.0 ± 0.2%	92.5 ± 0.3%	92.9 ± 0.3%

Destination IP. Including destination IPs runs into a similar risk as including source IPs. Certain portions of the network used for the data generation process are much more likely to be the target of attacks while other parts are always part of benign flows. The most prominent example would be malicious nodes which always attack on the internal network, while the benign data generation contacts servers outside the range of nodes controlled by the dataset authors (e.g. browsing the internet or exchanging emails). Again, for the included datasets, the effectiveness of just using destination IP ranges from 60 to 99+% accuracy.

Metadata Time Features. The labeling strategy of IDS datasets is typically based on a combination of strict role definition for nodes in the experimental network and precise bookkeeping of attack time frames. The CIC datasets have a Timestamp feature, CIDDS has a feature called date_first_seen, CTU-13 has starttime, ISCX-IDS2012 and UNSW-NB15 have start_date_time (stime) and stop_date_time (ltime). When using these features as single predictors, models with accuracies of 70% (UNSW-NB15) to 85% and above (all other datasets) can be expected. The models simply learn the time frames of the attacks.

5   Discussion

Performance on individual datasets and subsets (attack classes) varies, but the general trend is clear. Destination port (or its proxy service) can yield models which separate benign from malicious traffic with accuracies significantly better than random guessing. Put in terms of accuracy, the performance of the vast majority of models ranges between 70 and 100% accuracy.

The low end of this performance range is heavily correlated with greater overlap between the services that are attacked and which are also well-represented in user emulation. The top end of the performance range is characterized by models that were tasked with learning dataset (subsets, i.e. attack classes) where the attacks are scattered across many ports while the user emulation keeps to its narrow selection of emulated services.

Models that have included destination port suffer harder on datasets with pre-selected train and test splits, NSL-KDD and UNSW-NB15. The reason is that the dataset authors did not just take (stratified) samples from their total sample collection, but actively introduced new attacks (on unseen ports) in the test sets. These distributional differences between the preselected train/test sets are particularly detrimental for a categorical feature like destination port. It is yet another reason why it should not be included as a feature.

6   Conclusion

Modern network intrusion datasets, intended to be modeled by machine learning techniques, are often published with the inclusion of metadata features such as source and destination IP addresses, ports and time-based features used for sample labeling. Of these metadata features, destination port is most likely to be kept by researchers when training their models under the rationale that it contains useful information to identify service-specific attacks. This short article aims to demonstrate that the destination port or its proxy feature service are in fact contaminants that result in shortcut learning. This claim is demonstrated by showing the discriminative power of this feature by itself in models trained to classify ten state-of-the-art IDS datasets.

There is variability between the datasets, but the standard outcome is that destination port by itself can be used to generate models that are 70 to 100% accurate. The datasets in descending order of vulnerability to this effect are CIC-DDoS2019, CSE-CIC-IDS2018, CIC-IDS2017, CIDDS-002, UNSW-NB15, CIC-DoS2017, CIDDS-001, CTU-13 and ISCX-IDS2012.

The end result is a paradox for dataset publishers. If they equalize the proportion of benign and malicious samples on all represented ports, then the discriminating power of the feature is no better than random guessing. If they do not equalize representation across the ports, then the feature quickly rises to yield excellent, but ultimately meaningless models.

Based on this information, we propose that future dataset publications for intrusion detection omit this feature altogether. Reviewers evaluating newly proposed methods validated on the current datasets should inspect the list of included features. If destination port (or service) remained in the dataset, then the results have a near certain probability of being too optimistic. This potential for (unintended) inflation of the results is particularly poignant in this research domain where new proposals are considered more meritorious if they can demonstrate an increase in classification performance beyond the state-of-the-art.

7   Future Work

Settling the theoretical debate about whether intrusion detection models should include samples' destination port as a feature was the obvious first step in trying to improve the data handling by users of the state-of-the-art IDS datasets.

The conclusion of this article primarily targets other IDS researchers to interact more critically with the available datasets. In a secondary capacity it is addressed to dataset authors in the field to consider omitting the feature when publishing data.

The follow-up to this article will focus on finding less obvious contaminants in the state-of-the-art IDS datasets. We have already identified several high-impact features in the state-of-the-art datasets which may be the result of experimental design and execution, rather than a consequence of real attack behavior. The end goal is to also eliminate these features from the datasets to try to increase robustness and generalizability of ML-IDS models.

References

1. Abdulhammed, R., Faezipour, M., Abuzneid, A., AbuMallouh, A.: Deep and machine learning approaches for anomaly-based intrusion detection of imbalanced network traffic. IEEE Sensors Lett. **3**(1), 1–4 (2019). https://doi.org/10.1109/LSENS.2018.2879990
2. Althubiti, S.A., Jones, E.M., Roy, K.: LSTM for anomaly-based network intrusion detection. In: 2018 28th International Telecommunication Networks and Applications Conference (ITNAC), pp. 1–3 (2018). https://doi.org/10.1109/ATNAC.2018.8615300
3. Ammar, A., et al.: A decision tree classifier for intrusion detection priority tagging. J. Comput. Commun. **3**(04), 52 (2015)
4. Arp, D., et al.: Dos and don'ts of machine learning in computer security. In: Proceedings of the USENIX Security Symposium (2022)
5. Atli, B.G., Miche, Y., Jung, A.: Network intrusion detection using flow statistics. In: 2018 IEEE Statistical Signal Processing Workshop (SSP), pp. 70–74 (2018). https://doi.org/10.1109/SSP.2018.8450709
6. Bansal, A., Mahapatra, S.: A comparative analysis of machine learning techniques for botnet detection. In: Proceedings of the 10th International Conference on Security of Information and Networks, SIN 2017, pp. 91–98. Association for Computing Machinery, New York (2017). https://doi.org/10.1145/3136825.3136874
7. Farhat, S., Abdelkader, M., Meddeb-Makhlouf, A., Zarai, F.: Comparative study of classification algorithms for cloud ids using nsl-kdd dataset in weka. In: 2020 International Wireless Communications and Mobile Computing (IWCMC), pp. 445–450 (2020). https://doi.org/10.1109/IWCMC48107.2020.9148311
8. García, S., Grill, M., Stiborek, J., Zunino, A.: An empirical comparison of botnet detection methods. Comput. Secur. **45**, 100–123 (2014)
9. Geirhos, R., et al.: Shortcut learning in deep neural networks. Nat. Mach. Intell. **2**(11), 665–673 (2020). https://www.proquest.com/scholarly-journals/shortcut-learning-deep-neural-networks/docview/2621045756/se-2?accountid=11077, Springer Nature Limited 2020, Accessed 19 Jan 2022
10. He, W., Li, H., Li, J.: Ensemble feature selection for improving intrusion detection classification accuracy. In: Proceedings of the 2019 International Conference on Artificial Intelligence and Computer Science, AICS 2019, pp. 28–33. Association for Computing Machinery, New York (2019). https://doi.org/10.1145/3349341.3349364
11. Janarthanan, T., Zargari, S.: Feature selection in unsw-nb15 and kddcup'99 datasets. In: 2017 IEEE 26th International Symposium on Industrial Electronics (ISIE), pp. 1881–1886 (2017). https://doi.org/10.1109/ISIE.2017.8001537
12. Jazi, H.H., Gonzalez, H., Stakhanova, N., Ghorbani, A.A.: Detecting http-based application layer dos attacks on web servers in the presence of sampling. Comput. Netw. **121**, 25–36 (2017)
13. Ji, H., Kim, D., Shin, D., Shin, D.: A study on comparison of KDD CUP 99 and NSL-KDD using artificial neural network. In: Park, J.J., Loia, V., Yi, G., Sung, Y. (eds.) CUTE/CSA -2017. LNEE, vol. 474, pp. 452–457. Springer, Singapore (2018). https://doi.org/10.1007/978-981-10-7605-3_74
14. Jing, D., Chen, H.B.: SVM based network intrusion detection for the unsw-nb15 dataset. In: 2019 IEEE 13th International Conference on ASIC (ASICON), pp. 1–4 (2019). https://doi.org/10.1109/ASICON47005.2019.8983598

15. Karatas, G., Demir, O., Sahingoz, O.K.: Increasing the performance of machine learning-based idss on an imbalanced and up-to-date dataset. IEEE Access **8**, 32150–32162 (2020). https://doi.org/10.1109/ACCESS.2020.2973219
16. Kasongo, S.M., Sun, Y.: Performance analysis of intrusion detection systems using a feature selection method on the UNSW-NB15 dataset. J. Big Data **7**(1), 1–20 (2020). https://doi.org/10.1186/s40537-020-00379-6
17. Kim, J., Kim, J., Kim, H., Shim, M., Choi, E.: CNN-based network intrusion detection against denial-of-service attacks. Electronics **9**(6) (2020). https://doi.org/10.3390/electronics9060916, https://www.mdpi.com/2079-9292/9/6/916
18. Kurniabudi, S.D., Darmawijoyo, Bin Idris, M.Y., Bamhdi, A.M., Budiarto, R.: Cicids-2017 dataset feature analysis with information gain for anomaly detection. IEEE Access **8**, 132911–132921 (2020). https://doi.org/10.1109/ACCESS.2020.3009843
19. Kushwah, G.S., Ranga, V.: Optimized extreme learning machine for detecting ddos attacks in cloud computing. Comput. Secur. **105**, 102260 (2021)
20. Lohiya, R., Thakkar, A.: Intrusion detection using deep neural network with antirectifier layer. In: Thampi, S.M., Lloret Mauri, J., Fernando, X., Boppana, R., Geetha, S., Sikora, A. (eds.) Applied Soft Computing and Communication Networks. LNNS, vol. 187, pp. 89–105. Springer, Singapore (2021). https://doi.org/10.1007/978-981-33-6173-7_7
21. Moustafa, N., Slay, J.: Unsw-nb15: a comprehensive data set for network intrusion detection systems (unsw-nb15 network data set). In: 2015 Military Communications and Information Systems Conference (MilCIS), pp. 1–6 (2015). https://doi.org/10.1109/MilCIS.2015.7348942
22. Pendlebury, F., Pierazzi, F., Jordaney, R., Kinder, J., Cavallaro, L.: Tesseract: eliminating experimental bias in malware classification across space and time. In: Proceedings of the 28th USENIX Conference on Security Symposium, SEC 2019, pp. 729–746. USENIX Association, USA (2019)
23. Piskozub, M., Spolaor, R., Martinovic, I.: Malalert: detecting malware in large-scale network traffic using statistical features. SIGMETRICS Perform. Eval. Rev. **46**(3), 151–154 (2019). https://doi.org/10.1145/3308897.3308961
24. Priya Devi, A., Johnson Singh, K.: A machine learning approach to intrusion detection system using UNSW-NB-15 and CICDDoS2019 datasets. In: Satapathy, S.C., Bhateja, V., Favorskaya, M.N., Adilakshmi, T. (eds.) Smart Computing Techniques and Applications. SIST, vol. 225, pp. 195–205. Springer, Singapore (2021). https://doi.org/10.1007/978-981-16-0878-0_20
25. Ring, M., Wunderlich, S., Grüdl, D., Landes, D., Hotho, A.: Creation of flow-based data sets for intrusion detection. J. Inf. Warfare **16**, 40–53 (2017)
26. Ring, M., Wunderlich, S., Grüdl, D., Landes, D., Hotho, A.: Flow-based benchmark data sets for intrusion detection. In: Proceedings of the 16th European Conference on Cyber Warfare and Security (ECCWS), pp. 361–369. ACPI (2017)
27. Ryu, S., Yang, B., et al.: A comparative study of machine learning algorithms and their ensembles for botnet detection. J. Comput. Commun. **6**(05), 119 (2018). https://doi.org/10.4236/jcc.2018.65010
28. Sbai, O., El boukhari, M.: Data flooding intrusion detection system for manets using deep learning approach. In: Proceedings of the 13th International Conference on Intelligent Systems: Theories and Applications, SITA 2020. Association for Computing Machinery, New York (2020). https://doi.org/10.1145/3419604.3419777

29. Shamshirband, S., Chronopoulos, A.T.: A new malware detection system using a high performance-elm method. In: Proceedings of the 23rd International Database Applications; Engineering Symposium, IDEAS 2019. Association for Computing Machinery, New York (2019). https://doi.org/10.1145/3331076.3331119

30. Sharafaldin., I., Habibi Lashkari., A., Ghorbani., A.A.: Toward generating a new intrusion detection dataset and intrusion traffic characterization. In: Proceedings of the 4th International Conference on Information Systems Security and Privacy - ICISSP, pp. 108–116. INSTICC, SciTePress (2018). https://doi.org/10.5220/0006639801080116

31. Sharafaldin, I., Lashkari, A.H., Hakak, S., Ghorbani, A.A.: Developing realistic distributed denial of service (ddos) attack dataset and taxonomy. In: 2019 International Carnahan Conference on Security Technology (ICCST), pp. 1–8 (2019). https://doi.org/10.1109/CCST.2019.8888419

32. Shiravi, A., Shiravi, H., Tavallaee, M., Ghorbani, A.A.: Toward developing a systematic approach to generate benchmark datasets for intrusion detection. Comput. Secur. **31**(3), 357–374 (2012)

33. Su, T., Sun, H., Zhu, J., Wang, S., Li, Y.: Bat: deep learning methods on network intrusion detection using nsl-kdd dataset. IEEE Access **8**, 29575–29585 (2020). https://doi.org/10.1109/ACCESS.2020.2972627

34. Tavallaee, M., Bagheri, E., Lu, W., Ghorbani, A.A.: A detailed analysis of the kdd cup 99 data set. In: 2009 IEEE Symposium on Computational Intelligence for Security and Defense Applications, pp. 1–6 (2009). https://doi.org/10.1109/CISDA.2009.5356528

35. Thapa, N., Liu, Z., KC, D.B., Gokaraju, B., Roy, K.: Comparison of machine learning and deep learning models for network intrusion detection systems. Fut. Internet **12**(10) (2020). https://doi.org/10.3390/fi12100167, https://www.mdpi.com/1999-5903/12/10/167

36. Verma, A., Ranga, V.: Statistical analysis of cidds-001 dataset for network intrusion detection systems using distance-based machine learning. Procedia Comput. Sci. **125**, 709–716 (2018). https://doi.org/10.1016/j.procs.2017.12.091, https://www.sciencedirect.com/science/article/pii/S1877050917328594

37. Vuong, T.-H., Thi, C.-V.N., Ha, Q.-T.: N-tier machine learning-based architecture for DDoS attack detection. In: Nguyen, N.T., Chittayasothorn, S., Niyato, D., Trawiński, B. (eds.) ACIIDS 2021. LNCS (LNAI), vol. 12672, pp. 375–385. Springer, Cham (2021). https://doi.org/10.1007/978-3-030-73280-6_30

38. Xu, W., Jang-Jaccard, J., Singh, A., Wei, Y., Sabrina, F.: Improving performance of autoencoder-based network anomaly detection on nsl-kdd dataset. IEEE Access **9**, 140136–140146 (2021). https://doi.org/10.1109/ACCESS.2021.3116612

39. Yassin, W., Udzir, N.I., Muda, Z., Sulaiman, M.N., et al.: Anomaly-based intrusion detection through k-means clustering and naives bayes classification. In: Proceedings of 4th International Conference on Computer Informatics, ICOCI, vol. 49, pp. 298–303 (2013)

40. Zhiqiang, L., Mohi-Ud-Din, G., Bing, L., Jianchao, L., Ye, Z., Zhijun, L.: Modeling network intrusion detection system using feed-forward neural network using unsw-nb15 dataset. In: 2019 IEEE 7th International Conference on Smart Energy Grid Engineering (SEGE), pp. 299–303 (2019). https://doi.org/10.1109/SEGE.2019.8859773

41. Zhou, Y., Cheng, G., Jiang, S., Dai, M.: Building an efficient intrusion detection system based on feature selection and ensemble classifier. Comput. Netw. **174**, 107247 (2020)

Extended Abstract: Effective Call Graph Fingerprinting for the Analysis and Classification of Windows Malware

Francesco Meloni, Alessandro Sanna$^{(\boxtimes)}$, Davide Maiorca, and Giorgio Giacinto

Department of Electrical and Electronic Engineering, University of Cagliari,
Cagliari, Italy
{alessandro.sanna96,davide.maiorca,giacinto}@unica.it

Abstract. Malicious Windows executables still constitute one of the major threats to computer security. Various machine learning-based approaches have been proposed to distinguish them from benign applications or perform family classification, a critical task for threat intelligence. However, most of these techniques do not explicitly model the relationships between the various parts of the code. Additionally, the proposed systems, including deep learning ones, were vulnerable to adversarial attacks. This paper presents a novel, static learning-based method to detect and classify executables based on call graph fingerprinting. In particular, we generate a fingerprint for each call graph based on user-defined and library functions. Then, we represent the information sent to the classifier through a MinHash encoding that increases the overall system robustness against fine-grained modifications. The attained results show that our proposed approach can accurately distinguish malware families from each other by showing intriguing robustness properties. We claim that these results make this approach a promising research direction that deserves further exploration.

Keywords: Malware detection · Machine learning · Robustness · ×86

1 Introduction

Malware is a generic term to define malicious programs that perform actions that can compromise a digital system's confidentiality, integrity, and availability. Cyber attackers use malware to gain economic benefits from cyber attacks, targeting everyday users and state and industry computer systems. In particular, ×86 malware targeting MS Windows is still one of the most critical threats [1].

The rise and development of artificial intelligence (particularly machine learning) was employed as a plausible alternative to classical anti-malware signatures to perform malware and family classification [2–7]. However, using this technology also brought an entirely new set of challenges [8], mainly related to the necessity of devising feature sets embedding features strictly related to the sample maliciousness. An alternative approach to traditional systems has been, in these years, focusing on deep learning models [9].

L. Cavallaro et al. (Eds.): DIMVA 2022, LNCS 13358, pp. 42–52, 2022.
https://doi.org/10.1007/978-3-031-09484-2_3

However, both strategies exhibited so far two significant limitations. The first one is that they employ information that does not typically represent the *connections* between the various parts of the executable code (e.g., opcodes, network traces, and similar). The second limitation is the ease with which adversarial attacks can evade most of these systems, as attackers can perform simple modifications to the executable to achieve evasion.

To address the problems described above, we propose a novel approach to the *detection* and *discrimination of ×86 Windows malware families*. In particular, we defined a feature extraction technique based on a so-called *static behavioral fingerprint* for a given malware sample. A fingerprint is a compact representation of the function call graph of an executable, which synthesizes the operational characteristics of its procedures and their relationships. The fingerprint is encoded through a *MinHash* representation that constitutes the *feature set* that is fed to a traditional learning-based model. The idea here is to break the *direct relationship* between the functions and the feature representation that depends on the graph. In this way, even if the attacker knew the characteristic of each MinHash, it would be challenging to perform fine-grained modifications to obtain the desired representation. In other words, we are increasing the *practical challenges* that the attacker has to face to evade the system. The system will be released under an open-source license.

We tested the accuracy and robustness of our system on a dataset composed of more than 5000 executables divided into 20 families. Our preliminary experiments show that our system can accurately detect and classify them with encouraging computational performances. Moreover, we tested the robustness of our system on two practical black-box attacks, showing intriguing properties which would increase the attacker's effort to achieve effective evasion and confuse our system. The attained partial results are promising and demand more research to unravel this approach's potential entirely.

The rest of the paper is organized as follows: Sect. 2 provides the basics on Windows executables and the related work; Sect. 3 presents the methodology employed in this work; Sect. 4 shows the experimental results attained with our approach; Sect. 5 closes the paper by sketching possible future work.

2 Background and Related Work

Background. The structure and organization of binary executables strongly depend on the operating system they are running on. This paper focuses on Windows executables, also known as Portable Executable (PE) files.

A PE file is composed of a series of headers and sections. The headers contain the necessary information to characterize and navigate the file structure, while sections contain the real executable code and the executable's data to operate. Among the most important sections are the following [10]: *(i)* .text, which contains the executable code in terms of assembly instructions; *(ii)* .data, which contains the initialized read-write data marked as non-executable; *(iii)* .rdata, which contains read-only initialized data marked as non-executable. As it will be explained in the next sections, our approach focuses on analyzing the call-graph of malicious executables by extracting user-defined functions from the .text section.

Related Work. Machine learning techniques have been developed for over a decade to create a more substantial protection mechanism against new malware samples and detect their families. In the case of ×86 malware, the main idea is to identify common behavioral patterns in discriminant features extracted from the analysis of PE files. Two main categories of features are typically extracted from these files [7]: *(i) static features*, which characterize the behavior of a sample without requiring execution. This involves analyzing the PE header, data, and code sections to find potential threatening signs of malicious operation. A popular example is Ahmadi et al.'s work [5], where the authors extracted features from various executable parts (e.g., symbols, opcodes, sections) and combined them with measurements such as file entropy. *(ii) dynamic features*, which leverage file execution to acquire malicious traces from functional operations or specific data access. For example, Lin et al. [3] employed information extracted by calculating n-grams extracted from dynamic analysis reports. Mohaisen et al. [4] employed information extracted from the artifacts left on the system by the dynamic execution of each sample, including registry modifications, changes in the file system, and so forth.

Static analysis has also been employed with deep-learning systems in [11–13], especially in distinguishing between malicious and benign files.

3   Methodology

This work proposes a static malware classification system that can detect and classify non-packed executables. To classify a malicious sample, the system elaborates a fingerprint representation of the executable, using static analysis applied to a processed function call graph. In particular, this fingerprinting mechanism encodes the high-level behavioral features of the user-defined functions in the graph by collecting their respective library function calls. Moreover, it captures their relationships by compressing and clustering the structural graph information.

The system is composed of four processing modules: *(i) Pre-processing*, where the input executable is scanned to resolve all its user-defined and library functions. *(ii) Analysis*, which constructs the graph by using all the functions information collected in the previous phase. *(iii) Feature Extraction*, which computes the fingerprint of the graph. *(iv) Classification*, in which a learning model produces a label that can be used to classify executable graph fingerprints.

Each module will be further discussed in the following sections.

3.1   Pre-processing and Analysis

These two phases are devoted to graph construction. First, we distinguish library functions from user-defined ones. We minimize conflicts between library names by finding those wrongly characterized as user-defined functions and renaming them back to their original symbol in the executable. We used Ghidra and function databases to find as many library functions as possible, both statically and dynamically linked. In particular, the pre-processing module executes the following steps: *(i)* it performs signatures matching of the function by using Ghidra; *(ii)* it retrieves wrongly attributed user-defined function calls under library functions; *(iii)* it removes or renames the found results. The pre-processing module produces a list of user-defined functions and a set of library functions.

The analysis phase aims to construct the graph for a given sample by using this output. A graph is so defined: nodes represent user-defined functions, edges represent calls between said functions, and attributes represent library functions used by that node. This representation differs from other works in literature [14–17]. By not considering library functions as nodes but their attributes, we have two advantages: *(i)* the graph size is reduced, as all the calls involving library functions do not appear as node/edge pairs; *(ii)* libraries are treated as general operational characteristics of each function written by who developed the program. In this way, each node provides a general description of how each user-defined function operates.

3.2 Feature Extraction

The feature extraction module aims to encode and compress the processed graph information returned by the analysis stage. The final output is a compact matrix that retains the structure of the graph along with its attribute information, generating a so-called *malware behavior fingerprint*.

Background on Graphs and MinHash. The main components used to generate a fingerprint are graph theory and *MinHashing*. Given a graph $G = (V, E)$ where $V = \{v_1, v_2, ..., v_n\}$ is the set of nodes and $E = \{\{x, y\}|x, y \in V\}$ is the set of edges that link nodes together, the adjacency matrix A of G is defined as a square matrix $|V| \times |V|$ where $A_{i,j} = 1$ *if* $\{v_i, v_j\} \in E$ *else* $A_{i,j} = 0$.

From the adjacency matrix it is possible to extract the neighborhood N_{v_x} of a given node v_x, or in other words all the nodes directly adjacent with it, defined as $N_{v_x} = \{v_y|A_{x,y} \neq 0\}$.

Each node v_i can have a variable length set of attributes. $f(v_i) = \{l_1, .., l_x\}$. A graph signal can be defined as a vector s where $|s| = n$ and is defined as $[f(v_1)\ f(v_2)\ ...\ f(v_n)]^T$.

MinHash (or the min-wise independent permutations locality sensitive hashing scheme) is a technique for estimating the similarity of two sets. Its use in malware analysis has been initially introduced by Raff et al. [6]. It is considered as an approximation of the Jaccard similarity, which given two sets A, B is defined as $J(A, B) = \frac{|A \cap B|}{|A \cup B|}$.

The MinHash computation relies on the use of an hash functions h applied to m permutations of an input x such that:

$$MinHash_m(x) = [min(h(perm_i(x)))|i \in (1,m)] = [m_1, m_2, ..., m_m] \quad (1)$$

Given two sets A, B, we have that:

$$Pr[MinHash_m(A) = MinHash_m(B)] \simeq J(A,B) \quad (2)$$

In other words, the Jaccard similarity between two sets can be estimated by counting the common elements of their respective MinHash signature divided by the signature length. Another valuable property of MinHash is that multiple MinHashes can be merged, as long as they use the same permutation matrix. The resultant MinHash will capture the similarity-related properties of both. The merging operation consists in taking the minimum between each element of the MinHash signatures to be merged:

$$Merge(MinHash_m(A), MinHash_m(B))$$
$$= [min(m_{1_A}, m_{1_B}), ..., min(m_{m_A}, m_{m_B})] \quad (3)$$

Fingerprint Generation. A malware graph generated, as explained in the previous section, can be read as $G = (V, E)$, where the nodes in V are all the user-defined functions; the edges in E represent whether there is a call relationship between a node and another; the graph signal s contains the variable-length sets of strings $f(v_i)$ of library function names l_i that belong to each node. This information can be summed up into the adjacency matrix A of a malware sample and its graph signal s.

At the end of the feature extraction process, these two elements are compressed in a low sized $k \times m$ matrix F that we call fingerprint. The fingerprint extraction process follows these steps: *(i)* It computes the MinHash with m permutations of the attributes of each node; *(ii)* It merges the MinHashes of the nodes in each neighborhood; *(iii)* It performs a distributed merging of the MinHashes of each neighborhood; *(iv)* It selects k resultant MinHash signatures.

First, a MinHashing function $MinHash_m(x)$ (where m are the chosen number of permutations) is used to generate an embedding transformation $\hat{s}$ of a graph signal s of a given malware graph G with number of nodes $n = |V|$:

$$\hat{s} = \begin{bmatrix} MinHash_m(f(v_1)) \\ ... \\ MinHash_m(f(v_n)) \end{bmatrix} = \begin{bmatrix} \hat{f}(v_1) \\ ... \\ \hat{f}(v_n) \end{bmatrix} = \begin{bmatrix} m_{1,1} & m_{1,2} & ... & m_{1,m} \\ ... & ... & ... & ... \\ m_{n,1} & m_{n,2} & ... & m_{n,m} \end{bmatrix} \quad (4)$$

Since the MinHashing function returns a vector of fixed size m, we obtain that, at the end of this first process, the transformed $\hat{s}$ assumes a uniform shape of $n \times m$. Instead of the raw s that had its respective $f(v_i)$ as a set of strings, its transformed version $\hat{s}$ contains now $\hat{f}(v_i)$ that are m sized vectors of real numbers. In addition, thanks to the properties of MinHash, these vectors preserve the similarity of sets of library function calls with similar content, such that nodes having similar attributes reflect in similar vectors.

The second step aggregates the attributes of the neighborhood of each node by merging all the $\widehat{f}(v_i)$ of each N_{v_i}:

$$\widetilde{s} = \begin{bmatrix} Merge(\{\widehat{f}(v_i)|v_i \in N_{v_1}\}) \\ ... \\ Merge(\{\widehat{f}(v_i)|v_i \in N_{v_n}\})] \end{bmatrix} = \begin{bmatrix} \widetilde{f}(v_1) \\ ... \\ \widetilde{f}(v_n) \end{bmatrix} \tag{5}$$

The purpose of this operation is to compress the graph by considering the neighborhoods as nodes, thus reducing the overall structural complexity. This results in more descriptive signatures, which capture library function call sequences of complex node structures.

The last two steps produce the fingerprint F by merging all the information of the neighborhoods' MinHash signatures and keeping only k of the n signatures. The result is a compressed $k \times m$ matrix that retains the information of all neighborhoods while keeping only a small number of signatures. In order to follow a common way of merging all the neighborhood signatures together, each column of $\widetilde{s}$ is sorted. This is equivalent to merging each row i with the merge of all the signatures below it[1]. This operation synthesizes the common and distinctive characteristics of different node clusters, resulting in fingerprints that preserve similar dispositions of coefficients.

3.3   Classification

As the fingerprint for a given malware sample is constructed as an ensemble of MinHash signatures that embed the attributes of complex node clusters in its function call graph, a custom similarity metric between two fingerprints can be easily formulated as the average Jaccard similarity estimate between each of their MinHash signatures:

$$similarity(F_1, F_2) = \frac{1}{k} \sum_1^k Pr[F_{1_k} = F_{2_k}] \tag{6}$$

Malware samples of different sizes result in fingerprints with a number of signatures related to their graph structural complexity. In order not to consider padding, which could influence the similarity estimate, the metric is always computed on the region of coefficients of a size common to both fingerprints under comparison. This is possible because fingerprints follow the same disposition of coefficients after the last merging operation. We chose to classify fingerprint data using a Support Vector Machine that uses the similarity formulation as its custom kernel function.

---

[1] It derives from the equation3, as the merging operation of MinHash signatures takes the minimum between each element of each signature.

4   Experimental Evaluation

In this section, we provide the experimental results attained according to the methodology described in Sect. 3. First, we elaborate on the dataset employed for this evaluation. Then, we describe the detection results for the malware families belonging to the dataset. Finally, we discuss the robustness of the proposed system against possible evasion strategies.

Dataset. We used a dataset composed of 5735 ×86 Windows malware samples gathered from VirusTotal[2] in 2018. The malicious samples are organized in 20 popular families, whose composition is shown in Table 1. Additionally, we gathered another set of 784 benign ×86 executables from the Dike Dataset[3]. We selected malicious families from a larger dataset of 20, 000 samples as they did not show any evident traces of packers. In this way, we ensured that static analysis was not disrupted by the presence of strong obfuscation. We inspected each sample by using the popular tool PeID[4] to identify common packers. The table also reports the average number of nodes per family and its standard deviation. Note how each family features its specific node distribution.

Table 1. Number of samples, average number of nodes, and of neighbors for each malware family.

Family	#samples	#nodes ± σ	#neighbors ± σ	Family	#samples	#nodes ± σ	#neighbors ± σ
upatre	653	8.52 ± 17.68	0.60 ± 0.51	beebone	35	1610.0 ± 0.0	2.82 ± 0.0
shipup	631	27.33 ± 19.18	0.76 ± 0.19	downloadguide	23	811.91 ± 3.36	0.98 ± 0.01
sivis	615	43.53 ± 13.64	0.96 ± 0.43	tempedreve	21	6.0 ± 0.0	1.0 ± 0.0
autoit	611	1641.78 ± 255.51	2.75 ± 0.37	zbot	17	20.53 ± 31.74	0.75 ± 0.15
virlock	514	2.10 ± 1.06	0.04 ± 0.18	virut	17	306.94 ± 693.56	1.16 ± 0.58
ausiv	504	36.00 ± 0.00	0.72 ± 0.00	installmonster	17	1411.18 ± 5259.96	1.82 ± 0.21
gepys	496	30.00 ± 26.98	1.05 ± 0.22	miniduke	14	275.86 ± 137.04	0.56 ± 0.18
installcore	480	296.13 ± 24.72	1.59 ± 0.09	elemental	13	255.23 ± 45.26	1.23 ± 0.18
qqpass	220	1126.00 ± 0.00	1.46 ± 0.00	dapato	13	76.23 ± 56.23	1.42 ± 0.22
zusy	39	1524.5 ± 2522.04	0.58 ± 0.56	adposhel	13	138.69 ± 13.04	0.44 ± 0.04

Results. The whole system has been entirely developed in Python 3. We established and optimized the parameters of the Support Vector Machines with a custom kernel ($C = 1$ - see Sect. 3.3) by employing a 5-fold cross-validation. Then, we carried out two experiments: *(i) malware detection*, where the system is trained to detect benign and malicious samples (binary classification); *(ii) family classification*, where our dataset is only composed of malicious families, and the goal is to distinguish each malware family. We evaluated the performances of our model by randomly splitting our dataset in both experiments with an 80-20 proportion between training and test. We repeated this process

[2] https://www.virustotal.com.

[3] https://github.com/iosifache/DikeDataset.

[4] https://github.com/wolfram77web/app-peid.

five times to avoid any bias in the evaluation due to random splitting. We then built the average ROC curves (for family classification, we reported the ROC for the most popular families for clarity) and calculated the average F1 scores.

The attained results are reported in Fig. 1. Our system obtained excellent results in malware detection ($Precision = 97.4\%$; $Recall = 95.4\%$; $F1score = 95.8\%$) and auspicious ones in family classification ($Precision = 89.8\%$; $Recall = 85.2\%$; $F1score = 83.6\%$). Notably, we could not find other state-of-the-art tools that could be tested with the same dataset that we used. Thus, we plan to expand our analysis by testing our system on datasets used in other works.

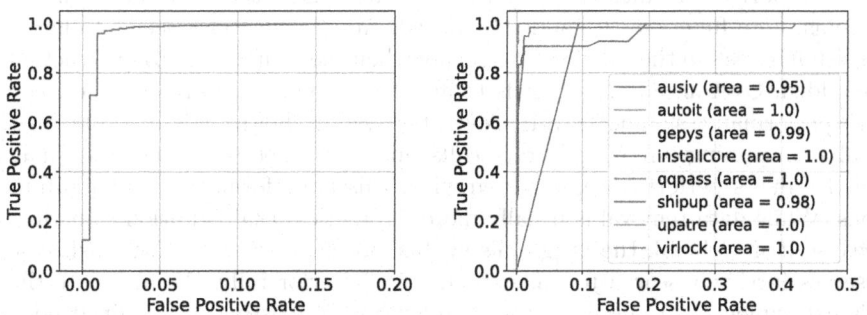

Fig. 1. *ROCs for malware detection (left) and family classification (right).*

We carried out our analysis on a Xeon X5660, 47 GB of RAM, and Debian 10. In this environment, our system timings performances were overall encouraging: the average time to completely analyze a single sample is less than a minute. Unsurprisingly, the most time-consuming step was graph computation.

As a final note, we observe that our preliminary evaluation and data are affected by both temporal and spatial bias that may affect the performances of our system [18,19]. The temporal bias can be mitigated in future work by re-organizing the training data so that it is always prior (in terms of release date) to the test data. The spatial bias can be mitigated by extending the dataset by significantly increasing the number of benign files to better reflect the real proportion of malicious and benign samples in the wild.

Evasion. In this experiment, we explored the performances of our system in terms of robustness against evasive attacks. We present a scenario in which the attacker does not know the characteristics of the targeted system (black-box scenario, according to the taxonomy described by [20]). The only information held by the attacker is that the system employs MinHash-based fingerprinting. We emphasize that this threat model was chosen referring to typical adversarial learning approaches. We acknowledge, however, that the attacker may have access to source code more often than not if this premise is void.

A viable strategy for the attacker would be to modify directly *library functions*, which constitute an essential component of our system, and which are used by all the analyzed malware samples. To this end, we calculated and ordered the most occurrent library functions in the whole dataset by considering the ones that appeared in at least the 75% of the data. From this analysis, we obtained 200 library functions. Then, we analyzed two scenarios: (i) *Function Addition*, where we incrementally removed the 200 most occurrent functions (starting from the most occurrent) from *all nodes* of each sample; (ii) *Function Removal*, where we incrementally removed the 200 most occurrent functions (starting from the most occurrent) from *all nodes* of each sample.

We report the results in Fig. 2, where we document the variation of the F1-score as more functions are added/removed. Adding functions seems to have a consistent effect on the classifier, especially when the 30 most occurrent functions are added. Overall, adding 50 calls to all nodes is enough to reduce the classifier's performance significantly. However, the system shows intriguing robustness results concerning removing library calls since this operation does not damage the classifier's performance, not even when this is performed with many functions. While data removal is usually more unpractical than addition to perform because it may break the program's syntax, we argue that the attained result deserves further research to understand this behavior fully. We also note that this experiment only discusses the modification of existing user-defined nodes by evaluating the impact of library function calls in existing user-defined nodes. Hence, we did not consider adding or removing user-defined nodes (by using, e.g., dead code injection or CFG flattening).

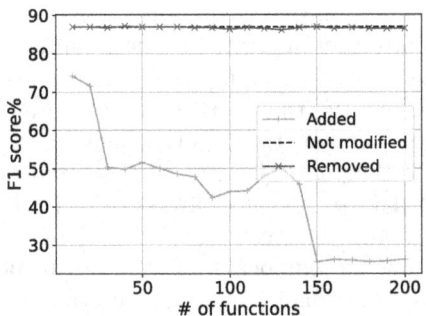

Fig. 2. *Variation of F1 score when two evasion strategies target the SVM.*

5   Conclusions and Future Work

This extended abstract proposed a novel learning-based approach to classify ×86 malware for the Windows platform. We identified each malware sample with a specific fingerprint generated from the call graph calculated on the user-defined functions, and we used library functions as attributes of the graph nodes. Our preliminary results are promising in terms of detection accuracy and show some uncommon robustness properties. However, there are also various limitations that we plan to address in a further extension of this work: *(i)* Our system has not been tested against packed executables; *(ii)* The amount of benign samples is limited in comparison to malicious samples (spatial bias); *iii* Training and test data are not temporarily organized (temporal bias); *(iv)* We did not explore the use of deep learning approaches as alternatives for detection; *(v)* We did not explore the addition/removal of user-defined nodes as a way to evade the system detection.

Acknowledgements. This work was partially supported by the project PON AIM Research and Innovation 2014–2020 - Attraction and International Mobility, funded by the Italian Ministry of Education, University and Research.

References

1. Malware Bytes: State of malware report (2021)
2. Nari, S., Ghorbani, A.: Automated malware classification based on network behavior, pp. 642–647 (2013)
3. Lin, C.-T., Wang, N.-J., Xiao, H., Eckert, C.: Feature selection and extraction for malware classification. J. Inf. Sci. Eng. **31**, 965–992 (2015)
4. Mohaisen, A., Alrawi, O., Mohaisen, M.: AMAL: high-fidelity, behavior-based automated malware analysis and classification. Comput. Secur. **52**, 251–266 (2015)
5. Ahmadi, M., Ulyanov, D., Semenov, S., Trofimov, M., Giacinto, G.: Novel feature extraction, selection and fusion for effective malware family classification. In: Proceedings of CODASPY 2016, pp. 183–194. ACM (2016)
6. Raff, E., Nicholas, C.: An alternative to NCD for large sequences, Lempel-Ziv Jaccard distance. In: Proceedings of KDD 2017, pp. 1007–1015. ACM (2017)
7. Ucci, D., Aniello, L., Baldoni, R.: Survey of machine learning techniques for malware analysis. Comput. Secur. **81**, 123–147 (2019)
8. Ye, Y., Li, T., Adjeroh, D., Iyengar, S.S.: A survey on malware detection using data mining techniques. ACM Comput. Surv. **50**, 1–40 (2017)
9. Raff, E., Barker, J., Sylvester, J., Brandon, R., Catanzaro, B., Nicholas, C.K.: Malware detection by eating a whole exe. In: AAAI Workshops (2018)
10. Sikorski, M., Honig, A.: Practical Malware Analysis: The Hands-On Guide to Dissecting Malicious Software, 1st edn. No Starch Press, San Francisco (2012)
11. Raff, E., Sylvester, J., Nicholas, C.: Learning the PE Header, Malware Detection with Minimal Domain Knowledge, pp. 121–132. ACM, USA (2017)
12. Nataraj, L., Yegneswaran, V., Porras, P., Zhang, J.: A comparative assessment of malware classification using binary texture analysis and dynamic analysis. In: Proceedings of AISec 2011, pp. 21–30. ACM, USA (2011)
13. Yakura, H., Shinozaki, S., Nishimura, R., Oyama, Y., Sakuma, J.: Malware analysis of imaged binary samples by convolutional neural network with attention mechanism. In: Proceedings of CODASPY 2018, pp. 127–134. ACM, USA (2018)
14. Yan, J., Yan, G., Jin, D.: Classifying malware represented as control flow graphs using deep graph convolutional neural network. In: DSN 2019, pp. 52–63 (2019)
15. Jiang, H., Turki, T., Wang, J.T.L.: DLGraph: malware detection using deep learning and graph embedding. In: Proceedings of ICMLA 2018, pp. 1029–1033 (2018)

16. Shang, S., Zheng, N., Xu, J., Xu, M., Zhang, H.: Detecting malware variants via function-call graph similarity. In: Proceedings of MALWARE 2010, pp. 113–120 (2010)

17. Mirzazadeh, R., Moattar, M.H., Jahan, M.V.: Metamorphic malware detection using linear discriminant analysis and graph similarity. In: Proceedings of ICCKE 2015, pp. 61–66 (2015)

18. Dos and don'ts of machine learning in computer security. In: 31st USENIX Security Symposium (USENIX Security 22). USENIX Association, Boston, August 2022

19. Pendlebury, F., Pierazzi, F., Jordaney, R., Kinder, J., Cavallaro, L.: TESSERACT: eliminating experimental bias in malware classification across space and time. In: 28th USENIX Security Symposium (USENIX Security 19), pp. 729–746. USENIX Association, Santa Clara August 2019

20. Biggio, B., Roli, F.: Wild patterns: ten years after the rise of adversarial machine learning. Pattern Recogn. **84**, 317–331 (2018)

COBRA-GCN: Contrastive Learning to Optimize Binary Representation Analysis with Graph Convolutional Networks

Michael Wang[✉], Alexander Interrante-Grant, Ryan Whelan, and Tim Leek

MIT Lincoln Laboratory, Lexington, USA
{michael.wang,ainterr,rwhelan,tleek}@ll.mit.edu

Abstract. The ability to quickly identify whether two binaries are similar is critical for many security applications, with use cases ranging from triaging millions of novel malware samples, to identifying whether a binary contains a known exploitable bug. There have been many program analysis approaches to solving this problem, however, most machine learning approaches in the last 5 years have focused on function similarity, and there have been no techniques released that are able to perform robust many to many comparisons of full programs. In this paper, we present the first machine learning approach capable of learning a robust representation of programs based on their similarity, using a combination of supervised natural language processing and graph learning. We name our prototype COBRA: Contrastive Learning to Optimize Binary Representation Analysis. We evaluate our model on several different metrics for program similarity, such as compiler optimizations, code obfuscations, and different pieces of semantically similar source code. Our approach outperforms current techniques for full binary diffing, achieving an F1 score and AUC .6 and .12, respectively, higher than BinDiff while also having the ability to perform many-to-many comparisons.

Keywords: Graph learning · Binary code · Similarity

DISTRIBUTION STATEMENT. Approved for public release. Distribution is unlimited. This material is based upon work supported by the Department of Defense under Air Force Contract No. FA8702-15-D-0001. Any opinions, findings, conclusions or recommendations expressed in this material are those of the author(s) and do not necessarily reflect the views of the Department of Defense. Delivered to the U.S. Government with Unlimited Rights, as defined in DFARS Part 252.227-7013 or 7014 (Feb 2014). Notwithstanding any copyright notice, U.S. Government rights in this work are defined by DFARS 252.227-7013 or DFARS 252.227-7014 as detailed above. Use of this work other than as specifically authorized by the U.S. Government may violate any copyrights that exist in this work.

1   Introduction

Detecting similar files is often used for tasks such as malware triage [30,34], patch analysis [23,26], and bug search [12,16–19,24]. However, identifying binary code similarity is very challenging – much of the program semantics can be lost during the compilation process. Many compiler optimizations such as function inlining will drastically change the syntax and structure of a binary even with the same source code. Figure 1 shows the *addr2line* program compiled with two different compilers and two different optimizations. As you can see, different compiler settings can cause identical source code to appear dramatically different at the binary level.

There has been a recent explosion in machine learning approaches to solve this issue. According to a recent survey of binary similarity techniques [28], 7/12 of the binary similarity papers since 2018 have been machine learning based, as opposed to 4/28 of the papers in the 3 years prior. However, recent solutions focus on one-to-one comparisons, and do not have the ability to perform efficient one-to-many or many-to-many comparisons of full programs.

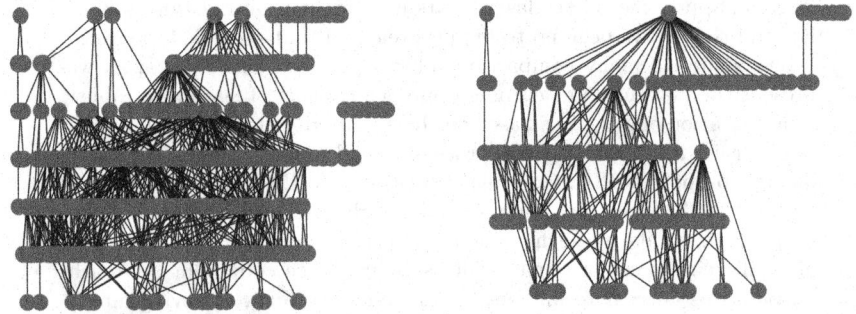

Fig. 1. Addr2line call graph compiled with two different optimizations and compilers. GCC and O0 on the left, Clang and Os on the right.

There are various levels of comparison granularity – some approaches only work at the function level, others only work with full programs. Additionally, there are various levels of comparisons – one-to-one, one-to-many, and many-to-many. One-to-one comparisons are often used for *binary code diffing* – they diff two different programs in order to determine the level of similarity. One-to-many comparisons compare one *query* piece of code to many target pieces of code in order to perform tasks such as bug searches. Many-to-many comparisons do not distinguish between source and target pieces. All inputs are considered equal, and many-to-many approaches often output *clusters* of similar binaries. In order to perform several tasks, such as malware clustering and triage, efficient many-to-many comparisons are needed. While one-to-one approaches could be used pairwise across an entire dataset to perform a one-to-many or many-to-many comparison, most one-to-many and many-to-many approaches avoid this due to inefficiency. None of the recent machine learning techniques are able to perform robust many to many matching at the full program level. We solve this problem by learning an *embedding*, i.e., a vector of numbers, for full programs. Similarity between two programs can be measured efficiently by taking the distance between their embeddings, allowing for fast one-to-many and many-to-many comparisons.

Approach. We propose a supervised siamese graph convolutional network to learn an embedding for a full program's call graph. Our approach has several stages. First, we learn embeddings for individual assembly instructions. Next, we aggregate these instruction embeddings to generate an embedding for a full function. Finally, we combine these function embeddings with the full program's call graph to generate an embedding for a full program. These embeddings contain information from both the function semantics as well as the full call graph structure. The primary benefit in utilizing function and instruction embeddings is the modularity - we can easily swap out the function and instruction similarity components for newer techniques as the field progresses. A full overview of our approach in action can be seen in Fig. 2.

We implement a prototype, COBRA, and conduct an evaluation on a program similarity dataset consisting of both compiler optimizations as well as obfuscations containing more than 8000 binaries. We also evaluate on more than 40,000 binaries from Google Code Jam, an annual programming competition. Binaries from Google Code Jam are different at both the source and binary level, making similarity detection much more difficult. Our evaluation shows that we outperform state of the art binary diffing tool BinDiff as well as locality sensitive hashing algorithms TLSH, SSDeep, SDHash.

Contributions. The contributions of this paper are as follows:

- We propose a supervised algorithm to learn robust representations for full programs. We leverage both natural language processing and graph learning techniques in order to generate high quality embeddings for full call graphs. To the best of our knowledge, it is the first supervised model able to perform many to many comparisons on full programs based on program similarity.
- We implement a prototype, COBRA, which takes as input a full binary and generates an embedding. It starts by learning embeddings for assembly instructions using fastText [9]. Next, it learns embeddings for functions using a bidirectional Recurrent Neural Network. Finally, we train a graph convolutional network [32] on the program's call graph which has been enriched with the previously learned function embeddings to learn an embedding for the full program.
- We show that our approach is able to outperform state-of-the-art binary diffing tools for cross-optimization, obfuscation, and different source code. In addition, we show that our model is capable of performing higher level tasks efficiently, such as clustering.
- We provide a brief comparison of Word2vec [39] and fastText [9]. Word2Vec has been a very popular method of representing instructions in the literature, but we believe fastText provides more robust representations for instructions.

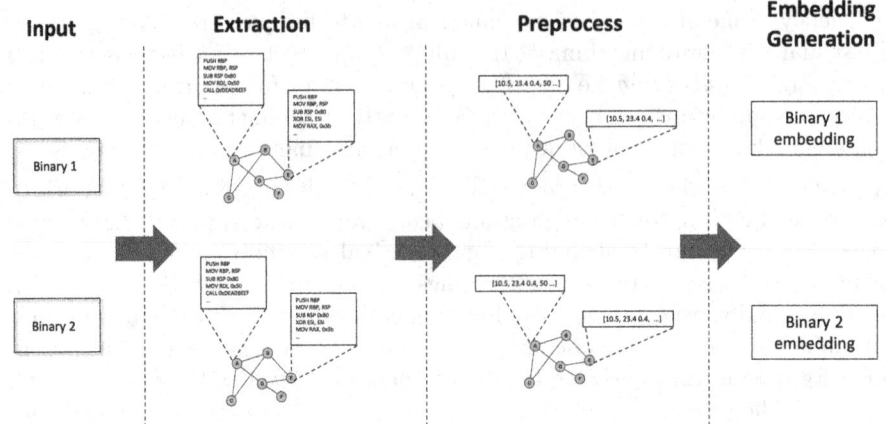

Fig. 2. An overview of COBRA.

2   Related Work

Non-learning Based Binary Similarity. One common technique to identify similar files is a similarity digest or "hash" [15,33,42,46,50]. This technique is commonly known as locality sensitive hashing or fuzzy hashing. These hashing functions convert a large byte string into a smaller, unique string similar to cryptographic hashes such as MD5 or SHA-1. However, locality sensitive hashing algorithms are designed to generate similar hashes for similar inputs. Thus, to quantify the similarity between two files, we can compare the similarity between their respective hashes rather than needing to compare the files themselves. The ability to generate a hash is extremely useful for malware triage, as it is much less computationally expensive to compare hashes and allows analysts to identify similar pieces of malware. Antivirus tools and engines such as VirusTotal [6] can generate the locality sensitive hash for a piece of malware once, and then use that hash in perpetuity to compare that piece of malware to other samples. Despite the widespread adoption of locality sensitive hashing algorithms, their effectiveness has been called into question by Pagani *et al.* [43]. Their results show that fuzzy hashes work well primarily due to matching the *.data* section, as the *.data* section often remains unchanged through compiler optimizations and obfuscations.

Other research approaches perform binary diffing using various data structures. BinDiff [1] performs graph isomorphism detection and matches basic blocks as well as functions. BinGold [7] extracts a novel data structure called a *semantic flow graph* using the data-flow graph as well as the control flow graph and uses several metrics such as graph edit distance for function similarity. Several approaches generate function signatures [51,54] for cross platform bug searches and patch detection. Another technique uses light emulation to generate traces, and performs a simple jaccard index on the traces of two functions in order to determine their similarity [12,29,55]. Additionally, Bingo [12] and Bingo-E [55] perform selective inlining of callee functions. In other words, when their target function calls another function, they inline the assembly of the called function to ensure that it's semantics are captured. Another common technique is to decompose a binary into *strands* - small sequences of instructions after a binary has been lifted into an intermediate representation [16–18], then find matching strands between two binaries. COP2017 [36] has the ability to perform comparisons of full programs, but is only able to perform one-to-one matching by taking the longest common subsequence of basic blocks.

Learning Based Binary Similarity. There have also been many learning-based approaches towards the problem of code diffing and similarity detection. However, many of these over the past five years focus on function similarity. According to Haq *et al.*, only 1/11 learning-based approaches are effective on full programs. DeepBinDiff [22], uses Text Associated DeepWalk [56] to learn embeddings for individual basic blocks. SAFE [38] uses a self-attentive recurrent neural network to generate function embeddings. ASM2Vec [21] learns a representation for functions using PV-DM [40] by converting each function into multiple sequences based on its control flow graph and using selective callee expansion. InnerEye [59] uses neural machine translation to generate embeddings for basic blocks. αdiff [35] combines two function's raw bytes, call graph, and imports to generate a similarity score between the two functions. Gemini [53] converts basic blocks into a vector of handcrafted features and uses Structure2vec [14] on a function's control flow graph to generate an embedding. Trex [45] first learns assembly instruction semantics by pre-training on sequences of assembly instructions similar to BERT [20] before finetuning on function pairs.

Malware Clustering. A common use of full program similarity is malware clustering and categorization. Clustering requires the ability to perform many to many comparisons. AMCS [57] uses instruction frequency and function based instruction sequences for categorization and clustering. Rieck *et al.* [49] clusters malware based on the reports generated from executing malware in CWSandbox. EC2 [11] uses ensemble clustering and classification on both static and dynamic features to generate malware clusters. Zhuang *et al.* [58] clusters websites together with malware binaries by using term frequency for websites and instruction frequency for binaries with an ensemble clustering scheme. Firma [47] clusters based on network traffic after executing malware in a sandbox. Bayer *et al.* [8] uses taint tracing to generate an execution trace for a piece of malware after executing in a sandbox, and then clusters with Jaccard Distance and Cosine Similarity.

3   Approach

3.1   Approach Overview

The full system can be broken down into the following stages. Each stage requires separate preprocessing before training:

1. *Assembly Instruction Embeddings*: We leverage fastText to learn embeddings to encapsulate similarities between single instructions.
2. *Function Embeddings*: We feed in a function represented as a sequence of instruction embeddings to a bidirectional recurrent neural network in order to generate embeddings for functions. Our approach is based largely off of SAFE[38].
3. *Call Graph Embeddings*: We first annotate each vertex of the program's call graph with the embedding for that function. We then feed this annotated call graph into a siamese graph convolutional network in order to generate embeddings for full programs.

3.2   Assembly Instruction Embeddings

In the first stage of our system, we learn an embedding $\vec{i}$ for each instruction i such that $\vec{i} \in \mathbb{R}^n$.

Preprocessing. Before training, we preprocess all instructions to reduce the vocabulary size. We process instructions very similarly to SAFE [38]. We replace all base memory addresses with the special symbol *MEM* and all immediate values whose absolute value is above 500 with the special symbol *IMM*. We then concatenate the mnemonic and operands into a single string after performing this filtering. Several examples are detailed below.

$$MOV\ EAX,\ 600\ \rightarrow\ MOVEAXIMM$$

$$MOV\ EAX,\ [0xdeadbeef]\ \rightarrow\ MOVEAXMEM$$

$$MOV\ EAX,\ [EBP+4]\ \rightarrow\ MOVEAX[EBP+4].$$

We implement this step using Ghidra to extract instructions before preprocessing.

fastText. Almost all machine learning models which generate instruction level embeddings use Word2vec [21,22,38,48,59]. However, Duan *et al.* showed in DeepBinDiff [22] that a Word2vec model trained on CoreUtils v8.29 compiled with gcc could only generate embeddings for 78.37% of instructions on Core-Utils v8.29 compiled with clang. In other words, 21.63% of instructions cannot be modeled on the same source code when a different compiler is used. Deep-Bindiff and some other algorithms solve this by modeling opcodes and operands separately. However, we feel that this limits the vocabulary size too much. In order to remedy these problems, we use fastText. We find that fastText offers both improved performance as well as the ability to generate embeddings for words that are not in the vocabulary. To the best of our knowledge, this is the first paper to use fastText to generate assembly instruction embeddings.

The primary difference between fastText and Word2vec is the use of character n-grams. Word2vec treats each word as an atomic unit, and can only learn embeddings for complete words. *MOV EAX 0x1* is treated as a completely separate word to *MOV EAX 0x2* despite being very similar, both using the same opcode and operand. However, fastText captures this relationship by learning embeddings for the n-grams that are within a word. For example, the word *MOVEAX1* and $n = 3$ can be broken down into the following ngrams:

$$<MO, MOV, OVE, VEA, EAX, AX1, X1>$$

as well as the special sequence

$$<MOVEAX1>.$$

The <and> signs are to denote the beginning and end of the sequence. For fastText, the distance between two words is an aggregate metric between their n-grams, as opposed to treating the entire word as an atomic unit. We find this beneficial for two reasons:

1. Semantically similar instructions will often have the same mnemonics and registers. In the example above, *MOV EAX 0x2* has many of the same n-grams as *MOV EAX 0x1* that are captured, whereas Word2vec treats them both as completely separate units. While there are cases in which Word2vec performs better, such as *MOV RAX 0* and *XOR RAX, RAX*, we have anecdotally observed these to be less common.
2. fastText is able to generate embeddings for out-of-vocabulary words by taking the seen n-grams of the word. Because Word2vec treats words as an atomic unit, it cannot generate embeddings for words that is has not seen during training. Given that there are a very large number of potential assembly instructions and the generated assembly instructions are often dependent on compilers, we find this to be an important characteristic.

3.3   Function Embeddings

In the second stage of our system, we learn an embedding $\vec{f}$ for each function f such that $\vec{f} \in \mathbb{R}^n$. We represent each function f as a sequence of instruction embeddings $\vec{i}$, and feed that into a bidirectional recurrent neural network with a siamese architecture. Using this, we are able to generate similarity-preserving embeddings which capture the semantic behavior of functions.

Siamese Architecture. The embedding model parameters are learned using a pairwise approach and a siamese architecture. At training time, the model is fed two functions $f1$, $f2$ separately, and outputs an embedding for each function. The functions can then be determined to be similar or different by calculating their cosine similarity with the formula below:

$$\cos(\vec{f1}, \vec{f2}) = \frac{\vec{f1}\vec{f2}}{\|\vec{f1}\|\|\vec{f2}\|} = \frac{\sum_{i=1}^{n} \vec{f1}_i \vec{f2}_i}{\sqrt{\sum_{i=1}^{n} (\vec{f1}_i)^2}\sqrt{\sum_{i=1}^{n} (\vec{f2}_i)^2}} \tag{1}$$

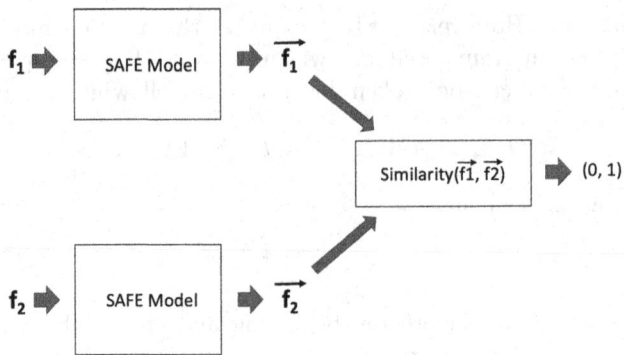

Fig. 3. The SAFE embedding network.

The network is trained using function pairs $< \overrightarrow{f1}, \overrightarrow{f2}>$, and labelled with ground truth $y_i \in \{+1, -1\}$. To train the network, we use the contrastive loss function proposed by Hadsell *et al.* [27] below:

$$L(Y, \overrightarrow{f1}, \overrightarrow{f2}) = (1 - Y)\frac{1}{2}(D_w)^2 + (Y)\frac{1}{2}\{max(0, m - D_w)\}^2 \qquad (2)$$

where D_w is defined as the cosine similarity between $\overrightarrow{f1}$ and $\overrightarrow{f2}$. m is the margin, meaning that dissimilar pairs only contribute to the loss if their euclidean distance is within this radius. An overview of SAFE can be seen in Fig. 3.

3.4   Program Embeddings

Finally, we learn an embedding $\overrightarrow{p}$ for each program p such that $\overrightarrow{p} \in \mathbb{R}^n$. In order to represent the entire program, we use the call graph. We represent each program p as two matrices using it's call graph. The first is an $N \times D$ matrix, where N is the number of functions, and D is the length of features associated with each node. The feature for each node is the function embedding for that node, of length 100 in our case. The second matrix is an adjacency matrix of the call graph.

Intuition. Two similar programs will often have similar call graph structures. There have been multiple efforts to using call graphs in order to determine program similarity [35,52]. However, using only the call graph structure does not encapsulate the contents of the functions themselves. Likewise, taking a purely function-based approach for binary similarity neglects information provided by the structure of the program as a whole. We aim to combine these two approaches by using a graph convolutional network. By annotating each node in the call graph with the embedding for that function, each node contains information about the semantics of that particular function. By passing in the full call graph structure, our model is able to learn from the holistic functionality of the program in order to generate full program embeddings. We then train a graph convolutional network, a model which learns from both node features and graph structure, in order to learn embeddings for full programs.

Graph Convolutional Networks. Traditional convolutional neural networks operate under the assumption that the input is grid-structured as opposed to arbitrarily structured graphs. However, Bruna *et al.* generalized convolutional networks to graphs, applying filters on a graph's frequency modes computed by graph Fourier transform [10]. Since then, graph convolutional networks have evolved and been used for many graph-based data problems, such as protein function prediction [25] and fake news detection [41]. Broadly speaking, graph convolutional networks learn a set of features from a graph taking as input:

- A feature vector x_i for every node i in the form of an $N \times D$ matrix, where N is the number of nodes and D is the number of features.
- The graph structure in matrix form, typically the adjacency matrix.

and outputs an $N \times F$ feature matrix, where F is the number of output features per node. We can then use normal pooling and fully connected layers across the full graph to train a siamese-style network. The high-level siamese architecture of this network is very similar to that of the function embedding network.

4 Datasets

We use four different datasets to train and evaluate our models. We refer to them as the *Android NDK* [3], *X86-SOK* [44], *VCPKG* [5], and *Google Code Jam* [4]. Each dataset contains binaries and functions that appear diverse but perform the same functionality. Our datasets are diversified primarily using compiler optimizations and obfuscations. We remove all duplicate functions as well as functions that do not have names.

Android NDK. The Android NDK is a toolset that allows developers to implement parts of their apps using native-code languages such as C and C++ in order to interact more directly with the kernel or the hardware. It includes a number of example programs for demonstration purposes that we use as a dataset for evaluation. We can compile these while introducing obfuscations from Obfuscator-LLVM [31] to generate software diversity. The obfuscations used are bogus control flow (*BCF*), instruction substitution (*SUB*), and control flow flattening (*FLA*) for a total of 2632 binaries and 27441 functions.:

- **BCF** obfuscates the program by modifying the control flow graph. It adds a large number of irrelevant control flow and basic blocks as well as merging and reordering existing blocks.
- **SUB** replaces standard binary operators with functionally equivalent sequences of instructions. For example, addition can be rewritten as $a = b - (-c)$, and subtraction can be written as $r = rand(); a = b + r; a = a - c; a = a - r$
- **FLA** completely flattens the control flow graph of a function by replacing conditional statements with switches, as well as modifying the instructions for entering and exiting basic blocks.

We can combine these in order to generate heavily obfuscated programs as well as varying the architecture (X86, X86-64).

X86-SOK. We also use the Linux binaries from the dataset provided by Pang *et al.* [44]. It is a dataset compiled with different compilers (GCC-8.1.0, LLVM 6.0.0) and optimizations (O1, O2, O3, O4, Os, Ofast), resulting in 3342 distinct binaries and 971,305 functions. Below are summaries of the optimization levels. More details on the optimization levels can be found on their website [2].

- *O0*: Reduces compilation time and ensures debugging information produces the correct results.
- *O1*: The compiler tries to reduce code size and execution time while minimizing compilation time.
- *O2*: The compiler performs all optimizations that do not involve a space-speed tradeoff. As opposed to *O1*, *O2* increases compilation time.
- *O3*: A superset of *O2* with even more aggressive optimizations enabled.
- *Os*: The compiler enables all optimizations except those that increase the code size.
- *Ofast*: The compiler enables all optimizations from *O3*, as well as additional options to increase speed.

VCPKG. VCPKG is a tool developed by Microsoft that acts as a package manager for various open-source libraries written in C and C++. We downloaded a dataset of 446 programs and compiled with MSVC with various optimizations(O1, O2, Od, Ox, Os) for a total of 2230 binaries and 20970 functions. All programs are 64 bit. Below are summaries of the optimization levels. More details about the optimizations can be found on their website [13].

- *O1*: The compiler creates the smallest code size possible.
- *O2*: The compiler optimizes for maximum speed.
- *Od*: The compiler disables all optimization.
- *Os*: The compiler favors optimizations that reduce size. This is a subset of *O1*.
- *Ox*: The compiler favors optimizations that increase speed. This is a subset of *O2*.

Google Code Jam. Google Code Jam is a programming competition run by Google each year. They are an interesting test case for program similarity - programs that solve the same problem have similar semantics and functionality, but are implemented differently by different authors. Unlike the previous datasets, these samples are different at both the source and binary level. However, because these binaries are much smaller and are meant to only be run from the command line, we consider these samples separate from our other three datasets. There are a total of 41573 unique solutions to 222 problems. Several examples of problems are listed below.

- Given a string of digits *S*, insert a minimum number of opening and closing parentheses into it such that the resulting string is balanced and each digit *d* is inside exactly *d* pairs of matching parentheses.

– Given a number **N** where **N** contains at least one digit that is a *4*, find two numbers *A* and *B* such that neither *A* nor *B* contains any digit that is a 4, and $A + B =$ **N**.

5   Evaluation and Results

5.1   Assembly Embeddings

The assembly instructions are difficult to evaluate objectively, as there does not exist a centralized dataset for comparing assembly instruction similarity. To show how fastText outperforms Word2vec, we generate a small dataset of 5 classes with 10 instructions each, with hand-written labels according to their semantic similarity. We then generate the corresponding embeddings for each, and plot it using *t-SNE* [37], a useful tool for dimensionality reduction. The five classes are *Subtraction instructions, Addition Instructions, XOR instructions, MOV instructions, Stack Operations*.

To evaluate, we generated all pairwise instruction comparisons between our dataset. As seen in a ROC curve in Fig. 4, fastText has a substantially higher AUC of *.93* compared to Word2vec's *.59*, as well as higher precision and recall as shown in Table 1. However, it is important to note that there are certain instructions that Word2Vec performs better on, such as *JZ MEMORY* and *JNZ MEMORY* which are both JUMP instructions. This is unsurprising, as they do not share ngrams. We leave a more robust evaluation of fastText against Word2vec with a larger dataset for future work.

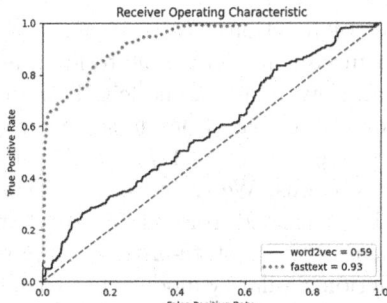

Fig. 4. ROC Curve of fastText compared to Word2vec.

Model	Precision	Recall	F1
fastText	.50	.84	.63
Word2vec	.19	.54	.28

Table 1. Precision and recall of W2V vs. FastText

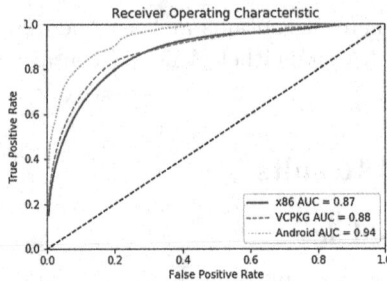

Fig. 5. ROC curves on each of our function datasets.

Dataset	Precision	Recall	F1
Android	.852	.867	.859
X86-SOK	.801	.778	.793
VCPKG	.815	.814	.815

Table 2. Precision and recall on each of our function datasets.

5.2   Function Embeddings

Android NDK, X86-SOK, VCPKG. We train our network on pairs of functions. For every function in our dataset, we generate a similar pair labeled as $+1$ and a dissimilar pair labeled as -1. A similar pair is the same function either compiled with a different optimization or a different obfuscation. A dissimilar pair is a different function entirely. This results in a total number of pairs twice that of our total number of functions. We test our performance on all three datasets separately to ensure our model is able to learn all three, using a 90-10 train-test split to train and evaluate our models. It is important to note that we split our training and test set based on classes before generating the pairs. For example, our dataset might consist of $f1, f2, f3, f4, f5$, where each function has several different versions. We train on pairs generated from functions $f1, f2, f3$ and test on pairs generated from $f4, f5$. We do not evaluate our function embedding model against other state-of-the-art approaches, as our goal is not to outperform all function similarity models, but to outperform full program similarity models. We are able to see in Table 2 as well as in Fig. 5 that our models are able to generate embeddings which capture function similarity, achieving F1 scores of *.859, .793, and .815* on the Android, X86-SOK, and VCPKG datasets respectively.

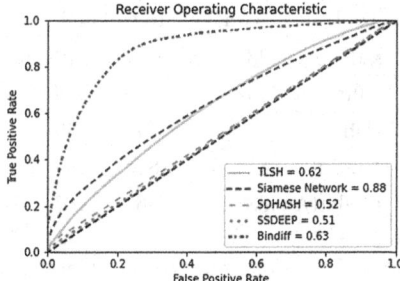

Fig. 6. ROC curves from Google Code Jam functions.

Google Code Jam. We also train and evaluate our function similarity model on the functions extracted from Google Code Jam and compare to some existing approaches. We find that our model is able to outperform some common tools used for program similarity, achieving an AUC of .88 as compared to the next highest of .63 by BinDiff. This suggests that machine learning models are capable of learning a higher level of semantic similarity than existing tools. The functions may not be noticeably similar at the assembly level, making it hard for tools such as *TLSH* which rely on heuristics such as shared instruction ngrams. A ROC curve can be seen in Fig. 6.

5.3   Program Similarity

For the full program similarity embeddings, we use a similar approach to our function embeddings. For each program, we extract the call graph, and annotate each node with the function embedding for that node. Then, for each call graph in our dataset, we generate similar pairs labelled as +1 and dissimilar pairs labelled as −1. Similar to learning our function embeddings, we split our training and test set based on classes before generating the pairs. We perform multiple experiments to test the robustness of our final embeddings:

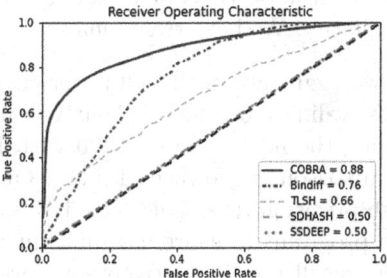

Fig. 7. ROC curve for COBRA compared to Bindiff, TLSH, SDHASH, and SSDEEP for samples from Coreutils.

Tool	Precision	Recall	F1
ssdeep	.33	1	.49
sdhash	.33	.999	.49
tlsh	.46	.54	.60
Bindiff	.81	.81	.81
COBRA	.88	.86	.87

Table 3. Precision and recall for Coreutils.

- We perform 10-fold Cross Validation using the X86-SOK dataset. We report results from the entire dataset, as well as isolating the test samples from GNU Coreutils. We select Coreutils as it is difficult for binary similarity as the programs share large amounts of library functions.
- We train on 90% of the X86-SOK dataset, validate on 10% of the X86-SOK dataset, and test on VCPKG and OLLVM obfuscations
- We perform a 90-10 train-test split on Google Code Jam.
- COBRA is the first tool able to generate many-many comparisons of full programs based on similarity, allowing for additional applications such as clustering. We showcase this using a dimensionality reduction algorithm t-SNE.

Our final model had two convolutional layers with sizes 64 and 32 with reLU activation functions, followed by two dense layers of size 256 and 128 with reLU activation functions. The final layer outputs the final embedding. The model is trained with contrastive loss and optimized with RMSProp on a Volta V100 GPU with 32 GB memory. We evaluate against Bindiff, TLSH, SDHash, and SSDeep. We would have liked to evaluate against COP2017 [36] but the authors did not respond to our email requesting to obtain the tool.

X86-SOK. For the X86-SOK dataset, we use 10-fold Cross Validation, and generated one positive pair and one negative pair during training. During testing, we generated two positive pairs and two negative pairs for each sample to ensure that we had sufficient results. We compared our approach to four existing techniques for binary similarity. We have two scenarios for testing.

- In the first scenario, we aggregate our results over each of our testing splits during our 10-fold cross validation. The ROC curve is shown in Fig. 9. We get .94 AUC, outperforming the next highest of .90 with Bindiff. The precision and recall of each comparison is shown in Table 4. One interesting result is TLSH's relatively high precision rate. This is likely because it is very uncommon for two different programs to share a significant number of instruction n-grams. However, the recall rate is relatively low given that compiler optimizations can cause significant perturbations at times. We also showcase the many-to-many capabilities of our tool by generating a visualization with t-SNE, shown in Fig. 8. We can see that many of the classes are in visibly distinct clusters.

Tool	Metric	O0O1	O0O2	O0O3	O0Os	O0Of	O1O2	O1O3	O1Os	O1Of	O2O3	O2Os	O2Of	O3Os	O3Of	OsOf	Avg
ssdeep	*Precision*	.54	.55	.54	.49	.46	.52	.53	.53	.50	.54	.50	.52	.48	.49	.51	**.51**
	Recall	1.0	1.0	1.0	1.0	1.0	1.0	1.0	1.0	1.0	1.0	1.0	1.0	1.0	1.0	1.0	**1.0**
	F1	.70	.71	.70	.66	.63	.69	.69	.69	.67	.70	.66	.69	.65	.66	.67	**.68**
sdhash	*Precision*	.54	.55	.54	.49	.47	.52	.53	.53	.50	.54	.50	.52	.48	.49	.51	**.51**
	Recall	1.0	1.0	1.0	1.0	1.0	1.0	1.0	1.0	1.0	1.0	1.0	1.0	1.0	1.0	1.0	**1.0**
	F1	.70	.71	.70	.66	.63	.69	.69	.69	.67	.70	.66	.69	.65	.66	.67	**.68**
TLSH	*Precision*	.87	.93	.85	.91	.84	.67	.76	.84	.85	.86	.77	.89	.89	.88	.69	**.83**
	Recall	.49	.59	.57	.50	.59	.77	.81	.68	.70	.60	.53	.60	.51	.74	.86	**.64**
	F1	.63	.72	.68	.65	.69	.72	.78	.75	.77	.71	.63	.71	.65	.80	.77	**.71**
BinDiff	*Precision*	.83	.85	.85	.80	.84	.80	.82	.79	.81	.79	.77	.87	.83	.77	.76	**.81**
	Recall	.80	.73	.71	.88	.76	.87	.84	.89	.85	.89	.92	.61	.80	.93	.94	**.83**
	F1	.82	.78	.77	.84	.80	.83	.83	.84	.83	.84	.84	.72	.81	.84	.84	**.81**
COBRA	*Precision*	.93	.86	.84	.85	.95	.92	.87	.81	.87	.84	.89	.84	.88	.91	.93	**.88**
	Recall	.90	.97	.93	.93	.78	.94	.95	.93	.96	.90	.93	.93	.91	.91	0.91	**.92**
	F1	.91	.91	.88	.89	.86	.93	.91	.87	.91	.87	.91	.88	.89	.91	.92	**.90**

Table 4. Detailed precision and recall across varying levels of optimization.

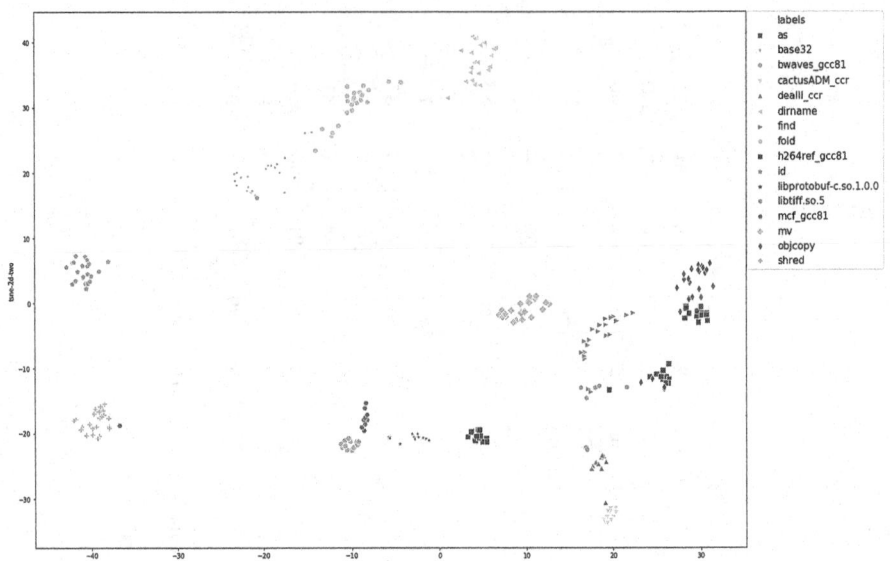

Fig. 8. Final embeddings of X86-SOK dataset with t-SNE.

- In the second scenario, we only test on Coreutils. The ROC curve is shown in Fig. 7. We get .88 AUC, outperforming the next highest of .76 again with BinDiff. The precision and recall is shown in Table 3. COBRA is still able to detect similarity despite Coreutils being notably harder than the rest of the dataset due to the amount of shared code.

Evaluation on Android and VCPKG. A concern of ours was that COBRA was simply memorizing the transformations in our datasets and would be unable to predict any new transformations or obfuscations in the future. In order to ensure that COBRA is capable of generalizing to new, unseen transformations, we train our model on 90% of the X86-SOK dataset, then test on the OLLVM obfuscations as well as Windows binaries. Details of these datasets can be seen in Sect. 4. This ensures that at testing time, the model has to predict whether two binaries are the same even when unseen transformations are applied. Precision, recall, and F1 can be seen in Tables 5 and 6. ROC curves can be seen in Figs. 10 and 11. Even evaluated against unseen transformations, COBRA is able to outperform all one-to-many and many-to-many approaches, and is only slightly worse than BinDiff. It is important to note that BinDiff has a significant advantage over COBRA in that it takes in two programs and directly computes a similarity score, whereas COBRA must learn a generic representation for each program, which is a significantly harder task.

Google Code Jam. Finally, we train and evaluate our model on a selection of 41573 solution files to 222 problems from Google Code Jam. We train it in a similar fashion, except similar samples are two solutions to the same problem, and dissimilar samples are two solutions to different problems. No special inlining

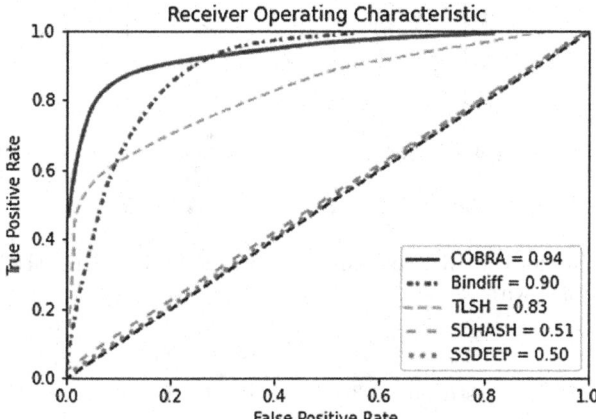

Fig. 9. ROC curve for COBRA compared to bindiff, TLSH, SDHASH, and SSDEEP across the entire X86-SOK dataset.

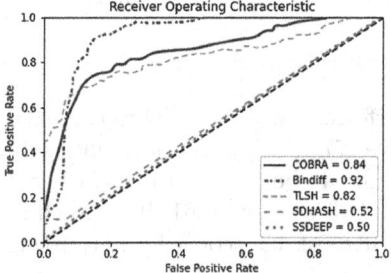

Fig. 10. ROC curve for COBRA compared to BinDiff, TLSH, SDHASH, and SSDEEP across the Android NDK compiled with OLLVM Obfuscations.

Tool	Precision	Recall	F1
ssdeep	.46	1	.63
sdhash	.46	.999	.63
tlsh	.87	.66	.75
COBRA	.77	.86	.81
BinDiff	.86	.91	.89

Table 5. Detailed COBRA precision and recall after being trained on X86-SOK and evaluated on Android.

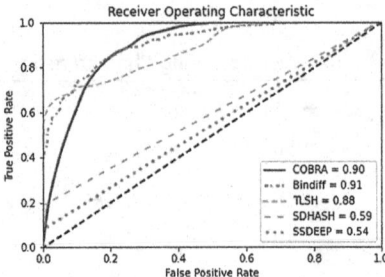

Fig. 11. ROC curve for COBRA compared to BinDiff, TLSH, SDHASH, and SSDEEP on VCPKG compiled with MSVC.

Tool	Precision	Recall	F1
ssdeep	.39	1	.64
sdhash	.48	.999	.64
tlsh	.93	.65	.77
BinDiff	.88	.85	.86
COBRA	.83	.82	.82

Table 6. Detailed COBRA precision and recall after being trained on X86-SOK and evaluated on vcpkg.

or preprocessing was performed with this dataset. A ROC curve can be seen in Fig. 12, where we achieve .77 AUC, outperforming the next highest of BinDiff at .66. Precision and recall can be seen in Table 7, where we achieve an F1 score of .73, outperforming BinDiff's score of .61. It is worth noting that SSDeep and SDHash have the next highest F1 scores by outputting a positive prediction every time.

Predicting whether two binaries are solutions to the same problem is much harder than our previous experiments using compiler optimizations and obfuscations, as the code is no longer identical at the source level. The performance of all tools is notably lower. This is likely both due to the inherent difficulty of the problem as well as the size of the binaries. The solution is implemented in a couple of functions at most, and so binaries are primarily comprised of compiler intrinsics and library functions, making it much harder to differentiate between classes at the binary level. However, we still believe these are promising results that our model can distinguish between high levels of semantic similarity at the binary level. Future work will address how we can improve our technique and training to better handle cases of semantic similarity, as seen in the Google Code Jam dataset.

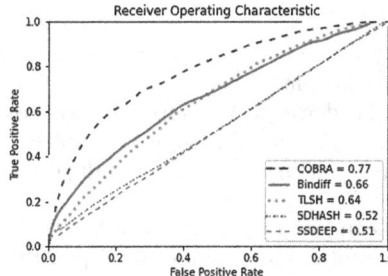

Fig. 12. Final ROC curve for full Google Code Jam programs.

Tool	Precision	Recall	F1
ssdeep	.51	.999	.67
sdhash	.51	.999	.67
tlsh	.61	.59	.60
BinDiff	.62	.60	.61
COBRA	.68	.80	.73

Table 7. Google Code Jam precision and recall

6   Limitations and Future Work

There are some limitations to our current approach. First, we are only able to handle the x86 and x86-64 architectures. Second, it has very limited interpretability. Given an embedding for a program, it is very difficult to know why the model generated that embedding. It will be interesting to incorporate some interpretability work into our model. Finally, our performance on Google Code Jam has room for improvement.

7   Conclusion

In this paper, we propose a novel graph learning algorithm to learn representations for full programs that are robust to syntactic changes. We start by learning function embeddings using natural language processing techniques, and then train a graph convolutional network over the program's full call graph while incorporating the function embeddings. We have found that our model outperforms current approaches on detecting the same code with various optimizations and transformations applied, and on detecting semantically similar source code written by different programmers.

References

1. https://www.zynamics.com/bindiff.html
2. https://gcc.gnu.org/onlinedocs/gcc/Optimize-Options.html
3. Android ndk. https://github.com/android/ndk-samples. Accessed 30 Sept 2010
4. Google Code Jam. https://codingcompetitions.withgoogle.com/codejam. Accessed 30 Sept 2010
5. Vcpkg. https://github.com/microsoft/vcpkg. Accessed 30 Sept 2010
6. Virustotal. https://virustotal.com. Accessed 30 Sept 2010
7. Alrabaee, S., Wang, L., Debbabi, M.: BinGold: Towards robust binary analysis by extracting the semantics of binary code as semantic flow graphs (SFGs)
8. Bayer, U., Comparetti, P.M., Hlauschek, C., Krügel, C., Kirda, E.: Scalable, behavior-based malware clustering
9. Bojanowski, P., Grave, E., Joulin, A., Mikolov, T.: Enriching word vectors with subword information
10. Bruna, J., Zaremba, W., Szlam, A., Lecun, Y.: Spectral networks and locally connected networks on graphs
11. Chakraborty, T., Pierazzi, F., Subrahmanian, V.S.: EC2: Ensemble clustering and classification for predicting android malware families. https://doi.org/10.1109/TDSC.2017.2739145
12. Chandramohan, M., Xue, Y., Xu, Z., Liu, Y., Cho, C.Y., Tan, H.B.K.: BinGo: Cross-architecture cross-OS binary search. https://doi.org/10.1145/2950290.2950350
13. Corob-Msft: /o options (optimize code). https://docs.microsoft.com/en-us/cpp/build/reference/o-options-optimize-code?view=msvc-160
14. Dai, H., Dai, B., Song, L.: Discriminative embeddings of latent variable models for structured data. http://arxiv.org/abs/1603.05629
15. Damiani, E., di Vimercati, S.D.C., Paraboschi, S., Samarati, P.: An open digest-based technique for spam detection
16. David, Y., Partush, N., Yahav, E.: Firmup: Precise static detection of common vulnerabilities in firmware. https://doi.org/10.1145/3173162.3177157
17. David, Y., Partush, N., Yahav, E.: Similarity of binaries through re-optimization. https://doi.org/10.1145/3062341.3062387
18. David, Y., Partush, N., Yahav, E.: Statistical similarity of binaries. https://doi.org/10.1145/2980983.2908126
19. David, Y., Yahav, E.: Tracelet-based code search in executables. https://doi.org/10.1145/2666356.2594343
20. Devlin, J., Chang, M., Lee, K., Toutanova, K.: BERT: pre-training of deep bidirectional transformers for language understanding. http://arxiv.org/abs/1810.04805
21. Ding, S.H.H., Fung, B.C.M., Charland, P.: Asm2vec: Boosting static representation robustness for binary clone search against code obfuscation and compiler optimization. https://doi.org/10.1109/SP.2019.00003
22. Duan, Y., Li, X., Wang, J., Yin, H.: DeepBinDiff: Learning program-wide code representations for binary diffing. https://doi.org/10.14722/ndss.2020.24311
23. Dullien, T.: Graph-based comparison of executable objects
24. Eschweiler, S., Yakdan, K., Gerhards-Padilla, E.: discovRE: Efficient cross-architecture identification of bugs in binary code
25. Fout, A., Byrd, J., Shariat, B., Ben-Hur, A.: Protein interface prediction using graph convolutional networks

26. Gao, D., Reiter, M., Song, D.: BinHunt: Automatically finding semantic differences in binary programs

27. Hadsell, R., Chopra, S., LeCun, Y.: Dimensionality reduction by learning an invariant mapping. https://doi.org/10.1109/CVPR.2006.100

28. Haq, I.U., Caballero, J.: A survey of binary code similarity. https://doi.org/10.1145/3446371

29. Hu, Y., Zhang, Y., Li, J., Gu, D.: Binary code clone detection across architectures and compiling configurations. https://doi.org/10.1109/ICPC.2017.22

30. Jang, J., Brumley, D., Venkataraman, S.: BitShred: feature hashing malware for scalable triage and semantic analysis

31. Junod, P., Rinaldini, J., Wehrli, J., Michielin, J.: Obfuscator-LLVM - software protection for the masses. https://doi.org/10.1109/SPRO.2015.10

32. Kipf, T.N., Welling, M.: Semi-supervised classification with graph convolutional networks

33. Kornblum, J.: Identifying almost identical files using context triggered piecewise hashing

34. Lakhotia, A., Walenstein, A., Miles, C., Singh, A.: VILO: a rapid learning nearest-neighbor classifier for malware triage

35. Liu, B., et al.: α diff: Cross-version binary code similarity detection with DNN. https://doi.org/10.1145/3238147.3238199

36. Luo, L., Ming, J., Wu, D., Liu, P., Zhu, S.: Semantics-based obfuscation-resilient binary code similarity comparison with applications to software and algorithm plagiarism detection. https://doi.org/10.1109/TSE.2017.2655046

37. van der Maaten, L., Hinton, G.: Visualizing data using t-SNE

38. Massarelli, L., Di Luna, G.A., Petroni, F., Baldoni, R., Querzoni, L.: SAFE: self-attentive function embeddings for binary similarity. In: Perdisci, R., Maurice, C., Giacinto, G., Almgren, M. (eds.) DIMVA 2019. LNCS, vol. 11543, pp. 309–329. Springer, Cham (2019). https://doi.org/10.1007/978-3-030-22038-9_15

39. Mikolov, T., Chen, K., Corrado, G., Dean, J.: Efficient estimation of word representations in vector space

40. Mikolov, T., Sutskever, I., Chen, K., Corrado, G., Dean, J.: Distributed representations of words and phrases and their compositionality

41. Monti, F., Frasca, F., Eynard, D., Mannion, D., Bronstein, M.M.: Fake news detection on social media using geometric deep learning. http://arxiv.org/abs/1902.06673

42. Oliver, J., Cheng, C., Chen, Y.: TLSH-a locality sensitive hash

43. Pagani, F., Dell'Amico, M., Balzarotti, D.: Beyond precision and recall: understanding uses (and misuses) of similarity hashes in binary analysis

44. Pang, C., et al.: SoK: All you ever wanted to know about ×86/×64 binary disassembly but were afraid to ask

45. Pei, K., Xuan, Z., Yang, J., Jana, S., Ray, B.: Trex: Learning execution semantics from micro-traces for binary similarity. https://arxiv.org/abs/2012.08680

46. Raff, E., Nicholas, C.: Lempel-Ziv Jaccard distance, an effective alternative to SSDeep and SDHash

47. Rafique, M.Z., Caballero, J.: FIRMA: malware clustering and network signature generation with mixed network behaviors. In: Stolfo, S.J., Stavrou, A., Wright, C.V. (eds.) RAID 2013. LNCS, vol. 8145, pp. 144–163. Springer, Heidelberg (2013). https://doi.org/10.1007/978-3-642-41284-4_8

48. Redmond, K., Luo, L., Zeng, Q.: A cross-architecture instruction embedding model for natural language processing-inspired binary code analysis

49. Rieck, K., Trinius, P., Willems, C., Holz, T.: Automatic analysis of malware behavior using machine learning
50. Roussev, V.: Data fingerprinting with similarity digests. In: Chow, K.-P., Shenoi, S. (eds.) DigitalForensics 2010. IAICT, vol. 337, pp. 207–226. Springer, Heidelberg (2010). https://doi.org/10.1007/978-3-642-15506-2_15
51. Shirani, P., Wang, L., Debbabi, M.: BinShape: scalable and robust binary library function identification using function shape. In: Polychronakis, M., Meier, M. (eds.) DIMVA 2017. LNCS, vol. 10327, pp. 301–324. Springer, Cham (2017). https://doi.org/10.1007/978-3-319-60876-1_14
52. Kim, T., Lee, Y.R., Kang, B.J., Im, E.G.: Binary executable file similarity calculation using function matching
53. Xu, X., Liu, C., Feng, Q., Yin, H., Song, L., Song, D.: Neural network-based graph embedding for cross-platform binary code similarity detection. http://arxiv.org/abs/1708.06525
54. Xu, Y., Xu, Z., Chen, B., Song, F., Liu, Y., Liu, T.: Patch based vulnerability matching for binary programs
55. Xue, Y., Xu, Z., Chandramohan, M., Liu, Y.: Accurate and scalable cross-architecture cross-OS binary code search with emulation. https://doi.org/10.1109/TSE.2018.2827379
56. Yang, C., Liu, Z., Zhao, D., Sun, M., Chang, E.Y.: Network representation learning with rich text information
57. Ye, Y., Li, T., Chen, Y., Jiang, Q.: Automatic malware categorization using cluster ensemble. https://doi.org/10.1145/1835804.1835820
58. Zhuang, W., Ye, Y., Chen, Y., Li, T.: Ensemble clustering for internet security applications. https://doi.org/10.1109/TSMCC.2012.2222025
59. Zuo, F., Li, X., Young, P., Luo, L., Zeng, Q., Zhang, Z.: Neural machine translation inspired binary code similarity comparison beyond function pairs. https://doi.org/10.14722/ndss.2019.23492

Prioritizing Antivirus Alerts on Internal Enterprise Machines

Shay Sakazi$^{(\boxtimes)}$, Yuval Elovici, and Asaf Shabtai

Ben -Gurion University of the Negev, Beer-Sheva, Israel
{sakazis,elovici,shabtaia}@bgu.ac.il

Abstract. Security analysts in large enterprises must handle hundreds or even thousands of alerts raised by antivirus (AV) solutions each day. Thus, a mechanism for analyzing, correlating, and prioritizing these alerts (events) is essential. In this paper, we present an unsupervised machine learning-based method for prioritizing AV alerts. The proposed method converts time windows that include sensitive (important) events to a vector of features and utilizes a set of autoencoder (AE) models, each of which is trained to rank a specific type of sensitive event; then it aggregates their results to identify abnormal and potentially critical machines (i.e., machine that require further examination). We evaluate our proposed method using real McAfee ePO datasets collected from a large organization over a four-month period. Security analysts manually inspected the machines for which an alert was raised by the proposed method, and on average 56% of the alerts were found to be relevant (i.e., require further investigation) compared with 43% raised by baseline models and 7% raised by random selection, thus demonstrating the proposed method's effectiveness at prioritizing AV events.

Keywords: Antivirus · Machine learning · Autoencoder · Big data

1   Introduction

Antivirus (AV) tools, such as McAfee antivirus, are installed on organizations' endpoints as a basic solution to protect the endpoints from malicious software. AV tools issue alerts from individual machines, which are aggregated by a centralized server (e.g., McAfee ePO server) for further investigation and processing. Usually, AV tools rely on an updated list of malware signatures. If a file containing a malware signature is downloaded to (or discovered on) the computer, an alert is raised. However, this technique can only detect known malware (attacks), and therefore, to improve their detection capabilities, such tools often offer the ability to define additional types of rules relating to a process's behavior; in this case, an alert is issued and logged if the monitored behavior matches a rule.

There are several types of rules (or alerts) at different levels of granularity. Some rules are at a low granularity level, indicating a potential security violation, such as *a process writing to the registry* or *an executable file running from*

L. Cavallaro et al. (Eds.): DIMVA 2022, LNCS 13358, pp. 75–95, 2022.
https://doi.org/10.1007/978-3-031-09484-2_5

a user folder. Such alerts are very difficult to analyze, since they can also be performed by legitimate applications and therefore are triggered often. Other rules defined by security experts are at a higher level of abstraction (based on other predefined events) to identify potentially malicious activity. Examples of such cases are *an Office tool loading an unsigned DLL component* and *Office creates or executes dangerous files.* Those rules are usually defined based on the MITRE ATT&CK [21] taxonomy and thus, represent specific malicious activities.

Due to the diversity, volume, and granularity level of detected events, it is difficult to manually analyze them and distinguish between critical alerts, which should be investigated, and those that are not important and can be ignored. In addition, since the alerts are triggered based on predefined rules, a malicious (or benign) activity that has been changed slightly may not be detected correctly. For these reasons, security analysts (who are considered a scarce resource) in the security operations centers (SOCs) of large organizations face a high rate of false alarms [23].

We propose an unsupervised machine learning-based approach for prioritizing AV alerts. We distinguish between two types of alerts: *sensitive, "important" alerts* that are triggered by rules defined by security experts and indicate potentially malicious activity and *contextual (low-level) alerts* that are triggered by rules that usually represent atomic operations, indicating potential security violations (e.g., writing to the registry). The goal of our research is to devise a data-driven approach for prioritizing AV alerts. Specifically, the proposed approach analyzes sensitive events and identifies anomalous and suspicious events, those that should be examined further, while utilizing all of the events in the dataset (including contextual events). This is done by extracting various features to represent time windows that include important events logged for a machine; then a set of pretrained autoencoder (AE) models are utilized to identify and rank anomalous time windows that include potentially critical important events. Note that for each type of important event a dedicated AE model is trained and used for ranking. In the last step, we apply a method for aggregating the anomalous events (time windows) detected (ranked) by the set of AE models for each machine, and prioritize the machines for investigation by a security analyst.

The proposed method was evaluated using real McAfee ePO datasets collected from a large organization for a period of four months. Our evaluation showed that when faced with millions of events each day, of which thousands are important events, the proposed method prioritized the events successfully issued alerts for suspicious events.

The alerts raised by the proposed method were manually inspected by a security analyst, and on average **56%** of them were found to be relevant (i.e., required further investigation), which is **30%** better than other baseline models, thus demonstrating the effectiveness of the proposed method in prioritizing AV events.

To summarize, our main contributions in this study are as follows:

- A contextual approach for representing AV alerts, and more specifically, sensitive alerts; although we applied and evaluated our approach on McAfee ePO data, it can be applied to any AV data and logs.
- An efficient unsupervised method for ranking AV alerts and prioritizing machines for investigation by security analysts.
- An explainability layer that provides complementary information enabling efficient analysis of the alerts.

2 Background

Traditionally, AV tools have used a repository of signatures manually extracted from known malicious files [1]. The advantage of this approach is a low (zero) false alarm rate, since each unique signature represents malicious code extracted from a malware file. However, the main drawback of this approach is its inability to cope with new, unknown malware and standard evasion techniques [6].

For this reason, today's AV tools have evolved into more sophisticated and comprehensive tools that monitor the applications and processes and look for suspicious activity, in addition to relying on signature techniques. Recent studies have shown that modern AV tools have shifted from signature detection to behavioral detection utilizing data mining techniques [28,34]. Although the behavioral approach yields better overall results, it raises new challenges that need to be addressed [34]. The false alarms raised represent one such challenge. This approach focuses on detecting anomalies in behavior that significantly deviate from the norm. However, not every suspicious behavior is malicious [12], and some false alarms can be due to unseen behavior associated with software updates, new applications, or even maintenance activities. For this reason, an additional analysis layer is required for correlating and ranking AV alerts.

In this study, we focus on the McAfee ePO logs. McAfee ePO events can be clustered into four main categories:

1. Dynamic Application Containment (DAC) - behavioral-based detection rules defined by McAfee. These rules are very specific and refer to atomic actions, e.g., allocating memory in another process or creating executable files.
2. Exploit Prevention (EP) - behavioral-based detection with predefined rules primarily based on the MITRE ATT&CK [21] taxonomy and other known attack patterns. These rules refer to a familiar attack pattern.
3. Joint Threat Intelligence (JTI) - cloud reputation-based malware detection. These rules are based on the file's reputation. McAfee stores information on files from which their reputation can be derived, e.g., digital signatures, download sources, and security alerts related to the files.
4. Malware Detection - signature-based malware detection. These rules are based on known malware signatures, as described before.

In this study, we specifically focus on ranking the EP rules created by the SOC analysts, as they represent a potential attack phase. In contrast, the other rule categories (i.e., DAC, JTI and malware detection) are more generic and do not imply specifically on a potential attack.

Each alert (event) triggered by one of the predefined McAfee rules includes a set of properties; Table 1 provides a description of a subset of such properties. Table 1 also present the equivalant features of two well known AVs, Microsoft Defender (denoted by MD) and Kaspersky (denoted by K).

Table 1. McAfee ePO alert properties.

#	Property	Description	Example	Other AVs properties
1	Rule ID	A unique ID assigned to each rule	#37280	MD (Event ID), K (Event ID)
2	Description	A short description of the rule/violation	Writing to another process memory	same
3	Timestamp	The date and time when the alert was triggered	22:20:30 2020-12-03	MD(Event ID), K(occurred)
4	Host ID	The unique ID of the monitored machine	U0ABCDE	MD (Machine ID), K (Device ID)
5	Category	The type of machine	Workstation, VM, Server	MD (osPlatform), K (Device type)
6	OS	The type of OS running on the machine	Windows 10, Windows server 2012	MD (version), K (OS)
7	Event category	The ePO McAfee event category	DAC, EP, JTI	MD (Category), K (task category)
8	Source name	The full path of the source process	C:\\ windows \ System32\ cmd.exe	MD (source file name), K(source file name)
9	Target name	The full path of the target process	C:\\ Program Files\ Internet Explorer \ iexplore.exe	MD (target file name), K (source file name)
10	Source hash	The source process md5 hash	3D19A66D0C C7DD593847 9978FC313C79	MD (source file hash), K (source file hash)
11	Target hash	The target process md5 hash	0550E1B8D3 501A0B9646 A7EF2D2CCFFA	MD(target file hash), K(source file hash)
12	Action	The action taken by the AV agent	Block or log the operation	MD (Action name), K (Action name)

3   Proposed Method

We propose an unsupervised machine learning-based method for prioritizing AV alerts. The proposed method converts time windows that include important events to vectors of features. These vectors of features are then used to train multiple autoencoder (AE) anomaly detection models (one AE model for each rule type) to identify abnormal and potentially malicious events.

3.1   Overview

We assume that a malicious activity is performed in an ongoing process that can be observed by specific, anomalous patterns identified when analyzing the logged AV events. We distinguish between two types of events:

- **Sensitive/important events** - events that are at a higher level of abstraction, defined by security experts, and indicate potentially malicious activity.
- **Contextual events** - events at a lower level of abstraction, usually representing atomic operations, indicating potential security violations (e.g., writing to the registry).

The proposed method analyzes sensitive events and identifies anomalous and potentially critical ones (i.e., those that should be examined further), by utilizing all other events in the dataset (including the contextual events). This is done by implementing the following steps: First, we represent the events recorded for a machine (e.g., computer or server) within predefined time windows, using various features (i.e., a vector of features). We specifically focus on time windows which include at least one important event. Then, in the second phase, we utilize a set of pretrained AE models to identify and rank anomalous time windows containing important events by their suspiciousness. Note that in our approach, each AE model is trained and used to rank a specific type of events. Finally, in the last phase, we aggregate the results (i.e., rankings) of the different AE models in order to prioritize and identify the machines that should be inspected.

3.2 Notations

In this section, we define the following notations:

- $e \in E$ - an event type for which the AV tool will raise an alert. E is the set of all possible types of events. Examples of two McAfee ePO event types are: *Writing to another process memory (ID #37280)* and *Office tool loads an unsigned DLL (ID #18060_20122)*.
- $e^* \in E^* \subset E$ - a sensitive (important) event type for which we generate a representation (in the form of a feature vector) and rank its alerts. E^* is the set of all types of sensitive events, which is a subset of E.
- $m \in M$ - a machine (e.g., computer, server, or tablet) monitored by the AV whose events are being logged. M is the set of all machines in the organization.
- w_i^m - a time window representing the i-th time window of machine m. The time window starts at timestamp t_i and ends at timestamp t_{i+1}. The time window contains a set of sensitive and contextual events.
- l - the size of the time window for which we compute the features ($|w_i^m| = l$).
- $f_{w,m,i}^{e^*}$ - the feature vector computed for machine m within time window w_i^m for the sensitive event type e^*.
- D_{train} - a dataset containing all events logged for machines in M that are used to train the AE models.
- $D_{train}^{e^*} \subset D_{train}$ - the set of feature vectors $\{f_{w,m,i}^{e^*} | \forall m \in M, \forall w_i\}$ extracted from the events in D_{train} for a selected e^*.
- AE_{e^*} - an AE model that was trained on $D_{train}^{e^*}$.
- tr_{e^*} - the threshold selected for AE_{e^*} when trained on $D_{train}^{e^*}$. The threshold is set to be the median of the reconstruction errors (root mean squared error) computed for all feature vectors in the training set. Feature vectors (i.e., time windows) with a reconstruction error that is higher than tr_{e^*} are considered as abnormal.

– D_{pred} - a dataset containing all events logged for machines in M. The interesting events in this dataset are processed by the AEs and ranked based on their anomaly level.

3.3 Training an AE Model (Ranker)

The process for training an AE model for $e^* \in E^*$ is presented in Fig. 1. In the following subsections, we elaborate on each step of the process (denoted by (a) to (i) in Fig. 1).

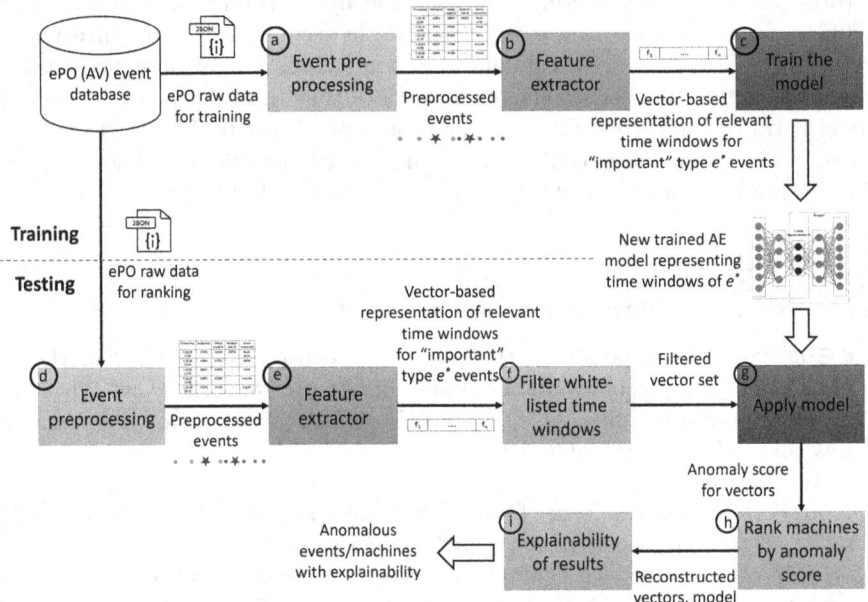

Fig. 1. The process of training an AE model and applying the trained model to rank machines.

Event Preprocessing (a): First, we retrieve all logged events for a predefined time period, which are used to train the model AE_{e^*}. Next, we aggregate the events based on the machines in M and time windows of size l. Finally, for each $e^* \in E^*$, we select only the time windows that include at least one type e^* event.

Figure 2 illustrates the data preprocessing phase. Important events of type e^* are denoted by the star icons, and all other events are denoted by the small circles (each color represents a different type of event). The figure illustrates nine time windows for three machines – $m1$, $m2$, and $m3$ (three time windows for each machine). As can be seen in the red rectangles, the $< t_{i+1}, t_{i+2} >$ of m_2 ($w_{i+1}^{m_2}$) and $< t_{i+2}, t_{i+3} >$ of m_3 ($w_{i+2}^{m_3}$) time windows do not contain any important type e^* events (no star icons), and therefore, they will be filtered out.

Feature Extraction (b): In this step, for a time window w_i of machine m, we extract a set of features to represent the e^* type events in that time window and construct the feature vector $f^{e^*}_{w,m,i}$. When computing the features in the feature vectors, only contextual events that have *the same source name attribute (i.e., event property #8 presented in Table 1) as one of the important events within the time window are used.*

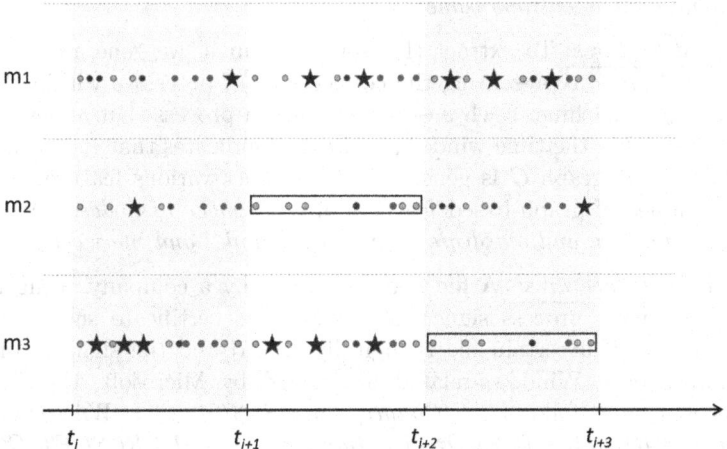

Fig. 2. An illustration of aggregating the events of three machines $m1$, $m2$, and $m3$ in the preprocessing phase. Important events of type e^* are denoted by the star icons, and all other events are denoted by the small circles (each color represents a different type of event).

We define $D^{e^*}_{train} = \{f^{e^*}_{t,w,i} | \forall m \in M, \forall w_i\}$ as the set of feature vectors extracted from the events in D_{train} for a selected e^*. Overall, we extract 146 features that can be categorized as follows.[1]

Statistical Features: These features represent statistical values, such as sum, max, min, mean, median, which are related to the occurrence and frequency of the events. Examples of statistical features are: *'Total number of events within the time window,' 'Total number of important events (i.e., of type e^*) within the time window,'* and *'Average time between events.'*

Activity-Based Features: These features leverage the information related to the behavior of the process in the monitored environment for which an AV event was triggered. Specifically, we utilize the type of action performed by the process on the target object (e.g., read, delete, write, execute) and the action taken by the AV as a result of the alert (e.g., blocked, logged, would block). Examples of activity-based features are: *'Percentage of important events with read access*

---

[1] The complete list of features is provided in the supplementary materials.

request within the time window' and *'Percentage of contextual events with a blocked action within the time window.'*

File and Directory-Based Features: This set of features represents important information related to the executed process's file type (e.g., exe, dll, bat), name (e.g., Entropy), and executed file path (system, users, program files, temp). Examples of file and directory features are: *'Percentage of important events in which the process was executed from the system folder within the time window'* and *'max file names' entropy value.'*

Graph-Based Features: To extract this set of features, we generate a directed graph $G = < V, E >$ representing the connections of processes within the time window for each machine. Each $v \in V$ represents a process that appears in one of the events within the time window, and $e \in E$ indicates that $v_i \in V$ accessed $v_j \in V$. Once the graph G is generated, we extract various features from the graph. Examples of graph-based features are: *'Number of nodes,'* *'Number of edges,'* *'max node in and out degree,'* *'max page-rank,'* and *'max centrality.'*

Certificate-Based Features: A file may be signed by a company, using its certificate. The target process signer, also known as certificate signing request (CSR), indicates if a certain file is digitally signed and the signing company. For instance, for a Windows-related file signed by Microsoft, the file's target signer will be as follows: *"C(Country) = US, S(State) = WASHINGTON, L(Locality) = REDMOND, O(Organization name) = MICROSOFT CORPORATION, CN(Common name) = MICROSOFT WINDOWS."*
The information on the signing entity provides an indication of the reputation of the file, and therefore, it is used by AV tools to verify whether a file is legitimate (i.e., signed by a known entity) or suspicious (may have been signed by an attacker). In order to extract the certificate-based features, we use an updated auxiliary table which, for each signing entity $signer_i$ previously logged in the McAfee ePO events, stores the following attributes: (A) number of events that contain files signed by $signer_i$, (B) number of distinct file names signed by $signer_i$, (C) number of distinct file hashes signed by $signer_i$, and (D) number of distinct machines that contain files signed by $signer_i$. Using this auxiliary table, we extract the following five features for each time window of a specific machine:
$min_{signer}\{signer_i | A_i/B_i, A_i/C_i, A_i/D_i, B_i/D_i, C_i/D_i\}$,
where $signer_i$ is a signer entity that appears in an important event e^* within the time window.

Context-Based Features: This set of features provides contextual information on the related user or host. Examples of contextual features are: *'user role (e.g., administrator, privilege, regular),'* *'host category (e.g., workstation or server),'* *'work hours (e.g., a flag for work hours or off hours),'* and *'weekdays (e.g., a flag for work day, holiday, or weekend).'*
An illustration of the feature extraction process is presented in Fig. 3.

Training the AE-Based Anomaly Detectors (c): Given a training set $D_{train}^{e^*}$, we train an AE model that learns the representation of the time windows.

An AE [15] is a special type of neural network which reconstructs the output values from the input values and is capable of discovering structure within data in order to develop a compressed representation. During training (compression), the bottleneck (hidden) layers of the AE extract the patterns essential for representing the input data in a latent space, while ignoring noise. To achieve this goal, the AE model is trained to minimize a reconstruction error. For example, we can calculate the reconstruction error by the root mean squared error (RMSE), shown in Eq. 1.

$$RMSE = \sqrt{\frac{1}{n}\sum_{n}^{i=1}(x_i - \hat{x}_i)^2}$$ (1)

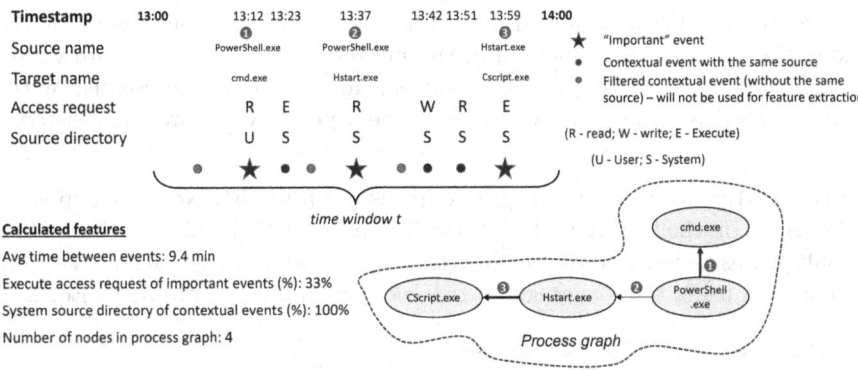

Fig. 3. An illustration of the feature extraction process for a one-hour time window between 13:00 and 14:00. The important events are marked by the star icons; the small red circles indicate contextual events with the same source name attribute as one of the important events within the time window, and the small blue circles indicate contextual events that are filtered out and not used for to calculate the features. The example shows four features calculated based on the information provided for each event (the timestamp, source name, target name, access request type, source directory of the process, and process graph).

where x_i is the input feature index i, and $\hat{x}_i$ is the reconstructed output feature index i. At the end of this step we have a set of AE models $\{AE_{e^*}|e^* \in E^*\}$, where each AE_{e^*} is the AE that models time windows related to the sensitive event e^*.

3.4 Applying the AE Models to Rank Sensitive Events

Given a dataset of events D_{pred}, we want to rank the sensitive events in D_{pred} according to their anomaly score. This is performed according to the steps presented in the lower part of Fig. 1.

Data Preprocessing and Feature Extraction (d) and (e): We start by preprocessing and extracting the features similarly to the way this is done when the model is trained (steps (a) and (b)). The output of these two steps is a set of feature vectors representing the time intervals for each event type e^*. We denote this set of feature vectors as $D^{e^*}_{pred}$.

Filtering (f): In some cases, the AV alerts manually inspected by a security analyst are identified as benign cases and are therefore added to a set of white-listed rules. The white-listed rules are defined as a set of conditions set for a specific alert's attributes (such as, the event type, organizational user name or process name) in cases where the alert is known to be not malicious (for example when the user is developer working on a machine and consequently creating alerts).

These white-listed events are not presented to the security analyst again, to minimize the number of false alarms. Similarly, we want to avoid analyzing and ranking time windows in which all of the interesting type e^* events are white-listed. Therefore, in this step, we filter out all time windows (represented by the feature vectors) from $D^{e^*}_{test}$ in which *all* of the type e^* events are white-listed.

Applying Models and Ranking Machines (g) and (h): Next, we apply the models AE_{e^*} on the feature vectors in the filtered set $D^{e^*}_{pred}$. Using the individual anomaly scores assigned to the vectors (time windows) for each machine, we rank the machines using to an aggregated risk score computed according to Eq. 2:

$$Score(m) = \sum_{i=1}^{|E^*|} \frac{1}{rank_i^{(m)}} * \alpha(d_i) \tag{2}$$

where m is one of the monitored machines in M, and $rank_i^{(m)}$ is the location of the event of type e_i^* (if exists) ranked by AE_i for machine m out of all the events ranked by AE_i for all machines in M. Thus, the higher an event is in the list, the higher the overall score for that machine.

Furthermore, in order to consider the distance of the anomaly score of an event from the model's threshold $(tr_{e_i^*})$, we multiply the rank of an event by an alpha factor $(\alpha(d_i))$, which is a function of the distance of the reconstruction error from the threshold of model AE_i, denoted by d_i.

We define the alpha factor according to the function presented in Eq. 3 (the distance d_i is normalized between zero and one). This function assigns (i) the value of zero - if the distance between the anomaly score and the threshold is below -0.667 (i.e., the event is *normal*); (ii) the value computed by a sigmoid function - if the distance between the anomaly score and the threshold is above -0.667 and below 0.667 (note that if the distance is zero, the alpha factor is one); and (iii) the maximal value of two - if the distance between the anomaly score and the threshold is above 0.667.

$$\alpha_i = \begin{cases} 0 & \text{if } d_i < -0.667 \\ \frac{2}{1+e^{-5d_i}} & \text{if } -0.667 \leq d_i \leq 0.667 \\ 2 & \text{if } d_i > 0.667 \end{cases} \tag{3}$$

Each day, alerts are issued for machines with the highest risk score (based on Eq. 2); those machines are analyzed by the security analyst.

Explainability (i): Finally, an explainability component is used to provide insights on the anomalous feature vectors (i.e., time windows) identified by each autoencoder (AE_{e^*}) and help in their subsequent investigation. In this step, the features of an anomalous feature vector are ranked based on their contribution to the overall reconstruction error. This is done based on the assumption that the features the model was unable to reconstruct properly are key indicators of the instance's classification as an anomaly.

The feature importance evaluation is performed as follows: given a feature vector $f^{e^*} = [f_1, f_2, ...f_i]$ and its reconstructed vector $\hat{f}^{e^*} = [\hat{f}_1, \hat{f}_2, ...\hat{f}_i]$, the reconstruction error for each feature is calculated individually as the squared distance between the real and reconstructed values: $|(f_1 - \hat{f}_1)^2|, |(f_2 - \hat{f}_2)^2|, ..., |(f_i - \hat{f}_i)^2|$. This list is sorted in descending order, and the top k features are selected.

4   Evaluation

This section describes the experiments performed to evaluate our proposed method. Our evaluation addresses the following research questions:

RQ1. How effective is the proposed method in ranking (prioritizing) machines, based on the AV events, for further investigation?

RQ2. What are the advantages of using the AE model to identify anomalous and potentially critical events, and what is the importance of the different groups of features suggested?

RQ3. How can the alerts (cases) raised by the proposed method be categorized?

RQ4. How does the performance of the proposed method compare to security expert-based ranking machines for inspection?

4.1   Experimental Setup

Datasets: In the evaluation, we used McAfee ePO event logs collected from a large enterprise for a period of six months from July to December 2021. At the end of each day, predictions were provided for all time windows at that day. Based on the preliminary experimental results, a one-hour window size was shown to represent the events most effectively. A larger window size introduced unwanted noise which led to high false alarms, and a shorter time window did not contain sufficient data. Thus, in our evaluation we set $l = 1\,hr$.

The AE models were trained on the data of two (consecutive) months and were applied on the data of the following month (for example, the AE models trained on the data of July and August were applied on the data of September.

A detailed description of the data is provided in Table 2. As explained in Sect. 3, only time windows that include at least one non-white-listed sensitive event are evaluated and ranked by the models; these time windows (i.e., feature vectors) are denoted by *#Non-white-listed time windows* in the table.

Modeling Sensitive Event Types: Based on the suggestion of the organization's SOC analysts, we selected 29 types of sensitive events for the evaluation. While the types of events selected relate to potential malicious activity, they also appear frequently in the logs and therefore are difficult to prioritize and analyze. For each of the selected event types we trained a dedicated AE model. In the evaluation we prioritize these 29 types of sensitive events (other types of events are considered contextual events). Examples of the sensitive event types selected include: (a) execute dangerous files from removable media; (b) rundll32 executes *cmd.exe*, *csc.exe*, or *cvtres.exe*; (c) create or execute *.js*, *.jar*, or *.class*; (d) Office creates or executes dangerous files; (e) Outlook executes scripting engine; (f) unmanaged powershell detected; and (g) Office application *startup:registry* modification.

Anomaly Detection Models: In the evaluation we tested two types of AE models implemented with Keras[2]: a standard AE model (AE) [15] and a denois-

Table 2. A description of the McAfee ePO event log datasets used for the evaluation.

Training set				
Dates	Jul–Aug	Aug–Sep	Sep–Oct	Oct–Nov
#Days	62	61	61	61
#Machines	50,095	51,186	49,985	52,131
#Events	64,761,192	51,221,172	65,482,009	48,582,848
#Sensitive events	4,178,323	4,425,060	5,945,807	4,251,690
#Time windows (feature vectors)	2,345,810	2,317,389	2,364,524	1,809,389
Test set				
Dates	Sep	Oct	Nov	Dec
#Days	30	31	30	30
#Machines	47,585	46,694	48,478	47,278
#Events	30,540,134	34,941,875	13,640,973	11,742,590
#Sensitive events	2,321,203	3,624,604	627,086	1,151,880
#Time windows (feature vectors)	1,167,948	1,196,576	612,813	913,995
#Non-white-listed time windows	972,948	903,170	555,639	840,886
#Potential alerts	776,304	620,651	505,683	782,164

---

[2] (https://keras.io/) version 2.2.5, Python 3.6.

ing AE (DAE) [32]. Table 3 summarizes the configuration parameters used to train the AE-based models. As a baseline, in addition to the two AE models, we trained a commonly used unsupervised anomaly detector, isolation forest (IF) [18]. IF is known for its good performance in anomaly detection tasks and for its ability to handle sparse feature vectors effectively [3]. The IF was implemented with scikit-learn[3], with 1,000 of base estimators in the ensemble.

To evaluate the effectiveness of the proposed features, each model was trained once using only the 11 statistical features and once on all of the 146 extracted features described in Sect. 3.3. Finally, in addition to the three anomaly detector algorithms (AE, DAE, and IF), we also evaluated another naive baseline approach that we refer to as random selection, which randomly selects alerts from the pool of potential alerts; the number of alerts selected is equal to the number of alerts detected by the AE model.

Evaluation Metrics: The alerts raised by the anomaly detector models were inspected by the SOC analysts (i.e., the domain experts) and labeled as a good alert, meaning that the alert requires further investigation, or a false alert, meaning that the alert should not be raised by the anomaly detector. Along with the alert, the following information was provided to the SOC analysts to facilitate the inspection process: *(i)* the sensitive event type; *(ii)* the machine's name; *(*iii) timestamp and *(iv)* the features that most contributed to the model's decision, which was part of the explainability phase (step (i) in Fig. 1). Based on this information, the SOC analyst could explore events of a specific machine provided by other sensors (e.g., active directory, firewall, and EDR) as well as to contact the user of that machine, in order to label the alert. Since the time of the SOC analysts is a very limited resource, the analysts were required to check and label only the alerts raised by our models, as well as the randomly selected alerts.

Table 3. Configuration of the autoencoders' parameters.

Configuration parameters	Value
Input & output size	146 (equal to the number of features used)
Size of dense layers	128, 64, and 32 for AE; 256 for DAE
Size of middle layer	16 for AE; 512 for DAE
Batch size	32
Epochs	100
Weight initialization	Sampled from normal distribution ($\mu = 0, \sigma = 0.01$)
Bias initialization	Sampled from normal distribution ($\mu = 0, \sigma = 0.01$)
Loss function	RMSE
Activation function	Sigmoid for the latent and output layers, ReLU for all other layers
Optimizer	Adam

---

[3] (https://scikit-learn.org/stable/) version 1.0 Python 3.6.

For the evaluation we defined the following metrics:

- **%Alerts** - the percentage of alerts raised per machine's time window out of the total number of potential alerts:

$$\%Alerts = \frac{\#Alerts}{\#PotentialAlerts} \qquad (4)$$

Low values for the *%Alerts* metric are preferable, since we want to minimize the number of alerts the SOC analysts need to analyze.

- **%GoodAlerts** - the percentage of alerted machines that were labeled as "good" alerts by the SOC analysts, which is also known as precision:

$$\%GoodAlerts = \frac{\#GoodAlerts}{\#Alerts} \qquad (5)$$

High values for the *%GoodAlerts* metric are preferable, since we want to maximize the number of alerts that could be a potential security breach.

- **%Local Recall** - the percentage of alerted machines that were labeled as "good" alerts by the SOC analysts, out of all known "good" alerts within the same time window:

$$\%LocalRecall = \frac{\#GoodAlerts}{\#KnownGoodAlert} \qquad (6)$$

High values of the *%LocalRecall* metric are preferable, since we want to cover all of the alerts that could be a potential security breach.

- **SOC Score** - a severity score manually assigned by the organization's SOC team for a machine based on the alerts raised for the machine. This score is based on AV data, as well as other data sources (e.g., DNS, Proxy, Carbon Black, Active Directory logs). The minimum value for the SOC score metric is zero, which means a legitimate case. A high SOC score value implies that there is a high chance that the machine has been compromised.

We were unable to report the global false negative cases (i.e., machines which, based on the AV events, should be checked by the SOC team but were missed by the models), due to the large number of events and because only the cases manually checked by the SOC analysts were labeled. Cases that our method could miss (i.e., false negatives) may occur, for example, when the malicious activity triggers a very small number of events (one or two events) within a short time interval, or when the attacker is using a valid certificate that the organization is considered as trusted.

4.2 Results

Method's Effectiveness (RQ1). The results of the evaluation are summarized in Table 4, which presents the total number of alerts raised ($\#A$), the percentage of alerts raised out of all possible alerts ($\%A$), and the percentage of good alerts ($\%GA$) for each anomaly detector algorithm and feature combination used by the model. As can be seen in the first row, the standard AE model trained with all features raised between 10 and 39 alerts (suspicious machines) per month, representing 0.001% to 0.005% of the potential alerts, and the model's good alert percentage ranged from 38% to 80%; the other baseline models' good alert percentage ranged from 27% to 75%, and the random selection model's good alert percentage ranged from 0% to 10.25%. These results demonstrate the proposed method's effectiveness.

Model Configuration (RQ2). From the results presented in Table 4 we can conclude that overall, the AE-based anomaly detector performed better than the DAE and IF detectors, while the DAE achieved competitive results, especially on the data from November and December. In addition, the use of The use of all groups of features was superior to using just the statistical features for all of the anomaly detector algorithms. This can be observed by the $\%GoodAlerts$ values, where the good alert percentage of the models trained with all groups of features was 40% to 80%, compared to the values of 25% to 65% obtained by the models trained with just statistical features.

Alert Categorization (RQ3). We analyzed the good alerts and found that they can be categorized into four types: (1) Ethical hack or red team activity - Since ethical hacking activity simulates real malicious activity, we expect our proposed method to identify and issue alerts regarding anomalous events logged for the machines on which the ethical hacking activity was conducted. (2) Should be white-listed - A suspicious activity of a legitimate program; this is an indication of a noisy rule, and for subsequent time periods, we can eliminate those events to reduce the number of false alarms. (3) Process activity that should be investigated - A suspicious activity of a process that was not observed in the data, which should be investigated (e.g., creation of files, reading credential files). (4) User activity that should be investigated - Suspicious behavior of a user that should be investigated (e.g., cmd.exe opened with an administrator privilege in a production machine, downloading suspicious files, or violation of policies such as downloading a program via the Internet instead of the company portal). Table 5 presents the number of alerts from the above mentioned categories for each month. As shown in the table, some categories are more common than others (e.g., process activities); it can also be seen that the model can capture ethical hacking activities, which are rare.

Table 4. Evaluation results for the #Alerts (#A), %Alerts (%A), %GoodAlerts (%GA), and %LocalRecall (%LR) metrics.

Month model	September	October	November	December
AE all features	#A = 10 %A = 0.001 **%GA = 70** %LR = 53.84	#A = 10 %A = 0.001 **%GA = 80** %LR = 57.14	#A = 16 %A = 0.003 **%GA = 68.75** **%LR = 91.67**	#A = 39 %A = 0.005 **%GA = 35.89** **%LR = 60.87**
AE statistical features	#A = 23 %A = 0.003 %GA = 47.8 **%LR = 84.61**	#A = 12 %A = 0.002 %GA = 66.67 %LR = 57.14	#A = 19 %A = 0.003 %GA = 47.36 %LR = 75	#A = 29 %A = 0.003 %GA = 34.48 %LR = 43.47
DAE all features	#A = 12 %A = 0.001 %GA = 66.67 %LR = 61.53	#A = 14 %A = 0.002 %GA = 71.42 %LR = 71.42	#A = 16 %A = 0.003 **%GA = 68.75** **%LR = 91.67**	#A = 21 %A = 0.002 **%GA = 38.1** %LR = 34.78
DAE statistical features	#A = 24 %A = 0.003 %GA = 45.83 **%LR = 84.61**	#A = 20 %A = 0.003 %GA = 65 **%LR = 92.85**	#A = 17 %A = 0.003 %GA = 41.17 %LR = 58.33	#A = 33 %A = 0.004 %GA = 27.27 %LR = 39.13
IF all features	#A = 24 %A = 0.003 %GA = 41.67 %LR = 76.92	#A = 13 %A = 0.002 %GA = 53.84 %LR = 50	#A = 8 %A = 0.001 **%GA = 75** %LR = 50	#A = 28 %A = 0.003 **%GA = 35.71** %LR = 43.47
IF statistical features	#A = 25 %A = 0.003 %LR = 69.23 %GA = 36	#A = 9 %A = 0.001 %GA = 44.44 %LR = 28.57	#A = 11 %A = 0.002 %GA = 54.54 %LR = 50	#A = 20 %A = 0.002 %GA = 30 %LR = 26.08
Random selection	#A = 10 %A = 0.001 %GA = 10 %LR = 7.69	#A = 10 %A = 0.001 %GA = 0 %LR = 0	#A = 16 %A = 0.003 %GA = 0 %LR = 0	#A = 39 %A = 0.005 %GA = 10.25 %LR = 17.39

Table 5. Number of good alerts per category.

Category/Month	Ethical hack	White-listed	Process	User
Sep	1	1	4	1
Oct	2	0	4	2
Nov	0	3	8	0
Dec	2	2	4	6

Security Expert Ranking Comparison (RQ4). Table 6 presents the average *SOC score* of the anomalous machines detected by each anomaly detector (algorithm and feature combination used by the model). The results presented in the table show that the AE anomaly detector trained using all features performed better than the DAE and IF models, with greater ability to identify machines that were assigned a high risk score by the SOC security analysts.

Table 6. Average (monthly) SOC analyst manual score for machines alerted by the models.

	September	October	November	December	Total (avg)
AE all features	**293.68**	**1810.24**	**429.53**	**2895.15**	**1357.14**
AE statistical features	190.69	1689.22	349.17	1064.68	823.43
DAE all features	**286.90**	1493.43	**428.90**	1407.63	904.21
DAE statistical features	182.70	1095.75	352.60	943.78	643.70
IF all features	175.37	1545.20	322.73	1099.11	785.60
IF statistical features	144.23	**1904.40**	241.18	512.23	700.51
Random selection	43.4	37.7	39.8	61.31	45.55

The proposed method was deployed and tested by the organization that provided the datasets for the research. According to the implemented pipeline, the AV logs were sent to a security information and event management system (i.e., SIEM system such as Sentinel or Splunk), and from the SIEM system, once a day to the centralized big data platform where our method was deployed and executed. The training phase was scheduled to run once a week, and the prediction and ranking task was executed once a day.

5   Related Work

Extensive research has been performed in the malware detection domain. Over the years, traditional AV tools have been shown to be prone to various evasion techniques such as reverse shell exploits [14] and user input simulation [11]. Consequently, prior research has focused on the use of machine learning (ML) and deep learning (DL) techniques to improve the detection capabilities of AV tools [5,9,24,29] (mainly of unknown malware). However, in recent years, ML models have been shown to be vulnerable to adversarial machine learning attack by which the adversary creates carefully crafted malware that can fool the ML-based detection model [10,25,26].

Such evasion techniques result in a high false alarm rate and therefore, to effectively utilize the capabilities of AV tools, a mechanism for analyzing, aggregating, and prioritizing alerts is essential. Alert prioritization is a known research area in the cyber security domain [13]. For example, Oprea et al. [22] utilized various external sources to prioritize suspicious domain names. Wu et al. [33] focused on intrusion detection alert correlation in cyber-physical systems, while McElwee et al. [19] proposed a deep learning-based model for prioritizing and responding to intrusion detection alerts in enterprise environments. Aminanto et al. [4] suggested an automated method based on a temporal isolation forest model for prioritizing intrusion detection system alerts. Shah et al. [30] presented a two-step approach for prioritizing alerts at a cyber security operations center. Carrasco et al. [7] used a deep learning approach to prioritize fraud detection system alerts, however their methods relied on a supervised (labeled) dataset containing both false alarms and real fraud cases, which is often difficult to obtain. These studies, however, do not fit our usecase, since they either use a manual expert-based scoring system or labeled datasets, or they are applied on datasets that do not share properties with the data used in this study (i.e., not related to anti-malware tools).

Since the data available is unlabeled, we opted to use unsupervised ML techniques for detecting anomalous cases. Methods proposed in previous studies provide scores for anomalies in unlabeled datasets; for example, Merrill et al. [20] presented cumulative error scoring (CES) which uses a deep AE to score anomalies between images, while only using their labels for evaluation. Cheng et al. [8] ranked casual anomalies via temporal and dynamical analysis on vanishing correlation, relying on graph features to rank anomalies based on bank information system logs. A collaborative alert ranking framework that exploits both temporal and content correlations from heterogeneous categorical alerts, based on intrusion detection logs (INET sockets), was presented by Lin et al. [17]. Kravchik and Shabtai [16] applied AE models to both the time and frequency domains of sensor data collected from three different industrial control systems environments for detecting anomalies that might indicate of cyber attacks.

Using a DAE for anomaly detection is also a well-known technique. particularly in the computer vision domain; Zhou et al. [35], for example, proposed a novel DAE that isolates noise and outliers in the computer vision domain. Mayu et al. [27] presented a DAE for the detection of anomalous telemetry data in spacecraft and found that an DAE is better at detecting anomalies than other dimension reduction algorithms like PCA. A DAE could be the best fit for anomaly detection on event logs, as this channel is influenced by many different factors and very noisy by nature [31].

Since AV alerts collected by vendors and organizational networks are considered proprietary and sensitive information [2], to the best of our knowledge, no previous research has attempted to analyze, correlate and prioritize AV alerts that might be part of the same malicious activity and prioritize them.

6   Conclusions

In this paper, we presented a method for prioritizing AV alerts. The proposed method has the following attributes: (1) it focuses on specific rules that are part of a relevant attack, (2) it ranks AV alerts in an unsupervised manner, and (3) it provides an explanation of the features that the model identified as abnormal. By prioritizing alerts and providing the feature-based explanations, the method enables an analyst to focus his/her attention on investigating the most meaningful alerts. Our evaluation using datasets that contain real-world data demonstrates our method's ability to identify malicious and relevant alerts that merit further investigation.

In future work, we suggest the following extensions to the proposed method: (1) integrating the security analyst's feedback (i.e., manual analysis results) in the model's training process; this may reduce the number of false alarms further, as the model will focus not only on the anomalous time windows but also on those windows most relevant to the security analyst;(2) adding more relevant features, such as sequential features, to model the inner dependencies between events in each time window; and (3) extending the proposed method for prioritizing AV alerts of other AV software (e.g., Microsoft Defender and Kaspersky).

References

1. Al-Asli, M., Ghaleb, T.A.: Review of signature-based techniques in antivirus products. In: 2019 International Conference on Computer and Information Sciences (ICCIS), pp. 1–6. IEEE, Sakaka (2019). https://doi.org/10.1109/ICCISci.2019.8716381
2. Al-Saleh, M.I., Hamdan, H.M.: On studying the antivirus behavior on kernel activities. In: Proceedings of the 2018 International Conference on Internet and E-Business, ICIEB 2018, pp. 158–161. Association for Computing Machinery, New York (2018). https://doi.org/10.1145/3230348.3230376
3. Aminanto, M.E., Ban, T., Isawa, R., Takahashi, T., Inoue, D.: Threat alert prioritization using isolation forest and stacked auto encoder with day-forward-chaining analysis. IEEE Access 8, 217977–217986 (2020). https://doi.org/10.1109/ACCESS.2020.3041837
4. Aminanto, M.E., Zhu, L., Ban, T., Isawa, R., Takahashi, T., Inoue, D.: Automated threat-alert screening for battling alert fatigue with temporal isolation forest. In: 2019 17th International Conference on Privacy, Security and Trust (PST), pp. 1–3. IEEE, Fredericton (2019)
5. Anderson, H.S., Roth, P.: Ember: an open dataset for training static pe malware machine learning models. CoRR abs/1804.04637 (2018). http://arxiv.org/abs/1804.04637
6. Barriga, J., Yoo, S.G.: Malware detection and evasion with machine learning techniques: a survey. Int. J. Appl. Eng. Res. 12, 7207–7214 (2017)
7. Carrasco, R.S.M., Sicilia-Urbán, M.Á.: Evaluation of deep neural networks for reduction of credit card fraud alerts. IEEE Access 8, 186421–186432 (2020)
8. Cheng, W., Zhang, K., Chen, H., Jiang, G., Chen, Z., Wang, W.: Ranking causal anomalies via temporal and dynamical analysis on vanishing correlations. In: Proceedings of the 22nd ACM SIGKDD International Conference on Knowledge Discovery and Data Mining, KDD 2016, pp. 805–814. Association for Computing Machinery, New York (2016). https://doi.org/10.1145/2939672.2939765
9. Delaney, J.: The Effectiveness of Antivirus Software. Ph.D. thesis, Utica College (2020)
10. Demetrio, L., Coull, S.E., Biggio, B., Lagorio, G., Armando, A., Roli, F.: Adversarial exemples: a survey and experimental evaluation of practical attacks on machine learning for windows malware detection. arXiv preprint arXiv:2008.07125 (2020)
11. Genç, Z.A., Lenzini, G., Sgandurra, D.: A game of "cut and mouse": Bypassing antivirus by simulating user inputs. In: Proceedings of the 35th Annual Computer Security Applications Conference, ACSAC 2019, pp. 456–465. Association for Computing Machinery, New York (2019). https://doi.org/10.1145/3359789.3359844
12. Grégio, A., Bonacin, R., Nabuco, O., Afonso, V.M., Lício De Geus, P., Jino, M.: Ontology for malware behavior: a core model proposal. In: 2014 IEEE 23rd International WETICE Conference, pp. 453–458. IEEE, Parma (2014). https://doi.org/10.1109/WETICE.2014.72

13. Hubballi, N., Suryanarayanan, V.: False alarm minimization techniques in signature-based intrusion detection systems: a survey. Comput. Commun. **49**, 1–17 (2014)
14. Johnson, A., Haddad, R.J.: Evading signature-based antivirus software using custom reverse shell exploit. In: SoutheastCon 2021, pp. 1–6 (2021). https://doi.org/10.1109/SoutheastCon45413.2021.9401881
15. Kramer, M.A.: Nonlinear principal component analysis using autoassociative neural networks. AIChE J. **37**(2), 233–243 (1991)
16. Kravchik, M., Shabtai, A.: Efficient cyber attack detection in industrial control systems using lightweight neural networks and PCA. IEEE Trans. Depend. Secure Comput. (2021)
17. Lin, Y., et al.: Collaborative alert ranking for anomaly detection. In: Proceedings of the 27th ACM International Conference on Information and Knowledge Management, CIKM 2018, pp. 1987–1995. Association for Computing Machinery, New York (2018). https://doi.org/10.1145/3269206.3272013
18. Liu, F.T., Ting, K.M., Zhou, Z.H.: Isolation forest. In: 2008 Eighth IEEE International Conference on Data Mining, pp. 413–422. IEEE (2008)
19. McElwee, S., Heaton, J., Fraley, J., Cannady, J.: Deep learning for prioritizing and responding to intrusion detection alerts. In: MILCOM 2017–2017 IEEE Military Communications Conference (MILCOM), pp. 1–5. IEEE, Baltimore (2017)
20. Merrill, N., Eskandarian, A.: Modified autoencoder training and scoring for robust unsupervised anomaly detection in deep learning. IEEE Access **8**, 101824–101833 (2020). https://doi.org/10.1109/ACCESS.2020.2997327
21. https://attack.mitre.org/ (2021)
22. Oprea, A., Li, Z., Norris, R., Bowers, K.: Made: security analytics for enterprise threat detection. In: Proceedings of the 34th Annual Computer Security Applications Conference, pp. 124–136. ACSAC, San Juan (2018)
23. Perera, A., Rathnayaka, S., Perera, N.D., Madushanka, W., Senarathne, A.N.: The next gen security operation center. In: 2021 6th International Conference for Convergence in Technology (I2CT), pp. 1–9 (2021). https://doi.org/10.1109/I2CT51068.2021.9418136
24. Raff, E., Barker, J., Sylvester, J., Brandon, R., Catanzaro, B., Nicholas, C.K.: Malware detection by eating a whole exe. In: Workshops at the Thirty-Second AAAI Conference on Artificial Intelligence (2018)
25. Rosenberg, I., Shabtai, A., Elovici, Y., Rokach, L.: Query-efficient black-box attack against sequence-based malware classifiers. In: Annual Computer Security Applications Conference, pp. 611–626 (2020)
26. Rosenberg, I., Shabtai, A., Rokach, L., Elovici, Y.: Generic black-box end-to-end attack against state of the art API call based malware classifiers. In: Bailey, M., Holz, T., Stamatogiannakis, M., Ioannidis, S. (eds.) RAID 2018. LNCS, vol. 11050, pp. 490–510. Springer, Cham (2018). https://doi.org/10.1007/978-3-030-00470-5_23
27. Sakurada, M., Yairi, T.: Anomaly detection using autoencoders with nonlinear dimensionality reduction. In: Proceedings of the MLSDA 2014 2nd Workshop on Machine Learning for Sensory Data Analysis, MLSDA 2014, pp. 4–11. Association for Computing Machinery, New York (2014). https://doi.org/10.1145/2689746.2689747
28. Scott, J.: Signature based malware detection is dead. Mob. Inf. Syst. **4**(1), 33–49 (2017)

29. Shabtai, A., Moskovitch, R., Elovici, Y., Glezer, C.: Detection of malicious code by applying machine learning classifiers on static features: a state-of-the-art survey. Inf. Secur. Tech. Rep. **14**(1), 16–29 (2009)
30. Shah, A., Ganesan, R., Jajodia, S., Cam, H.: A two-step approach to optimal selection of alerts for investigation in a CSOC. IEEE Trans. Inf. Forensics Secur. **14**(7), 1857–1870 (2018)
31. Sun, X., Hou, W., Yu, D., Wang, J., Pan, J.: Filtering out noise logs for process modelling based on event dependency. In: 2019 IEEE International Conference on Web Services (ICWS), pp. 388–392 (2019). https://doi.org/10.1109/ICWS.2019.00069
32. Vincent, P., Larochelle, H., Bengio, Y., Manzagol, P.A.: Extracting and composing robust features with denoising autoencoders. In: Proceedings of the 25th International Conference on Machine Learning, pp. 1096–1103 (2008)
33. Wu, M., Moon, Y.: Alert correlation for cyber-manufacturing intrusion detection. Procedia Manuf. **34**, 820–831 (2019)
34. Ye, Y., Li, T., Adjeroh, D., Iyengar, S.S.: A survey on malware detection using data mining techniques. ACM Comput. Surv. **50**(3) (2017). https://doi.org/10.1145/3073559
35. Zhou, C., Paffenroth, R.C.: Anomaly detection with robust deep autoencoders. In: Proceedings of the 23rd ACM SIGKDD International Conference on Knowledge Discovery and Data Mining,KDD 2017, pp. 665–674. Association for Computing Machinery, New York (2017). https://doi.org/10.1145/3097983.3098052

VANDALIR: Vulnerability Analyses Based on Datalog and LLVM-IR

Joschua Schilling[1](✉) and Tilo Müller[2]

[1] Friedrich -Alexander -Universität Erlangen -Nürnberg, Erlangen, Germany
joschua.schilling@fau.de
[2] Hof University of Applied Sciences, Hof, Germany
tilo.mueller@hof-university.de

Abstract. While modern-day static analysis tools are capable of finding standard vulnerabilities as well as complex patterns, implementing those tools is expensive regarding both development time and runtime performance. During the last years, domain specific languages like Datalog have gained popularity as they simplify the development process of analyses and rule sets dramatically. Similarly, intermediate representations like LLVM-IR are used to facilitate static source code analysis. In this paper, we present VANDALIR, a vulnerability analyzer and detector based on Datalog and LLVM-IR. VANDALIR is a static source code analyzer that allows to define and customize detection rules in a high-level, declarative way. We implement VANDALIR as a comprehensive static analysis tool, aiming to simplify vulnerability detection by a new combination of modern technologies. Besides the novel design of VANDALIR, we present a predefined detection rule set covering stack-based memory corruption, double free and format string vulnerabilities. As we show, our rule set achieves a detection rate of over 90% on test cases from the Juliet Test Suite, outperforming well-established vulnerability scanners such as the Clang Static Analyzer. Furthermore, we evaluated VANDALIR on open source projects and could reproduce existing vulnerabilities as well as identify previously unknown vulnerabilities.

Keywords: Vulnerability scanner · Static analysis · Datalog rule set

1 Introduction

Static analysis tools are extensively applied in today's software development process due to their integration in compilers, IDEs and CI solutions. Still, these tools cannot prevent all vulnerability issues due to various limitations. In static analysis, many interesting problems have been proven to be undecidable. Therefore, many tools detect all possible vulnerabilities and then apply heuristics to limit the number of detected cases and prevent exhaustion of the developers. While in recent years research has developed increasingly better heuristics to distinguish true and false positives, the used analyses and heuristics have become

L. Cavallaro et al. (Eds.): DIMVA 2022, LNCS 13358, pp. 96–115, 2022.
https://doi.org/10.1007/978-3-031-09484-2_6

increasingly complex. To manage this complexity, many modern tools separate detection rules from highly specialized static analysis frameworks. While frameworks, such as the Clang Static Analyzer [25], are a step in the right direction, the core problem remains in the complexity within the frameworks. Static analysis frameworks usually contain hundreds of thousands of lines of code, due to the complexity of modern-day static analysis algorithms, and can neither be easily understood nor customized. Also in the security domain, increasingly complex algorithms and frameworks make it hard to focus on the primary goal of vulnerability detection. To manage the complexity of static analysis, the use of *domain specific languages* (DSL) has risen during the last years, which counteract the complexity with high-level programming paradigms [29].

In this paper, we propose a static analyzer that relies on Datalog as a DSL to implement static analysis and perform vulnerability scans on LLVM-IR code. Reconstruction of IR semantics, static analyses and definition of rule sets exclusively happens on Datalog level.

Note that this work is not the first solution implementing static analysis based on Datalog rules [4,10,33,36]. Quite contrary, the Datalog engine *Soufflé* was designed with static analysis in mind. However, to the best of our knowledge, VANDALIR is the first comprehensive tool for security analyses which relies to this extent on Datalog to find different types of vulnerabilities based on LLVM-IR. To foster further research, our VANDALIR prototype is open source and available at https://github.com/vandaltool/vandalir.

In summary, we make the following contributions:

- We design and build VANDALIR, a static analysis tool that supports vulnerability patterns defined as declarative Datalog rules. Internally, we construct a VANDALIR pipeline searching for the defined rules on a lightweight knowledge base extracted from the LLVM-IR code of a source code project.
- We implement vulnerability detection rules for stack-based memory corruption, double free and format string vulnerabilities, and show the effectiveness of VANDALIR on the Juliet Test Suite. VANDALIR outperforms well-known tools like the Clang Static Analyzer, CppCheck and FlawFinder in all three categories.
- We demonstrate VANDALIR's effectiveness regarding real-world software code by showing that the implemented rules are able to detect existing as well as previously unknown vulnerabilities. More precisely, we identify 14 new issues in Open TFTP Server. Of these bugs, at least 2 are actually exploitable. One of them is a format string vulnerability, while the other is a buffer overflow. All relevant issues were reported to the developers.

2   Background

In this section we briefly introduce our key technologies, Datalog and LLVM-IR.

Datalog: Datalog is a declarative, logic programming language. It was specifically designed to query large, relational databases, which makes it a promising tool for static program analysis. The ability to express queries and analyses in a highly declarative manner aids and simplifies the development of complex analyses needed in static analysis. Development is usually sped up with Datalog, which reduces costs and manifests Datalog's reputation as a rapid-prototyping tool [11,29,32].

While the development speed is enhanced, the Datalog program itself cannot run natively. Instead, it is executed by a Datalog engine. It is generally accepted, that using Datalog as a DSL has usually worse runtime performance compared to hand-crafted C or C++ solutions. However, Datalog is still often chosen in static analysis [4,8,9,32] due to its other advantages. Furthermore, these performance weaknesses are challenged by new research in the field of Datalog engines. Soufflé [23] aims to enhance performance by synthesizing highly efficient, parallel C++ code from Datalog. This allows Datalog rules to run as monolithic, highly optimized programs, which was shown to increase the performance significantly. The term Soufflé also describes the Datalog dialect used in this paper. To avoid ambiguity, we refer to the Soufflé language just as Datalog [23,29].

A program in a logic programming language is made of a finite set of facts and rules. If all variables in a rule can be substituted by constants, this rule becomes *ground* and thereby new *deduced facts* are produced. These *deduced facts* can then be used to produce further *deduced facts*. Resolving all rules in a program and producing all *deduced facts* is done by the Datalog engine [9,14].

The *deduced facts* are also referred to as *intensional database* (IDB) predicates. They are distinguished from the *extensional database* (EDB) predicates, that contain all facts, that are known to the Datalog program at the beginning. These a-priori facts are also called input relations [16,29].

LLVM-IR: In static program analysis, the input program is often not directly processed by the analysis. Instead, a suitable intermediate representation (IR) is used. The goal is to simplify parsing and facilitate the analysis process [7].

LLVM-IR is an intermediate representation, which is used internally in the LLVM-IR compiler project. Due to different front ends of the LLVM project, various languages like C, C++, Rust or Haskell can be converted into this IR. LLVM-IR is independent of the underlying instruction set architecture, which allows program analysis independently of the used hardware. LLVM-IR itself has a reduced instruction set computer (RISC) architecture. This simplifies analysis as only a limited number of instruction has to be supported. Also, it is Static Single Assignment (SSA) based, which can be beneficial for data flow analysis. It supports a high level type system, that includes base types, derived types and structs. However, at the same time, high-level control flow constructs like loops are already resolved to basic blocks and conditional branching [5,7,15,22].

Altogether, LLVM-IR has many features, which are not only useful in compiler analysis, but also match the requirements of modern-day software analysis. This is why other static analysis tools [4,30,35] have previously used LLVM-IR.

3   Design

In this section, we describe the design of the VANDALIR pipeline. VANDALIR is designed to cover the following four design challenges.

Focus on Security: VANDALIR implements static analyses necessary for a large scope of security problems and also comes with a rule set for different types of vulnerabilities.

Modularization: To simplify extension of VANDALIR's current rule set, the static analyses (core) are separated from the vulnerability detection rule set.

Combination of Datalog and LLVM-IR: The combination of both technologies brings the rapid-prototyping approach of declarative Datalog rules to the broad spectrum of targets, which can be compiled to LLVM-IR. Similarly, the advantages of using Datalog can be combined with LLVM-IR features, that are well suited for static analysis.

Lightweight Relation Mapping: VANDALIR employs a lightweight approach to relations mapping to shift additional complexity to Datalog.

3.1 Overview

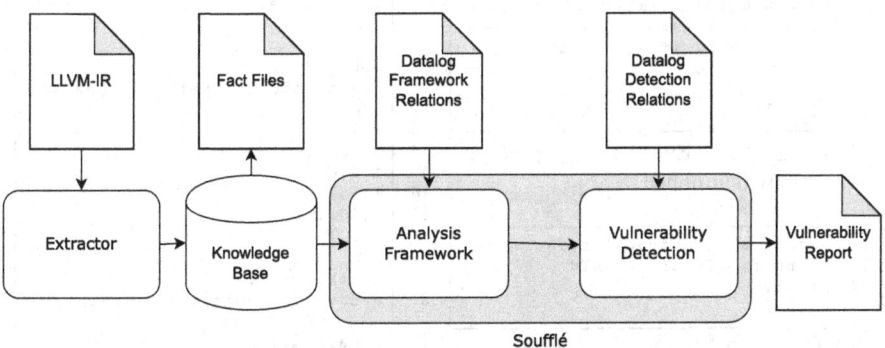

Fig. 1. Overview of the VANDALIR pipeline.

The VANDALIR pipeline consists of three major components, as shown in Fig. 1. It accepts the input program in LLVM-IR and uses the human-readable LLVM-IR assembly representation. However, LLVM bitcode files can also be used, which are then automatically converted into their human-readable counterparts. The extractor parses LLVM-IR and stores the extracted information in the knowledge base, which itself consists of fact files. The other two components, the static analysis core, as well as the vulnerability detection rule set are both implemented in Datalog and are therefore compiled by the Datalog engine Soufflé. Even though these components represent two separate logical steps, they are compiled into one binary and thus cannot be guaranteed to be executed in that order.

3.2   Knowledge Base

The knowledge base of our system consists of all facts, that are provided to the analysis.

Extractor: The knowledge base is generated by the extractor component. The extractor translates LLVM-IR code, which represents the input program, into Datalog facts, that can be accessed by the Datalog engine. The component is implemented as a lightweight Python3 script. It accepts human-readable as well as bitcode LLVM-IR files. To parse the LLVM-IR code, the extractor relies on the Python library LLVMLite [24]. However, as LLVMLite was neither designed for parsing complete LLVM-IR programs, nor does it support parsing of the full LLVM-IR instruction set, further custom parsing and processing steps were implemented.

```
1  [...]
2  define dso_local i32 @main() #0
       {
3      %1 = alloca i32, align 4
4      store i32 0, i32* %1, align 4
5      %2 = add nsw i32 %1, 1
6      call void @foo(i8* %2)
7      ret i32 0
8  }
9  [...]
```

Listing 1.1. Example program in LLVM-IR (simplified).

```
1  is_X_call_instruction.facts
2  Function;InstructionId
3  foo;1
4  [...]
```

Listing 1.2. Recreation of function call semantics in generated is_X_call_instruction fact.

```
1   instruction.facts:
2   BlockId;InstructionId;Instruct
3   0;0;%1;alloca
4   0;1;%-1;store
5   0;2;%2;add
6   0;3;%-1;call
7   0;4;%-1;ret
8   [...]
9
10  operand.facts:
11  InstructionId;OperandId;Operand
12  0;0;i32
13  0;1;1
14  1;2;i32
15  1;3;0
16  [...]
17  3;10;@foo
18  [...]
19
20  instruction.facts
21  FunctionId;Function;defdec;
        returnType
22  0;main;define;i32
23  1;foo;define;void
24  [...]
```

Listing 1.3. Excerpt from extracted fact files of the example program.

Relations Mapping: The mapping of LLVM-IR code to Datalog relations in VANDALIR does not model the semantics of LLVM-IR. Instead, the semantic information is retained as the input relations are directly derived and therefore closely resemble the structure and syntax of LLVM-IR code. This means for example that all operands of instructions are stored in a single Datalog relation. Operational semantics, whenever needed, are implemented in Datalog and are faithful to LLVM-IR semantics. This means that the extracted input relations are internally used by other Datalog relations to reproduce the semantics of the target and make them accessible for rule writing.

An example of our the process of relation mapping and semantics recovery can be seen in the following listings. Listing 1.1 shows an example program in LLVM-IR. The extractor maps this program to input relations and thereby produces facts, which are depicted in Listing 1.3. The *foo* function for example, which is called in line 6 in Listing 1.1 is stored in the operands relations (line 17), while the call instruction itself is stored in the instruction relation (line 6). To access function calls, the Datalog relation *is_X_call_instruction* is implemented, and the facts generated by it (Listing 1.2) recover the original semantics of the call instruction in LLVM-IR (line 3).

The lightweight mapping approach shifts complexity from the extractor to Datalog, which is in line with the original approach of utilizing Datalog to minimize complexity. This allows for easier modifications, as nearly all changes, even with newer LLVM versions, can likely be directly implemented in Datalog. Furthermore, any advances in Datalog processing [29] also apply to semantic reconstruction. Finally, debugging is also simplified, as the extracted input relations can be directly mapped to LLVM-IR code, which in our experience was very helpful during the implementation of VANDALIR and its rule sets.

3.3   Core Analyses

The VANDALIR core is a self-contained Datalog program. It receives a correctly formatted knowledge base from the extractor as input and aims to provide a solid foundation of static analyses, that are typically needed in the field of static security analysis. Therefore, a set of five distinguished analyses are currently implemented in Datalog.

```
1  .decl edge(functionid: _functionid, startblock: _blockid, endblock:
       _blockid)
2  edge(FID, START, END) :-
3      block(FID, START, STARTLABEL),
4      block(FID, END, ENDLABEL),
5      predecessor(FID, ENDLABEL, STARTLABEL)
```

Listing 1.4. Datalog relation that creates the edges of the CFG based on the label information within the predecessor relation.

Control Flow Analysis: The first step is the reconstruction of the control flow graph (CFG) of each function. This can be implemented by linking the correct basic blocks of a function which reconstructs the edges of the CFG. Listing 1.4 shows how VANDALIR utilizes Datalog to express the edges of a CFG in a very compact way. The relation constructs an edge from every block *START* to every block *END* if *START* is a *predecessor* to *END*. This short code fragment shows how powerful analysis operations can be implemented in compact Datalog.

Beyond this very basic example, VANDALIR's control flow analysis supports call graphs, interprocedural control flow and the detection and analysis of loops, conditions and paths. To handle the problem of indirect jumps and function pointers, VANDALIR's control flow analysis utilizes the pointer, alias and data flow analyses to statically determine additional edges in the interprocedural CFGs. If the necessary values cannot be determined statically, VANDALIR does not consider these edges in further analyses.

Data Flow Analysis: VANDALIR also implements a dedicated, interprocedural data flow analysis. It is based on the pointer and alias analyses and can utilize the control flow analysis to be partly context-sensitive. Context-sensitivity is currently only used partly with interprocedural analyses to keep runtime overheads manageable. VANDALIR's data flow analysis is based on constant and value propagation analysis. The constant value propagation algorithm supports basic mathematical operations (e.g. addition, multiplication, ...) of constants and can return calculated values. Furthermore, the data flow analysis relies heavily on the pointer and alias analysis to identify memory locations and their aliases, which may contain usable values. The main focus of the current capabilities was set on integer analysis, as well as on a dedicated buffer size analysis system. This analysis aims to identify the size of any type of memory allocations. For stack buffers with a fixed size, VANDALIR can extract the size directly from the operand of the *alloca* instruction. Similarly, are global variables supported. For heap allocations, however, VANDALIR scans for the functions *malloc*, *calloc* and *realloc* and tries to calculate the supplied size parameter with help of the integer value flow analysis.

Pointer Analysis: An Andersen style pointer analysis [1] was implemented, which is based on the concept of allocation-site abstraction and is similar to the work of Balatsouras and Smaragdakis [4]. The implemented analysis is context-sensitive and supports arrays as well as structs.

Alias Analysis: In general, the goal of this analysis is to identify pointers, which contain the same address and therefore point to the same object. Therefore, it is closely connected to the pointer analysis. To identify these pairs of pointers is useful for nearly any type of static analysis as it allows identifying objects, that reappear at different points in the program. This is especially important for LLVM-IR code as here the SSA-form often introduces additional virtual registers, that point to the same location as already existing virtual registers.

Taint Analysis: The algorithm aims to identify any inputs from outside into the program. This implementation assumes that outside input from the environment, the user, the network, the file system, etc. is processed and provided by a library function. To identify these entry points, the use of these functions is identified with a predefined extendable catalog of input functions. Additionally, this catalog contains the information, which parameters or return values contain pointers to the actual input and which parameters contain possible size restrictions. This catalog is then used to identify all points in the program where data from outside enters the program and taints these memory locations.

From there on, the tainted data is tracked through different mechanisms. In the most simple case, the alias and pointer analysis is utilized to taint aliases and handle use of tainted data in complex objects. To cover the use of typical library functions, like strcpy, a predefined set of transition functions is applied.

Library Mode: VANDALIR supports a special library taint mode in which all functions are assumed to be directly accessible by the user. Therefore, all parameters passed to these functions may contain unfiltered user input. Hence, all pointer type parameters as well as global variables are automatically tainted. While this approach has very negative assumptions, regarding the use of libraries and may introduce many false positives, it can help to identify user input related vulnerabilities in libraries, which are otherwise difficult to detect.

3.4   Vulnerability Detection

The second large Datalog component consists of the detection rule set, which uses the previously described analyses of VANDALIR's core to identify possible vulnerabilities. While these rules can be extended by others, VANDALIR also provides a rule set, which covers different types of vulnerabilities. Currently, 26 rules are implemented, which cover memory corruptions (19 rules), format string vulnerabilities (5 rules), double frees vulnerabilities (2 rules). These rules were implemented based on Common Weakness Enumerator (CWE) definitions and the practical examples provided there.

Buffer Overflows: The detection of buffer overflows is arguably one of the easiest applications for VANDALIR, as its core provides dedicated functionality, which is useful in this use case. The typical example of overflows based by misuse of standard C functions follows a simple pattern: The contents of one memory location are transferred to a buffer, which is not sufficiently sized to hold these values.

```
1   is_vulnerable_strcpy_call_instruction(IID, LEVEL, MESSAGE) :-
2       is_strcpy_call_instruction(IID),
3       block(FID, BID, _), instruction(BID, IID, _, _),
4       get_first_operand(IID, DEST), get_second_operand(IID, SRC),
5       get_buffsize_by_vreg(DEST_SIZE, FID, DEST),
6       get_buffsize_by_vreg(SRC_SIZE, FID, SRC),
7       DEST_SIZE < SRC_SIZE,
8       MESSAGE = "strcpy:␣insufficient␣buffer␣size␣[...]",
9       LEVEL = "Vulnerability".
```

Listing 1.5. Simple Buffer overflow detection rule to catch overflows related to strcpy.

A simple example is the *strcpy* function, for which a detection rule is depicted in Listing 1.5. Uses of the function are identified by the rule in line 2. Then, the source and destination locations are assessed (line 4), their sizes are calculated (line 5–6) and if the destination size is smaller than the source size (line 7), a vulnerability message (line 8) is reported.

This simple example shows how VANDALIR can be used to construct simple and intuitive rules for security issues. Of course, this example can and was further extended to cover also more complex cases. For example, additional analysis of size parameters, as used in *strncpy*, was implemented with the help of the integer value analysis. Also, rules for functions that use format strings like *sprintf* were implemented.

Beyond these basic memory corruption cases also memory corruption for arrays or within loops is supported. Here, the typical issue of out-of-bounds accesses is targeted. In LLVM-IR, accesses to arrays, structs or other complex objects are handled by the *getelementptr* instruction, which receives an operand with the targeted data object as well as possible indices. This design feature of LLVM-IR can be utilized to craft a very compact rule set for the detection of out-of-bounds accesses. The Datalog rules first calculate the size of the targeted object, with the help of the buffer size detection relation. Then, they evaluate for each index, which may be either hard coded or evaluated via the integer value analysis, whether this index is in-bounds or not.

A similar approach was implemented to detect memory corruption within loops. Conceptually, objects over which are iterated are detected, and their size is calculated. Then, the bounds of the loop are analyzed, and it is determined whether the calculated minimal or maximal index accesses may be out of bounds of the iterated memory object.

Format String Vulnerabilities: Regarding the detection of externally-controlled format strings, two different detection mechanisms were implemented. The first, traditional method assumes, that all format strings should be constant. If format strings are constant values, they cannot be used for format string attacks. Therefore, this approach flags all format strings, which are not constant values. However, this traditional approach may result in false positives as not all format strings, that are not constant values, can actually be used for attacks. Instead, attacks can only be successfully executed if the format string can actually be controlled by an attacker. To identify these cases, the second detection approach relies on VANDALIR's taint analysis to detect format strings, which may contain user input.

Double Frees: VANDALIR is also capable of detecting typical heap vulnerabilities, like double frees. The implemented rules rely on the interprocedural alias analysis to identify memory objects, which are freed multiple times within the program. Then, the interprocedural control flow analysis is used to identify paths, which contain at least two free operations on the same memory.

4   Evaluation

To verify, whether our implemented system is capable of detecting vulnerabilities, we evaluated VANDALIR in two ways. First we tested the system with more than 12,000 positive and negative test cases from the Juliet Test Suite [34] and compared the results of rules implemented in VANDALIR against commonly used, state-of-the-art static source code vulnerability detectors. Furthermore, we evaluated whether our proposed system is capable of detecting vulnerabilities in real software products. Since the decision to use the Juliet Suite was made, the detection rules were not amended or extended to avoid possible overfitting of the implemented rule set. However, bug fixes have been applied to the VANDALIR core during any time in the development process.

4.1 Juliet Test Suite Results

Data Set: For the evaluation of the implemented system, we chose the Juliet Test Suite for C and C++ in version 1.3 [34]. The Juliet Test Suite is commonly used in academic work [13,37] as a benchmark test suite for static analysis. The Juliet Test Suite features more than 64,000 artificially created, vulnerable Juliet test cases for C and C++. The cases contained in the suite are ordered by CWE [34]. Our rule set contains detection rules for stack-based memory corruption, format string vulnerabilities and double free vulnerabilities. Hence, we decided to use only test cases from the 9 CWEs, that fall into these categories. We included C test cases for a Linux environment in our test set. An overview of the test set is shown in Table 1.

Table 1. Overview of the chosen CWEs.

CWE	Description	Bad cases	Good cases	All cases
121	Stack-based buffer overflow	324	478	802
129	Improper validation of array index	228	678	906
131	Incorrect calculation of buffer size	102	147	249
193	Off-by-one error	340	490	830
242	Use of inherently dangerous function (gets)	18	31	49
805	Buffer access with incorrect length value	1020	1470	2490
806	Buffer access using size of source buffer	456	660	1116
134	Use of externally-controlled format string	950	3785	4735
415	Double free	190	678	868
Total		**3628**	**8417**	**12045**

Metrics: The bad test cases contain a vulnerability from the given category, while the good test cases contain a patched version of the same code. This allows us to measure not only the number of true positives, but also the number of false positives produced by each tool. The *detection rate* (DR) is defined as the fraction of all bad test cases, which are detected, while the *false positive rate* (FPR) is defined as the fraction of all good test cases, that are falsely detected. Furthermore, we computed a *productivity score* (PR) [3,31], which balances both DR and FPR and is defined as follows.

$$PR = \sqrt{DR * (1 - FPR)}$$

The *robust detection rate* (RDR) shows how many of the test cases are handled robustly. If a test case is handled robustly, the vulnerable version of it is detected (true positive), while the patched version of the same vulnerability is not detected (true negative). Based on this metric *Uniques* (U) can be calculated, which give an absolute number of test cases, which are robustly handled only by one tool in the comparison [3].

Comparison Tools: To verify if our system can compete with the current state of static analysis tools, we used three common static vulnerability scanners for comparison, that have previously been used in the industry as well as in academic research [3,28]. To reflect the broad spectrum of currently used scanners, we opted for three very different tools.

CppCheck (CC) [17] is a tool, that uses unsound flow sensitive analysis to detect a broad range of bugs. According to the developers, the focus is to detect bugs, that other tools do not detect, as well as to minimize false positives.

Contrary to this, Flawfinder (FF) [38] aims to detect as many vulnerabilities as possible with the minimal amount of computational power needed. Therefore, it uses simple pattern matching directly on the source code and is thus especially prone to false positives. Hence, the option by the tool to exclude hits, that are likely false positives, was used during the analysis.

The last tool is the one with the most complex static analysis engine. Here, the capabilities of Clang (CL) in the form of the Clang Static Analyzer [25] and Clang-tidy [26] are leveraged to detect vulnerabilities. Both combined cover a broad spectrum of defects and offer the most sophisticated analysis engine of the compared tools, which also makes it the slowest. Clang was selected as it has proven in a comparative study [3] to excel many other static analysis tools in various categories. The Clang Static analyzer and Clang-tidy were both run together via the tool CodeChecker [20]. In addition to the default core option, the checkers in the group named *security* as well as *alpha.security* were all enabled. To minimize the number of false positives, only findings of the severity level *HIGH* and *MEDIUM* are considered in this paper, which improves Clang's performance in our evaluation.

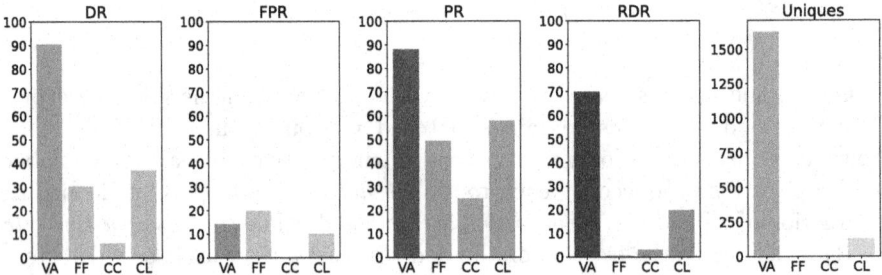

Fig. 2. This bar chart shows the overall performance metrics of the compared tools.

Results: Table 2 shows how the implemented VANDALIR rule set performed throughout our data set. For memory corruption vulnerabilities, the detection rate is over 88%. The large performance differences between different CWEs cannot be explained with different rules, as nearly the same rules apply for all memory corruption test cases. Instead, the differences show, that some CWE categories (e.g. 806) are in general harder to detect in static analysis than others.

This assumption was later confirmed by the results of the other tools, which show similar differences between CWEs.

Both approaches for format string vulnerability detection are able to detect nearly all vulnerabilities and score a 97.4% (taint) respectively 100.0% (static) detection rate. However, as expected, the differences of both approaches become apparent when analyzing the false positives. Here, the traditional approach of format string detection has a relative high false positive rate of over 34%, while the taint based approach did not detect any false positives in the data set. In total, our proposed rules score a detection rate of over 90% and have a false positive rate of less than 15%, which equals a productivity score of over 88%.

Table 2. Overview of the VANDALIR results grouped by CWE category. The tables show the absolute numbers of evaluated test cases in the form of true positives (TP), false negatives (FN), false positives (FP) and true negatives (TN). Also, the detection score (DR), the false positive rate (FPR) and the productivity rate (PR), which combines both metrics, is given. The robustly handled test cases (RO), the robust detection rate (RDR) and Uniques (U) show how robust the detection of our tool is. MC summarizes all categories related to stack based memory corruption. In the all category, the taint based format string vulnerability detection method is used.

CWE	TP	FN	FP	TN	RO	DR	FPR	PR	RDR	U
121	316	8	208	270	172	97.5%	43.5%	74.2%	53.1%	112
129	176	52	163	515	84	77.2%	24.0%	76.6%	36.8%	64
131	64	38	0	147	66	62.7%	0.0%	79.2%	64.7%	22
193	324	16	0	490	334	95.3%	0.0%	97.6%	98.2%	158
242	18	0	0	31	18	100.0%	0.0%	100.0%	100.0%	0
805	852	168	202	1268	724	83.5%	13.7%	84.9%	71.0%	501
806	444	12	624	36	0	97.4%	94.5%	23.0%	0.0%	0
MC	2194	294	1197	2757	1398	88.2%	30.3%	78.4%	56.2%	857
134 (static)	950	0	1290	2495	0	100.0%	34.1%	81.2%	0.0%	0
134 (taint)	925	25	0	3785	950	97.4%	0.0%	98.7%	100.0%	725
415	169	21	0	678	169	88.9%	0.0%	94.3%	88.9%	45
All	3288	340	1197	7220	2535	90.6%	14.2%	88.2%	69.9%	1627

The comparison with other tools, as seen in Fig. 2, shows that the VANDALIR rules produce by far the highest detection rate. No other tool in the comparison comes close. Clang is second best with 37.2% and FlawFinder third with about 30%. However, FlawFinder does not support double free vulnerabilities, which are therefore excluded from its rating. Similarly, CppCheck does not support format string vulnerabilities. Even after exclusion of this category, CppCheck's detection rate is still the lowest with 6.2%. This low rate can be explained as CppCheck focuses more strictly than the other tools only on vulnerabilities it can detect without false positives.

The different designs of the tools become even more apparent in the false positive rates. Here, CppCheck does not detect any false positives in the whole data set. Clang follows with a false positive rate of about 10%, which is only slightly lower than that of our rule set. As expected, FlawFinder has the worst FPR with a rating of almost 20%. As some tools in the comparison have a larger scope than the current VANDALIR rule set, all false positives produced by the comparison tools, which are out of VANDALIR's current scope, are not counted during the evaluation.

Another important finding is, that VANDALIR's current rule set is able to robustly detect 2535 test cases (nearly 70% of all test cases). Of those, 1627 (44.8% of all test cases) are only detected by our tool. The next best tools in this category are Clang with 129 Uniques and CppCheck with only 3 Uniques, while FlawFinder has not detected any Uniques at all.

In summary, our results show that VANDALIR outperforms all other tools in the comparison. Not only does it detect more vulnerabilities and other vulnerabilities than the other tools, but in combination with its relative low FPR, it also achieves the best productivity score. This is not only true for the whole data set, but also for all three different types of vulnerabilities. Our tool also scores the best results in all CWEs, except for CWE 131, where Clang's productivity is slightly higher. Altogether, VANDALIR seems to strike the best balance between vulnerability detection and false positive prevention. As this applies to such a wide variety of test cases, we assume that the good results are not caused by specific detection rules, but show that our chosen approach of combining Datalog and LLVM-IR for vulnerability analysis is in general very promising.

4.2   Real World Results

While test suites can be very useful for evaluation and comparison of different tools, the source code in these test cases may be fundamentally different from vulnerable code in real world software. Test cases are often constructed much simpler. Even though the Juliet Test Suite tries to avoid this shortcoming by generating complex contexts for their test cases, the total program size is still much smaller and has a much higher frequency of vulnerabilities. Even though the Juliet Test Suite offered more relevant test cases in our scope than any other test suite we could find, test suites can usually not cover all possible vulnerabilities from a certain field. Therefore, real world vulnerabilities are often much harder to detect than vulnerabilities in test suites, which leads to tools that may excel in benchmarks, but can hardly find vulnerabilities in real applications [37]. This is why we decided to evaluate VANDALIR also with real world, open source software. Below, we present three showcases, of which each one focuses on a different aspect important to evaluate VANDALIR.

GattLib: The first program of interest is the GattLib library [21], which implements the Generic Attribute Profile (GATT) protocol of Bluetooth Low Energy. In version 0.2 it contained CVE-2019-6498 [19], which is a typical buffer over-read vulnerability (CWE-126) caused by the misuse of the *strncpy* function. This means, it is in our scope of memory corruption vulnerabilities and especially interesting as no similar vulnerability is contained in the Juliet Test Suite.

The *strncpy* function copies n byte from a source to a destination buffer. However, it does not enforce a terminating null byte. So if the destination buffer has the size n and n bytes are copied, but the source buffer contains n or more non-null bytes, the resulting string is not null terminated, which might induce further problems like in the case of this vulnerability.

```
1   gatt_connection_t *gattlib_connect(const char *src, const char *dst, ...)
2   {
3       char device_address_str[20];
4           [...]
5       strncpy(device_address_str, dst, sizeof(device_address_str));
6       for (i = 0; i < strlen(device_address_str); i++) {
7           [...]
```

Listing 1.6. C implementation of the vulnerable function gattlib_connect.

The implemented rule set contained a rule, which should be able to identify this vulnerability. However, as can be seen in Listing 1.6, a pointer received as a function parameter was used as the source buffer. As this function was not called within the library, but exported to be used by other programs, the size of the source buffer could not be calculated by VANDALIR's data flow analysis. While the vulnerability was originally detected using fuzzing, VANDALIR with its existing rules was also able to detect this vulnerability due to library mode, which correctly assumed the source buffer might include user input of an arbitrary length and was able to detect this vulnerability statically. Even though library mode is by design especially prone to false positives, only a single false positive result was detected by VANDALIR [19].

Baron Samedit: This shows that the implemented VANDALIR rules are not limited to test benches, but can also detect vulnerabilities in real world conditions, even if the vulnerabilities are different from those in the Juliet Test Suite. However, we also wanted to verify, how VANDALIR could be used by developers to craft rules for more specific vulnerabilities. Therefore, we decided to design a detection rule for the *Baron Samedit* vulnerability (CVE-2021-3156) [12]. This vulnerability is a heap overflow vulnerability found in 2021 in the then current version (1.9.5) of the sudoers plugin, which is part of the widely used sudo utility. Analysis showed, that the vulnerability has been included in sudo for almost a decade, before it was found by researchers. As sudo is a security-critical, open source tool used in many Linux distributions, it can be assumed, that the code base has been undergone a lot of security testing before. Hence, no current tools are efficient in detecting this vulnerability.

The relevant code fragment is shown in Listing 1.7. The *from* pointer references an argument containing escaped characters, from which these characters should be unescaped by the following while loop (line 3). However, if the provided argument ends with a backslash, the next character behind it is the terminating null byte, which does not count as white space. Therefore, the backslash character is skipped by increasing the pointer value by one. Now, the pointer points to the terminating null byte, which is copied to the buffer to which *to* points to. Then the pointer is increased again and now points to memory behind this terminating

```
1   if (ISSET(sudo_mode, MODE_SHELL|MODE_LOGIN_SHELL)) {
2       for (to = user_args, av = NewArgv + 1; (from = *av); av++) {
3           while (*from) {
4                   if (from[0] == '\\' && !isspace((unsigned char)from[1]))
5                       from++;
6                   *to++ = *from++;
7           }
8           *to++ = '␣';
9       }
10      *--to = '\0';
11  }
```

Listing 1.7. Vulnerable C Code from the sudoers.c file.

null byte. Thus, the while loop is not left and out-of-bounds characters are read and copied to the buffer, pointed to by the variable *to* [12,18].

The underlying problem is that the pointer variable over which the loop iterates is increased more than once within one iteration of the loop. If this happens during the last iteration, the previously described issue occurs. Therefore, to detect this vulnerability as well as similar issues, the designed rule focuses to identify multiple loop variable increases within one loop iterations.

```
1   is_loop_with_duplicate_increase(CBIID, LEVEL, MESSAGE) :-
2       TYPE = "head-controlled",
3       loop(FID, CB, TYPE),
4       loopCondition(FID, LASTBLOCK, CB, CBIID, TYPE),
5       instruction(CB, CBIID, _, _),
6       downwardPath(FID, CB, LASTBLOCK),
7       blockInDownwardPath(FID, CB, LASTBLOCK, BLOCK),
8       blockInDownwardPath(FID, CB, LASTBLOCK, BLOCK2),
9       loop_variable(CB, FID, VAR),
10      is_increase_instruction_of_var(BLOCK, IID, VAR),
11      is_increase_instruction_of_var(BLOCK2, IID2, VAR),
12      IID != IID2,
13      MESSAGE = "duplicate␣loop␣variable␣increase␣in␣loop[...]",
14      LEVEL = "Vulnerability".
```

Listing 1.8. This listing shows the new Datalog rule developed to detect vulnerabilities related to double increases within loops similar to the vulnerability found in sudo.

One version of such a rule is seen in Listing 1.8. The depicted rule supports only head-controlled loops, while of course a similar variant for foot-controlled loops was implemented as well. The rule identifies the loop (line 3) and its terminating condition (line 4). Then, it identifies all syntactically feasible paths within the body's loop (line 6) and searches for instructions, which increase the loop variable (line 10–11). If at least two of these instructions are found and these instructions are not identical (line 12), the issue is detected (line 13–14). Applying this new rule successfully identifies the vulnerability. The other more general rule sets previously implemented for VANDALIR produced one false positive hit on the tested code.

Open TFTP Server: After covering real world memory corruption vulnerabilities, we also evaluated the implemented rule set for format string vulnerability detection. We decided to test the rule set on the current version (1.66) of Open TFTP Server [6]. The program is open source and contains two fairly recent, critical format string vulnerabilities (CVE-2018-10388 and CVE-2018-10389). Both issues misuse the function *syslog* and therefore allow format string attacks. As the existent rule set was applied to the program, both issues were successfully detected. However, in the single-threaded version of the program alone, 15 other possible issues were also detected. Of these issues, only one could be confirmed false positives, 14 were identified as actual bugs and from these at least two are actually exploitable. One of them is an additional format string vulnerability, while the second one is a buffer overflow vulnerability. All relevant issues, were reported to the developers.

4.3 Performance

Table 3. Performance of VANDALIR on real world programs with file size, lines of code (LoC) and number of produced facts of the LLVM-IR file. Also, extraction time (ET), analysis time (AT) and total runtime (RT) is given.

Test case	Size	LoC	Facts	ET	AT	RT
GattLib	120 KB	2,327	7,446	0.28 s	3.63 s	3.91 s
Baron Samedit	557 KB	8,949	19,832	1.39 s	11.00 s	12.39 s
Open TFTP	868 KB	14,561	47,607	2.99 s	74.72	77.71
Sha512sum	1.5 MB	25,426	61,414	11.49 s	192.78 s	204.27 s

Performance and scalability can become problems for Datalog based implementations. Our evaluation was performed using a general purpose quad-core CPU and 8 GB of RAM. In comparison with VANDALIR, FlawFinder and CppCheck are both very fast, with an average time of 0.4 and 0.5 s for 100 Juliet test cases. Due to the complexity of its analysis, VANDALIR is slower with an average time of 8.5 s, while Clang is by far the slowest with an average of 30.0 s. As the Juliet test cases tend to be small with an average IR file size of around 10 KB and produce only a limited number of often less than 1,000 facts, we also measured the performance on real programs with our case studies and programs from *GNU Coreutils*. The largest IR file tested was the *sha512sum* program, which has a size of 1.5 MB and when extracted produces over 61,000 facts. The analysis of this file, with all analyses and rule sets activated, took 204 s and did not produce any vulnerabilities nor false positives. A representative list of programs and execution times can be seen in Table 3.

Our results show, that extraction time is not a major factor, due to our lightweight mapping approach. Additional tests, with different rule sets, did not have much impact on runtime behavior. Instead, the majority of computational effort is needed for the interconnected core analyses of VANDALIR.

5 Limitations

The current VANDALIR prototype is only implemented for and tested with LLVM-IR files generated from C code. However, due to our generic approach to parsing LLVM-IR, we assume that other languages, which can be converted to LLVM-IR, can be analyzed similarly. Also, further research has to show how well our approach scales to large applications. Currently, VANDALIR does not scale to larger programs on our chosen lightweight hardware setup. While large targets were not the current focus of VANDALIR, various tools based on Souf-flé [2,4,9] have been shown to scale to large code bases. These tools assume much higher computational resources and often limit the depth of their interprocedural analyses, which would likely also benefit VANDALIR. Furthermore, Soufflé offers options for optimization via a performance profiling tool as well as external functors, which so far have only been used sparsely during the development of VANDALIR. Additionally, our approach of shifting complexity to Datalog processing is designed to benefit from any advantages made in large-scale Datalog processing [29]. Finally, source code analysis is inherently limited by the availability of source code. Also, unsound, incomplete static analysis tools like VANDALIR will always be prone to false positives. While the current rule set of VANDALIR showed good performance in that regard, this might be different if the rule set and the scale of the analyzed code base are extended.

6   Related Work

Various other approaches have successfully utilized Datalog for static analysis before. Smaragdakis and Bravenboer (2010) [32] presented Doop, a static analysis framework, which focuses on points-to analysis of Java code. In the security domain, Datalog is also utilized in numerous publications. For example, Tsankov (2018) [36] used stratified Datalog for a fully automated security analyzer for Ethereum smart contracts. Another example from the security domain encompasses the work of Garmany et al. (2019) [10], where a Datalog based approach is presented to detect uninitialized stack variables in binary code.

However, these tools can not utilize the benefits of LLVM-IR as the combination of Datalog as an analysis tool and LLVM-IR as an intermediate language is quite rare. Balatsouras and Smaragdakis (2016) [4] presented a structure-sensitive, partly array-sensitive points-to analysis for C and C++ code, which retains much of the available high-level structure information by utilizing type information contained in the LLVM-IR code. Their cclyzer tool implements a successful pointer and alias analysis algorithm. However, it does not include further analyses (like e.g. data flow or taint analysis), that are important for security analysis. Also, it does not support vulnerability detection. For their tool, they also implemented a complex extraction tool in C++, which mapped LLVM-IR to relational Datalog representations [27]. To our knowledge, this tool is the only other LLVM-IR extractor for Datalog applications. Compared to our extractor, their tool focuses more on replicating LLVM-IR semantics, which makes it hardly comparable to our lightweight approach. We believe, that our extractor can be more easily modified or ported to upcoming versions of LLVM-IR. Also, our lightweight approach shifts more complexity to Datalog to fully utilize its benefits. In the work of Gao et al. (2018) [8] a comprehensive detection system for memory corruption vulnerabilities for C/C++ is presented. In this approach, a flow-sensitive pointer analysis is combined with additional information from abstract syntax trees to identify possibly vulnerable operations. However, the false positive rate is not quantified by the authors and the tool has not been open sourced, which is why we could not include it in our comparison. Furthermore, their approach is not suitable for other types of vulnerabilities.

7   Conclusion

We introduce VANDALIR, a Datalog driven, static vulnerability detection tool for LLVM-IR. VANDALIR shows how the benefits of LLVM-IR as an intermediate representation and Datalog as a domain specific language can be combined to create static analyses tools, which use simple, declarative rules to efficiently detect vulnerabilities. VANDALIR's current rule set outperforms other static analysis tools in test cases from the Juliet Test Suite, where it achieved a detection rate of over 90% and identified vulnerabilities, which no other tool in the comparison detected. On real-world open source software, VANDALIR's rule set was capable of detecting known as well as previously unknown vulnerabilities, while maintaining a reasonably low number of false positives.

Acknowledgments. We would like to thank Behrad Garmany for his support during the creation of VANDALIR, as well as Sam L. Thomas, and the anonymous reviewers for helping us improve this paper.

References

1. Andersen, L.O.: Program analysis and specialization for the C programming language. Ph.D. thesis, Citeseer (1994)
2. Antoniadis, T., Triantafyllou, K., Smaragdakis, Y.: Porting doop to soufflé: a tale of inter-engine portability for datalog-based analyses. In: Proceedings of the 6th ACM SIGPLAN International Workshop on State Of the Art in Program Analysis, pp. 25–30 (2017)
3. Arusoaie, A., Ciobâca, S., Craciun, V., Gavrilut, D., Lucanu, D.: A comparison of open-source static analysis tools for vulnerability detection in c/c++ code. In: 2017 19th International Symposium on Symbolic and Numeric Algorithms for Scientific Computing (SYNASC), pp. 161–168. IEEE (2017)
4. Balatsouras, G., Smaragdakis, Y.: Structure-sensitive points-to analysis for C and C++. In: Rival, X. (ed.) SAS 2016. LNCS, vol. 9837, pp. 84–104. Springer, Heidelberg (2016). https://doi.org/10.1007/978-3-662-53413-7_5
5. Criswell, J., Johnson, E., Pronovost, C.: Tutorial: Llvm for security practitioners. In: IEEE Secure Development Conference (2020)
6. Dhir, A.: Open TFTP Server - Project Website (2019). https://sourceforge.net/projects/tftp-server/, Accessed 22 May 2021
7. Dillig, I., Dillig, T., Aiken, A.: Sail: static analysis intermediate language with a two-level representation. Technical report (2009)

8. Gao, Y., Chen, L., Shi, G., Zhang, F.: A comprehensive detection of memory corruption vulnerabilities for c/c++ programs. In: 2018 IEEE International Conference on Parallel & Distributed Processing with Applications, Ubiquitous Computing & Communications, Big Data & Cloud Computing, Social Computing & Networking, Sustainable Computing & Communications (ISPA/IUCC/BDCloud/-SocialCom/SustainCom), pp. 354–360. IEEE (2018)
9. Garmany, B.: Mentalese-an architecture-agnostic analysis framework for binary executables (2021)
10. Garmany, B., Stoffel, M., Gawlik, R., Holz, T.: Static detection of uninitialized stack variables in binary code. In: Sako, K., Schneider, S., Ryan, P.Y.A. (eds.) ESORICS 2019. LNCS, vol. 11736, pp. 68–87. Springer, Cham (2019). https://doi.org/10.1007/978-3-030-29962-0_4
11. Green, T.J., Huang, S.S., Loo, B.T., Zhou, W., et al.: Datalog and Recursive Query Processing. Now Publishers, Norwell (2013)
12. Jain, A.: CVE-2021-3156: heap-based buffer overflow in sudo (baron samedit) (2021). https://blog.qualys.com/vulnerabilities-threat-research/2021/01/26/cve-2021-3156-heap-based-buffer-overflow-in-sudo-baron-samedit, Accessed 21 Apr 2021
13. Kaur, A., Nayyar, R.: A comparative study of static code analysis tools for vulnerability detection in c/c++ and java source code. Procedia Comput. Sci. **171**, 2023–2029 (2020)
14. Kowalski, R.A.: Logic programming. Comput. Logic **9**, 523–569 (2014)
15. Lattner, C.: Llvm. In: Brown, A., Wilson, G. (eds.) The Architecture of Open Source Applications: Elegance, Evolution, and a Few Fearless Hacks, vol. 1. Lulu.com (2011)
16. Lifschitz, V.: Datalog programs and their stable models. In: de Moor, O., Gottlob, G., Furche, T., Sellers, A. (eds.) Datalog 2.0 2010. LNCS, vol. 6702, pp. 78–87. Springer, Heidelberg (2011). https://doi.org/10.1007/978-3-642-24206-9_5
17. Marjamäki, D.: Cppcheck - a tool for static C/C++ code analysis (2021). http://cppcheck.sourceforge.net/, Accessed 17 July 2021
18. Miller, T.C.: Buffer overflow in command line unescaping (2021). Accessed 12 Mar 2021
19. Mishra, D.: GattLib 0.2 - stack buffer overflow. https://www.exploit-db.com/exploits/46215, Accessed 21 June 2021
20. Open Source Software of Telefonaktiebolaget LM Ericsson: CodeChecker Website (2021). https://codechecker.readthedocs.io/en/latest/, Accessed 17 July 2021
21. Part, L.A.: GattLib - GitHub repository. Lab A Part. https://github.com/labapart/gattlib, Accessed 21 June 2021
22. Project, L.: LLVM Language Reference Manual - LLVM 12 documentation. LLVM Project (2021). https://llvm.org/docs/LangRef.html, Accessed 21 Jan 2021
23. Project, S.: Soufflé. A Datalog Synthesis Tool for Static Analysis. Soufflé Project. https://souffle-lang.github.io/, Accessed 22 Jan 2021
24. llvmlite Project, T.: A Lightweight LLVM Python Binding for Writing JIT Compilers - GitHub repository. The llvmlite Project. https://github.com/numba/llvmlite, Accessed 07 Feb 2021
25. Project, T.C.: Clang Static Analyzer. The Clang Project (2021). https://clang-analyzer.llvm.org/, Accessed 17 July 2021
26. Project, T.C.: Clang-Tidy. The Clang Project (2021). https://clang.llvm.org/extra/clang-tidy/, Accessed 17 July 2021
27. Psallida, E.I., Balatsouras, G.: Relational representation of the LLVM intermediate language. Ph.D. thesis, BS Thesis, University of Athens (2014)

28. Russell, R., et al.: Automated vulnerability detection in source code using deep representation learning. In: 2018 17th IEEE International Conference on Machine Learning and Applications (ICMLA), pp. 757–762 (2018). https://doi.org/10.1109/ICMLA.2018.00120

29. Scholz, B., Jordan, H., Subotić, P., Westmann, T.: On fast large-scale program analysis in datalog. In: Proceedings of the 25th International Conference on Compiler Construction, pp. 196–206 (2016)

30. Schubert, P.D., Hermann, B., Bodden, E.: Phasar: an inter-procedural static analysis framework for c/c++. In: TACAS, vol. 2, pp. 393–410 (2019)

31. Shiraishi, S., Mohan, V., Marimuthu, H.: Test suites for benchmarks of static analysis tools. In: 2015 IEEE International Symposium on Software Reliability Engineering Workshops (ISSREW), pp. 12–15 (2015). https://doi.org/10.1109/ISSREW.2015.7392027

32. Smaragdakis, Y., Bravenboer, M.: Using datalog for fast and easy program analysis. In: de Moor, O., Gottlob, G., Furche, T., Sellers, A. (eds.) Datalog 2.0 2010. LNCS, vol. 6702, pp. 245–251. Springer, Heidelberg (2011). https://doi.org/10.1007/978-3-642-24206-9_14

33. St Amour, L.: Interactive synthesis of code level security rules. Northeastern University Boston United States, Technical report (2017)

34. N.I., Technology of Standards: Juliet Test Suite v1.2for C/C++User Guide. National Institute of Standards and Technology (2012). Accessed 12 June 2021

35. Sui, Y., Xue, J.: SVF: interprocedural static value-flow analysis in llvm. In: Proceedings of the 25th International Conference on Compiler Construction, pp. 265–266 (2016)

36. Tsankov, P.: Security analysis of smart contracts in datalog. In: Margaria, T., Steffen, B. (eds.) ISoLA 2018. LNCS, vol. 11247, pp. 316–322. Springer, Cham (2018). https://doi.org/10.1007/978-3-030-03427-6_24

37. Wagner, A., Sametinger, J.: Using the juliet test suite to compare static security scanners. In: 2014 11th International Conference on Security and Cryptography (SECRYPT), pp. 1–9. IEEE (2014)

38. Wheeler, D.A.: Flawfinder - Project Website (2021). https://dwheeler.com/flawfinder/, Accessed 17 July 2021

Branch Different - Spectre Attacks
on Apple Silicon

Lorenz Hetterich[✉] and Michael Schwarz

CISPA Helmholtz Center for Information Security, Saarbrücken, Germany
s8lohett@stud.uni-saarland.de

Abstract. Since the disclosure of Spectre, extensive research has been conducted on both new attacks, attack variants, and mitigations. However, most research focuses on ×86 CPUs, with only very few insights on ARM CPUs, despite their huge market share. In this paper, we focus on the ARMv8-based Apple CPUs and demonstrate a reliable Spectre attack. For this, we solve several challenges specific to Apple CPUs and their operating system. We systematically evaluate alternative high-resolution timing primitives, as timers used for microarchitectural attacks on other ARM CPUs are unavailable. As cache-maintenance instructions are ineffective, we demonstrate a reliable eviction-set generation from an unprivileged application. Based on these building blocks, we demonstrate a fast Evict+Reload cross-core covert channel, and a Spectre-PHT attack leaking more than 1500 B/s on an iPhone. Without mitigations for all Spectre variants and the rising market share of ARM CPUs, more research on ARM CPUs is required.

1 Introduction

With the discovery of Spectre [16] and Meltdown [20], a new class of so-called transient-execution attacks has been introduced [7]. Follow-up works discovered several such attacks classified into Spectre-type and Meltdown-type [7] attacks. Spectre-type attacks exploit speculative execution, a performance optimization found in most CPUs [16]. Meltdown-type attacks exploit vulnerabilities in the exception handling during out-of-order execution [20]. In both cases, transiently-executed instructions, i.e., instructions without architectural effect, have temporary access to data inaccessible in the architectural program flow.

While these transient executions are not visible on an architectural level, they may leave microarchitectural traces such as a modified cache state. Hence, to make the transiently-accessed data visible, these attacks rely on microarchitectural side channels to convert the microarchitectural state to an architectural state. Most implementations rely on the cache as a microarchitectural element to encode the leaked data, and on cache side channels to retrieve them [7,16,20]. Cache side channels are well researched and robust [38]. Even before transient-execution attacks, cache side channels have been used to attack implementations of cryptographic algorithms [21,22,27,38], covertly transmit data in the cloud [25,37], or spy on user behavior [11,19].

L. Cavallaro et al. (Eds.): DIMVA 2022, LNCS 13358, pp. 116–135, 2022.
https://doi.org/10.1007/978-3-031-09484-2_7

Although both cache side channels and transient-execution attacks have been researched for multiple years, the main focus is still on ×86 CPUs. While ×86 undoubtedly plays a big role in computers and servers, ARM chips become more and more popular in PC chips. By the end of 2021, ARM has an estimated market share in the PC chip market of 8%, mostly due to Apple's M1 chip [32]. Moreover, ×86 does not play a large role in mobile devices such as smartphones. These devices are typically powered by ARM CPUs. In this market, Apple CPUs are leading with a market share of 23.4% in 2022.[1] Still, there is next to no research on these CPUs designed by Apple.

In this paper, we analyze Apple ARMv8 CPUs for their susceptibility to Spectre and cache attacks. We rely on 3 different CPUs designed by Apple, the A10 and A11 used in iPhones, and the M1 used in Macbooks and the Mac mini. Our evaluation runs on the stock operating system, i.e., iOS and macOS. In contrast to previous cache attacks on the A10 [12], we do not require a bootrom exploit or a jailbreak. We show that cache attacks are possible from unprivileged applications.

While cache attacks have been shown on other ARMv8 CPUs [19], we face several new challenges on Apple CPUs. Compared to other ARMv8 CPUs, the ISA is limited. For example, the timestamp counter cannot be used in user space, and the flush instructions cannot be used to flush arbitrary addresses. Both are essential building blocks that have been used for side-channel attacks on ARM [19]. Moreover, there is no documentation on the CPU, experiments on the A10 and A11 are tedious as they have to be executed on smartphones, and the operating system is more limited in terms of low-level functionality than, e.g., Linux or Android.

To enable microarchitectural attacks, we investigate different timing primitives on Apple CPUs. For this, we evaluate system registers available to unprivileged users and analyze system libraries. We demonstrate that there are stable timers that can be used by unprivileged users. However, while they can measure microarchitectural states, their resolution is insufficient for efficient attacks. Thus, we rely on a handcrafted counting thread, similarly as previously shown on ×86 CPUs [30], achieving a nano-second resolution.

In addition to the timing primitive, we analyze cache-maintenance instructions on Apple CPUs. We show that, although available, the cache-flush instructions cannot be used in attack settings. Except for the low-power mode of the A10, the flush instructions silently fail, leaving the target data cached. Hence, we show how state-of-the-art eviction-set-generation algorithms can be modified to work on Apple CPUs. Our eviction sets can be generated in less than a second and do not require knowledge of physical addresses. We demonstrate the efficacy of our eviction sets by building a cross-core Evict+Reload covert channel transmitting 3 kB/s with error rates below 13%.

By combining our building blocks, we show a Spectre-PHT and Spectre-BTB implementation on two iPhones and an M1 Mac mini. Our Spectre attack leaks up to 1500 B/s, which is in the same range as the fastest proof of concepts on

---

[1] https://www.statista.com/statistics/216459/global-market-share-of-apple-iphone/.

×86 [31]. Our proof-of-concept implementations also demonstrate that efficient
Spectre attacks can be mounted without requiring a detailed understanding of
the branch-prediction structures. We show that memory barriers, which are the
recommended mitigation by ARM [4], do not behave the same on all tested
CPUs, impeding the efficient mitigation of Spectre gadgets. Moreover, there are
no hardware or software mitigations against our same-address-space, in-place
Spectre-BTB implementation.

We release our entire code as open source:
https://github.com/cispa/BranchDifferent.

Contributions. The main contributions of this work are:

1. We systematically evaluate unprivileged timing primitives on Apple CPUs.
2. We study cache maintenance primitives and provide fast and effective
   eviction-set generation from unprivileged code.
3. We demonstrate that unprivileged cache side-channel attacks on iOS are feasible by implementing a cross-core Evict+Reload covert channel.
4. We show that Spectre-type attacks are possible on Apple CPUs with a proof-
   of-concept attack leaking up to 1500 B/s.

Structure. The paper is organized as follows. Section 2 covers the required
background knowledge. Section 3 discusses the building blocks on Apple CPUs.
Section 4 demonstrates a cross-core Evict+Reload cache covert channel on Apple
devices. Section 5 describes our Spectre proof of concept. Section 6 evaluates proposed timers, cache maintenance methods, and the Spectre proof of concept.
Section 7 discusses mitigations on Apple CPUs. Section 8 concludes the paper.

2   Background and Related Work

Caches. Modern CPUs feature a hierarchy of set-associative caches with N levels. Each cache level has S cache sets each consisting of W ways. Every way
stores a single cache line of a fixed size. When a memory location is cached,
the cache set is determined by the address, while the cache way is decided by a
cache-replacement strategy. The cache line is additionally tagged with the physical address of the memory location. On a cache lookup, all ways of the target
set are checked by comparing the stored tag to the address. If the tag matches,
the cache line can be used and the memory access is done. Otherwise, the next
level in the hierarchy is checked. If a matching cache line is found (cache hit) no
access to main memory is performed, otherwise (cache miss) the value has to be
fetched from main memory. On multi-core CPUs, the hierarchy usually features
at least one level of small but fast caches that are private to each core and a level
with a bigger but slower shared last-level cache (LLC). A cache level is inclusive if its content is a subset of the next-higher cache level. In inclusive cache
hierarchies, cache lines not present in the LLC are not present in any cache.

Cache Attacks. Cache attacks exploit the timing differences between accessing memory that is cached, and memory that is not cached. The best-known cache attack is Flush+Reload [38], which relies on read-only shared memory between attacker and victim. On ×86 CPUs, Flush+Reload uses the unprivileged `clflush` instruction to remove the targeted data from all cache hierarchies. If the victim accesses the target data, it is again cached. The attacker can measure the access time to the target data, based on that time infer whether the victim accessed the data. This suffices to recover cryptographic keys [11,38] or spy on users [19].

To measure the cache state, an accurate timer is used to time memory accesses and distinguish cache hits from cache misses. ×86 provides the unprivileged `rdtsc` instruction to obtain a high-resolution timestamp. If this instruction is unavailable, e.g., as an attacker runs in a restricted environment, a counting thread has been shown as an alternative timing primitive [9,19,28,30]. Depending on the environment and the implementation, the resolution of such a counting thread is in the same range as the native timestamp counter [28].

On ×86, an unprivileged user can remove any accessible memory location from the cache hierarchy using `clflush`. In contrast to ×86, the ARM instruction set does not necessarily provide an unprivileged flush instruction. A slower alternative to flushing is eviction. By accessing a set of addresses mapping to the same cache set, a so-called eviction set, the target cache line is evicted from the cache. Depending on the replacement strategy implemented in the processor, the addresses are accessed multiple times in special patterns to achieve good eviction rates [19]. Using eviction instead of flushing, Flush+Reload can be modified to Evict+Reload. Moreover, a vendor can also decide to prevent unprivileged access to the timestamp counter. As a result, cache attacks on ARM devices are more challenging [8,19]. Green et al. [10] also showed that cache attacks on some ARM devices are harder than anticipated due to Autolock, a performance optimization locking cache lines in the LLC if they are present in a core-private cache. Lipp et al. [19] demonstrate cache attacks on some ARM devices using system calls to access otherwise privileged performance counters. To maintain the cache state, they rely on flushing if available and on eviction otherwise. As Android exposed virtual to physical address mappings at the time of their research, finding eviction sets was straightforward as the physical address determines the cache set. Haas et al. [12] also demonstrate cache side-channel attacks on an Apple A10 CPU. However, they rely on privileged code to do so.

Transient Execution. To improve the performance, modern CPUs rely on out-of-order and speculative execution. These performance optimizations allow executing instructions in a different order than specified in the application to reduce pipeline stalls. However, to ensure correctness, instructions retire in application order, i.e., architecturally, it seems that the instructions are executed in the order specified in the application. The umbrella term for out-of-order and speculative execution is *transient execution*, and instructions executed during transient execution are called *transient instructions* [7,16,20]. Transient instructions that are wrongly executed, e.g., due to a previous misprediction of the control flow, are discarded. Similarly, exceptions during transient execution are not raised architecturally but only result in a pipeline flush. However, microarchitectural state changes, e.g., cache states, are not reverted. Transient-execution attacks exploit these microarchitectural traces to leak data that is not accessible during normal architectural program execution. Transient-execution attacks are categorized into Spectre-type attacks, which exploit control- or data-flow mispredictions [16], and Meltdown-type attacks, which exploit vulnerabilities in delayed exception handling during out-of-order execution [20].

Spectre. Spectre [16] is a transient-execution attack that exploits speculative execution. To avoid pipeline stalls on, e.g., branches, CPUs try to predict the outcome of branches based on previous observations. For correct predictions, the CPU successfully avoids stalling, resulting in an improved performance. However, for wrong predictions, the CPU executes a code path that would not be executed during architectural execution. Such a code path can, e.g., be an out-of-bounds access of a data structure. A *Spectre gadget* is a special piece of code that encodes such illegitimately accessed data into a microarchitectural state. An attacker relies on side channels to bring this microarchitectural state to the architectural state, ultimately leaking the data. Even though several techniques for encoding the data exist [5,18,29,36], most Spectre attacks rely on cache covert channels. Spectre attacks are classified by the target predictor [7]. The variants that received the most attention are Spectre-PHT and Spectre-BTB. Spectre-PHT (also known as Spectre Variant 1) exploits the pattern history table used for predicting whether a conditional branch is taken or not [7]. Spectre-BTB exploits the branch-target buffer predicting the target of indirect branches.

3   Building Blocks

In this section, we introduce the building blocks required for Spectre attacks on Apple CPUs. We focus on Spectre-PHT with a cache-based covert channel. The reason is that Spectre-PHT is widespread [15], not mitigated in hardware [4], and not mitigated via automated software workarounds [34]. However, these building blocks can also be used for different Spectre variants, as we describe in Sect. 7. The main building blocks required are as follows.

1. **Accurate timing**: To distinguish cache hits from cache misses, we require a high-resolution timing source. Previous work [12,19] often relies on platform-specific instructions or APIs that are not available to unprivileged users on Apple CPUs running iOS or macOS.
2. **Cache maintenance**: To continuously probe a cache line, we need an efficient way to remove certain cache lines from the cache. Previous work [19] typically relies on the flush instructions which does not work in unprivileged code on Apple CPUs. Also, the mapping of virtual to physical addresses [12,19] is not available, preventing the direct calculation of eviction sets.
3. **Speculative execution and mistraining**: For a successful Spectre attack, we must mistrain a predictor and obtain a long enough transient-execution window to leak information with a Spectre gadget.

Table 1. Devices used for testing.

	iPhone 7	iPhone 8 plus	M1 Mac mini
CPU	Apple A10 fusion	Apple A11 bionic	Apple M1
OS version	iOS 14.3	iOS 14.2	macOS 11.2.1

In the remaining paper, we use an iPhone 7, iPhone 8 Plus, and M1 Mac mini as listed in Table 1. All these devices feature an ARM-based CPU designed by Apple and run the stock Apple operating system, i.e., iOS on the iPhones and macOS on the M1. All building blocks are evaluated on all of the devices.

3.1 High-resolution Timing

Distinguishing cache hits from cache misses by timing a memory access requires a high-resolution timing source with a resolution of several nanoseconds. Based on a systematic analysis of available timers, we identify and evaluate three possible timing sources discussed in more detail in this section. First, we investigate *system control registers* provided by the CPU. Amongst other functionality, these registers provide different timing sources. Second, we analyze *library functions* provided by the operating system. Such functions sometimes rely on undocumented syscalls or instructions that can be used for precise timing measurement. Third, we implement a *dedicated counting thread* to emulate a high-resolution timer. This approach has also been used in restricted environments for mounting microarchitectural attacks [9,30].

System Control Registers. On ARMv8, system control registers can be read using the `mrs` instruction. While some registers can only be read by privileged users, others are accessible by unprivileged users. We identify two promising registers: the system counter registers (`CNTPCT_ELx`, `CNTVCT_ELx`) [3] as well as performance counters (`PMCCNTR_ELx`) [2]. However, reading the performance counters as unprivileged user results in an illegal-instruction exception on all tested devices. This is in contrast to previous work [19], which used this performance counter via a syscall to mount cache attacks on Android-based ARM devices. We could not find similar unprivileged system calls on Apple devices, hence we cannot use this known high-resolution counter. As unprivileged user, only `CNTPCT_EL0` and `CNTVCT_EL0` are accessible. Apart from a possible fixed offset, `CNTVCT_EL0` is the same counter as `CNTPCT_EL0` [3]. Our evaluation of the counter resolution (cf. Sect. 6) shows that while the counter is stable, its resolution is not sufficient to reliably distinguish cache hits from misses. However, it might still be useful for attacks that distinguish larger timing differences, or when combining it with amplification methods [31].

Library Functions. Library functions provide another source of accurate timing. They may use undocumented system calls or instructions to access a high-resolution timer. We analyze system libraries on iOS and macOS for timing-related functions. According to Singh [33], `mach_absolute_time` is the function with the highest resolution on macOS. We also identify `clock_get_time` as an alternative to `clock_gettime` used in previous research. However, further analysis shows that both functions internally use the `CNTVCT_EL0` system register (cf. Fig. 7 in Appendix B). Hence, these functions do not provide a higher resolution than directly accessing the system register. Consequently, they are not accurate enough to be used as building blocks.

The `clock_gettime` syscall used in previous work [19] is only available on macOS and not on iOS. In contrast to Android, macOS only provides a microsecond resolution instead of a nanosecond resolution. Although the `CLOCK_MONOTONIC_RAW` should provide nanosecond resolution, it again falls back to `CNTVCT_EL0`.

Counting Thread. As an alternative to using an existing timer, we create our own timer by incrementing a shared variable in a background thread. Previous work also used such counting threads for microarchitectural attacks [19,30]. As in previous work [30], we handcraft the counting thread in Assembly to ensure that we achieve the highest-possible update frequency. Using the counting thread, we can distinguish cache hits from cache misses reliably, as evaluated in Sect. 6.

3.2   Cache Maintenance

To remove cache lines from the cache, several flush instructions are available on the ARMv8 architecture. They differ in whether they flush or just invalidate, target instructions (`IC`) or data (`DC`) and which levels of caches are flushed. Also, some determine the cache line to flush by virtual address, while others flush by cache set and way. According to the ARM manual [1], they may or may not be available to unprivileged users. On ARM CPUs where these instructions are available, Lipp et al. [19] demonstrate that they can be used for cache attacks. Specifically, they rely on `DC CIVAC`. This instruction flushes data by virtual address from all CPU cache levels, similar to the `clflush` instruction on ×86 CPUs. While this instruction is available to unprivileged users on Apple CPUs, it does not flush the target address. Similarly, none of the other flush instructions raises an illegal-instruction exception. However, they also fail to flush the targeted cache line. In Sect. 6, we evaluate the effects of the instructions, showing that they are not ignored but also do not work as expected.

As an alternative to flushing, eviction can remove cache lines from the cache by accessing multiple addresses mapping to the cache set of the target cache line. With access to physical addresses, generating an eviction set is straightforward, as parts of the physical address determine the cache set. However, there is no unprivileged way to read the mapping from virtual to physical addresses on iOS or macOS. Thus, we cannot calculate eviction sets as shown previously by Lipp et al. [19]. Lipp et al. [19] relied on the `/proc/self/pagemap` file, which exposed this information on older Android versions. This Linux-specific (pseudo) file is not available on iOS or macOS.

Our eviction is based on the fast eviction-set generation using group testing introduced by Vila et al. [35]. This approach starts from a large set of addresses

```
1  uint64_t cachemiss(char* page){
2    /* page is a fresh page */
3    memory_access(page + rand()
4      % (PAGE / 2));
5    return probe(
6      page + PAGE / 2 +
7      rand() % (PAGE / 2));
8  }
```

```
1  uint64_t cachehit(char* page){
2    memory_access(page);
3    memory_access(page);
4    return probe(page);
5  }
```

Listing 1: Code to produce cache hits and misses without flushing or eviction.

that likely form an eviction set and reduces it until a minimal eviction set is reached. The original implementation is only available for ×86 and does not work on ARM CPUs. The main reason is the usage of low-level ×86 functions, e.g., clflush and rdtsc, which are unavailable on ARM. Moreover, it only supports the eviction strategies of Intel CPUs. However, these strategies are not efficient on ARM due to the different cache-replacement strategy [12,19].

As the eviction-set generation relies on timing to distinguish cache hits from misses, it calibrates a threshold initially. Without a flush instruction available, we would have to resort to eviction for the calibration, resulting in a chicken-and-egg problem. We can easily measure cache hits by accessing the same address multiple times. Accesses after the first access are most likely L1 cache hits. To reliably measure cache misses without flushing or eviction, we rely on the property that a newly-allocated page is not cached. To ensure that the page is physically backed and the translation is cached in the TLB, we access one cache line of the page. Accessing any of the remaining cache lines results in a cache miss. As generating multiple cache misses on a page can trigger the hardware prefetcher [13], we only measure one other cache line on the page before freeing the buffer again. Listing 1 shows the code for measuring cache hits and misses without relying on flushing or eviction. For measuring the time, we rely on a counting thread, as it provides the highest resolution (cf. Sect. 6.1).

4   Fast Covert Channel

In this section, we rely on our building blocks to implement a fast cross-core Evict+Reload covert channel. As our Spectre PoC attack uses Evict+Reload to transfer information from the microarchitectural to the architectural state, this covert channel provides an approximate upper bound for the leakage rate in a cross-core scenario. We evaluate the covert channel on the devices listed in Table 1.

Setup. Sender and receiver are both unprivileged applications running in parallel on different CPU cores. They both map the same read-only shared file into their virtual address space. The data transmission uses two cache lines in

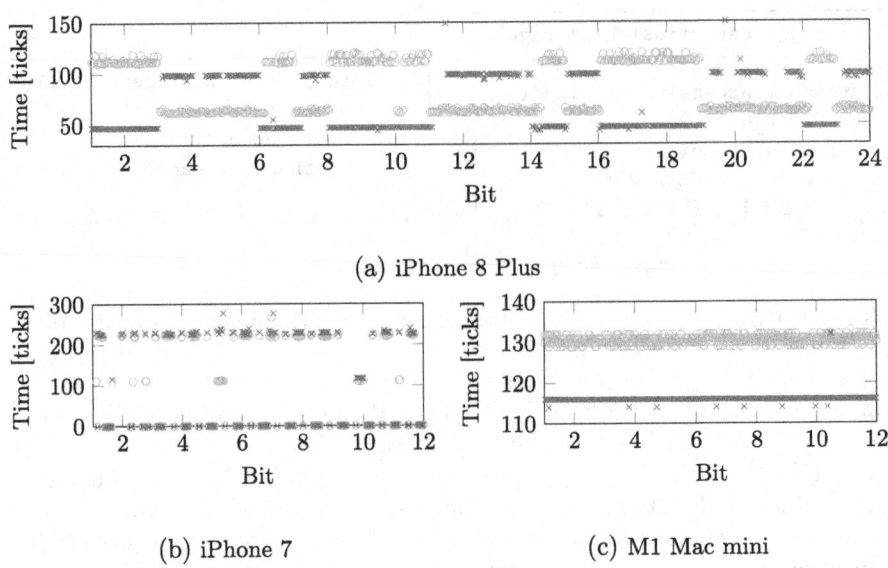

(a) iPhone 8 Plus

(b) iPhone 7

(c) M1 Mac mini

Fig. 1. Covert channel repeatedly transmitting 01110001 with 48 bit/s. Timing on data 1 cache line (red) and data 0 cache line (blue). (Color figure online)

this shared file to transmit data. Depending on the bit to send, one of the two lines is repeatedly accessed while the other one is not accessed. Relying on two cache lines already provides a simple form of error detection. With this encoding, we can detect if either the sender or receiver is not scheduled, a common cause for errors in covert channels [26]. The receiver alternatingly mounts an Evict+Reload attack on both cache lines.

Evaluation. On the iPhone 8 Plus, the covert channel works well with low transfer rates as seen in Fig. 1. As the receiver was started at an arbitrary point in the transmission sequence, the received bit sequence is offset (11100010). On the iPhone 7, the covert channel does not work reliably as pictured in Fig. 1. The figure shows that many measurements are zero. This is due to the limited amount of available cores: On the iPhone 7, only two cores can be active at the same time and no simultaneous multithreading is available. Since our setup requires three threads in parallel, namely one for sending, one for the timer and one to mount the Evict+Reload attack, two cores do not suffice. As a result, we cannot accurately measure memory access times, as the counting thread is not always scheduled.

On the M1 Mac mini (Fig. 1) as well as for increased transfer rates on the iPhone 8 Plus, we observe an interesting phenomenon: We measure cache hits even though the cache line is not accessed by the sender. One reason is that ARM devices can have non-inclusive caches [10,19] which is also the case for the M1 as reported by Handley [13]. On non-inclusive cache hierarchies, a cache line might

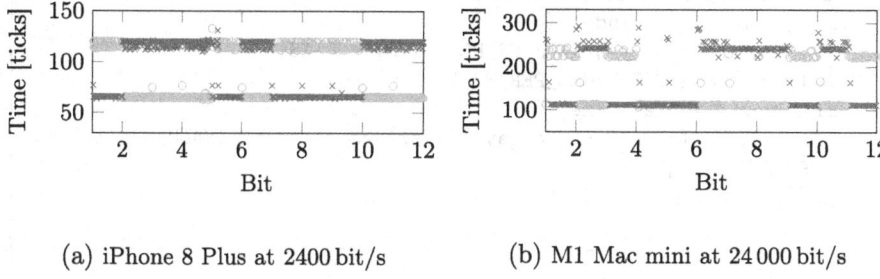

(a) iPhone 8 Plus at 2400 bit/s   (b) M1 Mac mini at 24 000 bit/s

Fig. 2. Optimized covert channel repeatedly transmitting 01110001. Timing on data 1 cache line (red) and data 0 cache line (blue). (Color figure online)

be present in a private cache of a different core even if it is not present in the shared LLC. Instead of fetching the value from memory, it can be served from the private cache instead. Additionally, with AutoLock [10], there is a performance optimization on ARM CPUs. AutoLock prevents a cache line present in a core-private cache from being evicted from shared cache levels. While these effects are problematic for cache attacks [10], we can counteract them as we control both sender and receiver. After transmitting a bit by repeatedly accessing one of the cache lines, the sender evicts that cache line from its private cache. This makes sure that the receiver does not measure cache hits caused by cross-core cache lookups or cache lines locked by AutoLock. With this modification, the phenomenon disappears and we can increase the transfer rate (cf. Fig. 2).

On the M1 Mac mini, we can increase the transfer rate up to 24 000 bit/s as shown in Fig. 2. At this transfer rate, we achieve a bit-error rate of 12.67% without any error correction in place. This results in a true capacity of 10 840 bit/s, which is slightly faster than the fastest Evict+Reload covert channel on ARM demonstrated by Lipp et al. [19]. On the iPhone 8 Plus, we achieve a transfer rate of 2400 bit/s with an error rate of 7.84%, resulting in a true capacity of 1448 bit/s. As shown by Maurice et al. [26], an error-free transmission via such cache-based channels is possible by using error correction.

5 Spectre Exploit

In this section, we describe our Spectre-PHT proof-of-concept implementation using a cache side channel to extract the leaked data. The attack runs as unprivileged applications and leaks up to 1500 B/s on the tested devices (Table 1).

Threat Model. For our proof of concept, we assume an attacker can reliably trigger the execution of a Spectre gadget in the victim. In line with previous work [6,23,29,31], we rely on a bit-wise leakage gadget. Finding such Spectre gadgets in existing code is orthogonal to our work [16,17,24,29]. Hence, we follow best practices for the evaluation and inject our own gadget into the victim application [16,17,24,29]. Listing 2 shows a generic gadget that we use for the

```
1  void victim(size_t index){
2    int shift = (index % INDICES_PER_BYTE) * BITS;
3    index = index / INDICES_PER_BYTE;
4    if(index < *array_size) {
5      mem_access(array2 + ((array1[index] >> shift) & (VALUES - 1)) *
       ENTRY_SIZE);
6    }
7  }
```

Listing 2: The Spectre gadget of the PoC allows leaking 1, 2, 4, or 8-bit values.

evaluation. This gadget allows selecting the number of bits to leak per invocation. Generally, the gadget can either be in the same process, e.g., in a sandbox environment or a different process. In the case of different processes, we also assume shared memory for the array indexed by the leaked value such that the leakage can be recovered using Evict+Reload.

Attack. The attacking code can be divided into four steps:

1. **Mistraining**: To induce a misprediction, we need to mistrain the branch predictor in a way that it predicts the bound check in our Spectre gadget to be true even though the index is out of bounds.
2. **Leaking a value**: With the mistrained branch predictor, we provide an out-of-bound index to access a normally inaccessible value and encode it into the cache. We rely on the same cache-encoding technique as previous work [16].
3. **Retrieving the leaked value**: As the leaked value is only visible in the microarchtiectural state, we rely on a cache covert channel, namely Evict+Reload, to make it visible in the architectural state.
4. **Repeat**: We reset the microarchitectural state by evicting the cache set used for the encoding. With this fresh state, we can repeat the attack for every target bit.

Mistraining and Leaking a Value. For the mistraining, we rely on in-place mistraining [7]. We call the gadget with an in-bound value 9 times to bias the prediction to predict that the provided index is always in bounds. We refer to these invocations of the gadget as training calls. In the 10th call to the gadget, we provide an out-of-bounds index to access memory located after the array. The illegitimately accessed data is encoded in the cache by accessing a memory location that depends on the leaked value [16]. The in-place mistraining has two advantages. First, potential hardware countermeasures cannot prevent this mistraining strategy [7]. Second, we do not have to reverse engineer the intricate details of the branch-prediction structures to find colliding virtual addresses. The mistraining happens at exactly the same virtual address as the misprediction, resulting in a portable and stable way of exploiting Spectre-PHT.

```
1  for(int i = 40; i >= 0; i--) {
2    // leak_index every 10 iterations, training_index otherwise
3    size_t x = (!(i % 10)) * (leak_index - training_index)
4        + training_index; // avoid branches
5    cache_remove(array2); // remove from cache
6    victim(x); // training (in-bound) or attack (out-of-bounds) call
7  }
```

Listing 3: Mistraining and out-of-bounds call to leak a value speculatively.

The training calls each encode the values from the target array (array1) into the cache state (array2). Since we train on a null byte in array1, array2[0] is always cached. For the leakage, a cache line of array2 is accessed that depends on the leaked value. To increase the speculative execution window, we evict the size of the array (array_size) that is used for the bound check from the cache. Listing 3 shows the loop that calls the Spectre gadget. To deal with the non-perfect misprediction rate, we try to leak every value 4 times.

Retrieving the Leaked Value and Repeat. To retrieve the leaked value from the cache state, we probe all entries of array2 and remember indices where a cache hit was measured. A cache hit at a non-zero index directly reveals the leaked value. A cache hit on index zero does not directly provide information, as this index is always cached due to the training calls. However, if there is no other cache hit, we infer that the leaked value must be '0'. To reset the cache state of array2, we require an eviction set for every entry that we probe. These eviction sets are generated once and then used for every repetition.

Section 6 evaluates our proof-of-concept implementation.

6 Evaluation

In this section, we evaluate our implementation. We analyze the building blocks, i.e., the timing sources and cache-maintenance functions (cf. Sect. 3). We evaluate the Spectre-PHT proof-of-concept implementation, demonstrating leakage rates of up to 1500 B/s. All evaluations are done on three devices (2 iPhones, 1 Mac mini), as shown in Table 1.

6.1 High-Resolution Timing

Accurate timing allows distinguishing cache hits from cache misses and serves as a powerful primitive for cache side channels. Section 3.1 introduces three different methods for accurate timing, based on directly reading system-control registers, via syscalls, and using a counting thread. In this section, we analyze the resolution of these different timing sources. We show that a dedicated counting thread is the most reliable method for distinguishing cache hits from misses on all tested devices.

System Control Registers. The system control register of the system timer can be accessed directly via inline assembly (cf. Listing 4 in Appendix A). We do this to benchmark the timer on both iPhones and the M1 Mac mini. The measured frequency for all three devices is approximately 25 MHz (40 ns per increment). This measurement aligns with the 24 MHz (41.67 ns per increment) reported by the system counter frequency register CNTFRQ_EL0. This resolution is in the same range as the difference between cache hits and misses. However, based on when the register is read, misclassifications can happen in both directions, i.e., cache hits can be classified as misses and vice versa. While this is tolerable for the Spectre attack, it is not tolerable for the eviction-set generation. In this process, the timing has to reliably distinguish cache hits from misses to ensure that the algorithm converges. Using this system counter as a timer, we are unable to find eviction sets due to these misclassifications. This indicates that the timer is not accurate enough for measuring single events.

Library Functions. Section 3.1 introduces two candidates for accurate timing through library functions: clock_get_time and mach_absolute_time. However, the analysis of these functions (cf. Fig. 7 in Appendix B) shows that internally, they rely on reading the system counter. We also evaluate this empirically, showing the expected update frequency of approximately 25 MHz. Hence, these functions are no improvement over directly accessing the system control register.

Counting Thread. We implement the counting thread purely in inline assembly to ensure the highest-possible update frequency (cf. Listing 5 in Appendix A). To measure the resolution, we evaluate the number of increments per second. The counting thread achieves approximately 800 MHz (1.25 ns per increment) on the iPhone 8 Plus, 2.4 GHz (0.42 ns per increment) on the iPhone 7, and 3 GHz (0.33 ns per increment) on the M1 Mac mini. In addition to the update frequency, we evaluate how well the timer is suited for distinguishing cache hits and misses. To evaluate this, we measure individual cache hits and misses to verify that we can distinguish them. For ensuring that an address is a cache hit or miss, we use the method shown in Listing 1 that we also use to calibrate the eviction-set generation. Using this method, we ensure that we do not inadvertently see the effects of imperfect eviction.

Figure 3 shows that we can clearly distinguish most cache hits from misses. However, in fewer than 1% of the measurements, we measure an access time of zero for both cache hits and misses. This happens if the counting thread is not scheduled and, thus, the counter is not incremented. As zero is never a valid access time, we can mark measurements of zero as invalid instead of cache hits to decrease the number of false positives. We observe less than 0.6% false positives and negatives on both iPhones, excluding invalid measurements of zero.

6.2   Cache Maintenance

In this section, we evaluate the native cache-flush instructions and cache eviction on Apple CPUs.

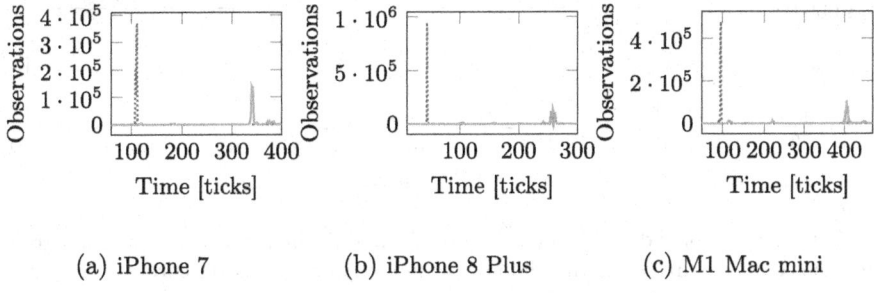

(a) iPhone 7   (b) iPhone 8 Plus   (c) M1 Mac mini

Fig. 3. Counting thread cache hit (blue dotted) and miss (red solid) timings. (Color figure online)

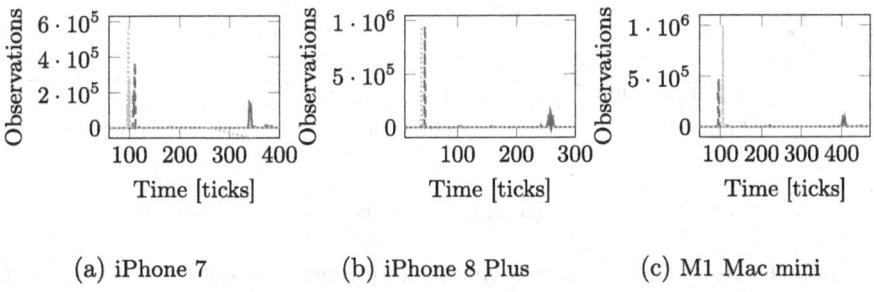

(a) iPhone 7   (b) iPhone 8 Plus   (c) M1 Mac mini

Fig. 4. Cache hit (blue dashed), miss (red solid), and flushed (green dotted) histogram using the counting thread. (Color figure online)

Flushing. We evaluate the flush instructions by timing 1 000 000 accesses to cached cache lines and flushed cache lines using the counting thread as the timing source. While we expect a timing difference between cache hits and cache misses, the average access times for flushed and non-flushed cache lines are the same, as shown in Fig. 4. However, if we only measure 200 accesses on the iPhone 7, we see a timing difference for accessing flushed and cached cache lines (Fig. 5). Increasing the run time of the evaluation code by prepending a busy-wait loop reveals that flushing does not work if the execution time of the code exceeds approximately 25 ms. This is likely caused by the processor switching from low-power to high-power cores and flushing only working on low-power cores. Thus, the native flush instructions cannot be used for generic cache attacks on Apple CPUs. Interestingly, this silent-fail behavior is undocumented. The flush instructions can throw an exception, e.g., if the target address is not readable or if the instruction is not enabled for unprivileged users. Based on the documentation, the instruction is successful if no such exception is thrown.

Eviction. For the eviction, we use the eviction-set-generation algorithm from Sect. 3.2. For both iPhones, an eviction set size of size 16 works reliably. For the M1 Mac mini, the set contains 32 addresses. We do not require minimal eviction

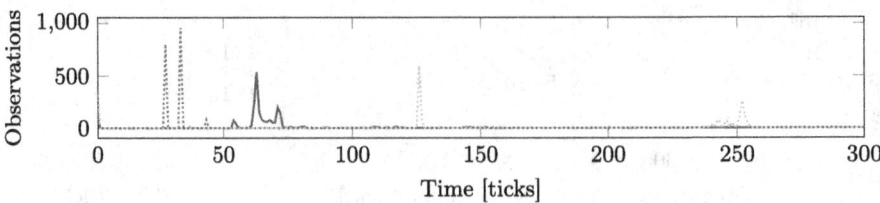

Fig. 5. Cache hit (blue dashed), miss (red solid), and flushed (green dotted) histogram using the counting thread on an iPhone 7 presumably on low-power core. (Color figure online)

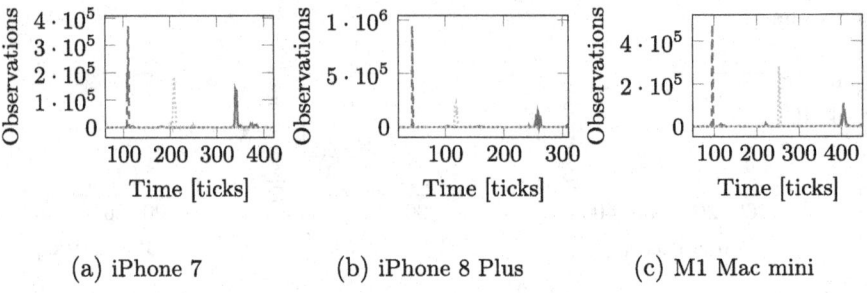

| (a) iPhone 7 | (b) iPhone 8 Plus | (c) M1 Mac mini |

Fig. 6. Cache hit (blue dashed), miss (red solid), evicted (green dotted). (Color figure online)

sets for our Evict+Reload attack as this only affects the leakage rate but not the success of the attack. Thus, trading some performance for greater reliability by increasing the number of addresses is reasonable. Figure 6 shows the access times for data in the cache, not in the cache, and evicted. Accessing evicted data is faster than data not in the cache, as it might not have been evicted from all caches. Still, the timing difference is large enough to distinguish evicted data from cached data reliably.

Eviction takes on average 904 ticks on the iPhone 7, 820 ticks on the iPhone 8, and 987 ticks on the M1 Mac mini. For each device, we measure one million evictions and calculate the eviction rate by dividing the number of cache misses by the number of valid measurements. We achieve eviction rates above 98.5% on all devices, as shown in Table 2.

Table 2. Eviction rates tested with 1 000 000 measurements.

Device	Threshold	Cache hits	Cache misses	Invalid	Eviction rate
iPhone 7	100	14	996 968	3018	99.999%
iPhone 8 plus	80	13 868	976 748	9384	98.600%
M1 Mac mini	140	6	999 223	771	99.999%

Table 3. Spectre PoC leakage and error rate.

Device	Leakage rate	Error rate	Setup time
iPhone 7	1522 B/s	6.18%	804 ms
iPhone 8 plus	1590 B/s	4.89%	852 ms
M1 Mac mini	1109 B/s	13.66%	957 ms

6.3   Spectre-PHT Proof of Concept

In this section, we evaluate the Spectre-PHT proof of concept (cf. Sect. 5). For the evaluation, we use a Spectre gadget leaking 4 bit per invocation on both iPhones and 2 bit per invocation on the M1 Mac mini. Those values resulted in the highest leakage rate in our testing. To evaluate throughput and error rate, we leak 10 kB of data. As the setup time has a significant impact on the total runtime, we measure the setup time additionally. The setup time mainly consists of creating the eviction sets used for the cache encoding. On all devices, the setup time is slightly below 1s. Note that the setup time is independent of the size of the secret and thus always in the same range.

The results are summarized in Table 3. We measure leakage rates above 1000 B/s on all devices, with up to 1590 B/s on the iPhone 8 Plus. Our leakage rates are in the same range as state-of-the-art Spectre proof-of-concept implementations on ×86 [31]. These results not only show that our building blocks are robust but also that Apple CPUs are not inherently more secure against Spectre than Intel or AMD CPUs.

7   Discussion

Other Spectre Variants. For our proof of concept, we focus on Spectre-PHT, as it is difficult to mitigate and a widespread issue [15,19]. However, our building blocks can also be combined for other Spectre variants. We experimentally verify that our proof of concept also works with a Spectre-BTB [16] gadget, which mispredicts the destination of an indirect branch. As our code is open source, it can be used to test a variety of transient-execution attacks on Apple CPUs. Testing other Spectre variants is simply a matter of replacing the victim gadget.

Mitigations. To prevent Spectre-PHT attacks, the state-of-the-art mitigation technique on all CPUs is to add memory fences between conditional jumps and subsequent memory accesses [4,14]. ARM introduced a new barrier instruction CSDB. This barrier is also used in higher-level functions provided by ARM[2], such as load_no_speculate_fail that load a value from a bounded buffer without speculatively accessing values out of bounds. However, we experimentally verify that on both iPhones, the CSDB instruction has no effect on speculative execution.

---

[2] https://github.com/ARM-software/speculation-barrier

Adding `CSDB` to the Spectre-PHT gadget does not mitigate the exploit. On the M1 Mac mini, `CSDB` is available and stops the leakage in our proof of concept. ARM also suggests to use a Data Synchronization Barrier (DSB) together with an `ISB`. The `ISB` instruction prevents exploitation on both iPhones and the M1 Mac mini. Data Memory Barriers (DMB) or `DSB` alone do not stop speculative execution.

Other Spectre variants, such as Spectre-BTB, can be mitigated in an automated way on ×86 using retpolines [34]. However, this workaround does not work on ARM CPUs [4]. Hence, our Spectre-BTB proof of concept can currently not be mitigated on Apple CPUs.

8   Conclusion

We demonstrated a reliable Spectre attack on the ARMv8-based Apple CPUs with leakage rates up to 1500 B/s. Our attack solves several challenges specific to Apple CPUs and their operating system. We showed that no unprivileged high-resolution timer is available but that a counting thread is highly reliable for microarchitectural attacks. We demonstrated a reliable eviction-set-generation implementation to enable cache attacks despite the unavailability of cache-maintenance instructions. The incomplete software workarounds for Spectre variants on these CPUs combined with the rising market share shows that more research on ARM, and especially Apple CPUs, is required.

Acknowledgments. We thank the anonymous reviewers for their valuable feedback and suggestions that helped to improve the paper. Furthermore, we thank the Saarbrücken Graduate School of Computer Science for their funding and support of Lorenz Hetterich.

A   Code

```
1 uint64_t read_system_counter() {
2   uint64_t result;
3   asm volatile("MRS %[result], CNTPCT_EL0": [result] "=r" (result));
4   return result;
5 }
```

Listing 4: Reading the system counter control register.

Listing 4 shows the code for directly accessing the system control register of the system timer. Listing 5 shows the code used for the counting thread. This code is executed in a thread running on its own CPU core.

B   Library Functions

Figure 7 shows the call graph of library functions providing high-resolution times-tamps. All functions internally use the CNTVCT_EL0 system register.

```
1 static void* counter_thread(void* arg) {
2   asm volatile(
3     "LDR x10, [%[counter]]\n" // load counter once
4     "loop:\n"                 // while(true) {
5     "ADD x10, x10, #1\n"      //    increment counter
6     "STR x10, [%[counter]]\n" //    store counter to memory
7     "B loop\n"                // }
8     :: [counter] "r" (arg) : "x10", "memory");
9 }
```

Listing 5: The counting thread used for accurate timing.

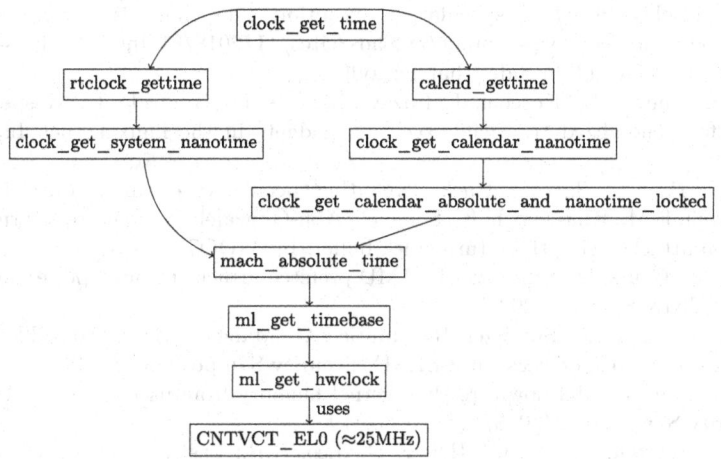

Fig. 7. Call hierarchy of timer library functions.

References

1. ARM: ARM Architecture Reference Manual ARMv8. ARM Limited (2013)
2. ARM: Arm coresight performance monitoring unit architecture (2020). https://developer.arm.com/documentation/ihi0091/a-a
3. ARM: Learn the architecture: Generic timer (2021). https://developer.arm.com/documentation/102379/0000/The-processor-timers

4. ARM: Whitepaper Cache Speculation Side-channels (2018). https://developer.arm.com/support/arm-security-updates/speculative-processor-vulnerability/download-the-whitepaper

5. Bhattacharyya, A., et al.: SMoTherSpectre: exploiting speculative execution through port contention. In: CCS (2019)

6. Bhattacharyya, A., et al.: SMoTherSpectre: exploiting speculative execution through port contention. arXiv:1903.01843 (2019)

7. Canella, C., et al.: A systematic evaluation of transient execution attacks and defenses. In: USENIX Security Symposium (2019). extended classification tree and PoCs at https://transient.fail/

8. Easdon, C., Schwarz, M., Schwarzl, M., Gruss, D.: Rapid prototyping for microarchitectural attacks. In: USENIX Security (2022)

9. Gras, B., Razavi, K.: ASLR on the line: practical cache attacks on the MMU. In: NDSS (2017)

10. Green, M., Rodrigues-Lima, L., Zankl, A., Irazoqui, G., Heyszl, J., Eisenbarth, T.: AutoLock: why cache attacks on ARM are harder than you think. In: USENIX Security Symposium (2017)

11. Gruss, D., Spreitzer, R., Mangard, S.: Cache template attacks: automating attacks on inclusive last-level caches. In: USENIX Security Symposium (2015)

12. Haas, G., Potluri, S., Aysu, A.: itimed: Cache attacks on the apple a10 fusion soc. Cryptology ePrint Archive (2021)

13. Handley, M.: M1 Exploration - v0.70 (2021)

14. Intel: Intel analysis of speculative execution side channels (2018). https://newsroom.intel.com/wp-content/uploads/sites/11/2018/01/Intel-Analysis-of-Speculative-Execution-Side-Channels.pdf

15. Johannesmeyer, B., Koschel, J., Razavi, K., Bos, H., Giuffrida, C.: Kasper: scanning for generalized transient execution gadgets in the linux kernel. In: NDSS (2022)

16. Kocher, P., et al.: Spectre attacks: exploiting speculative execution. In: S&P (2019)

17. Koruyeh, E.M., Khasawneh, K., Song, C., Abu-Ghazaleh, N.: Spectre returns! speculation attacks using the return stack buffer. In: WOOT (2018)

18. Lipp, M., Gruss, D., Schwarz, M.: AMD prefetch attacks through power and time. In: USENIX Security (2022)

19. Lipp, M., Gruss, D., Spreitzer, R., Maurice, C., Mangard, S.: ARMageddon: cache attacks on mobile devices. In: USENIX Security Symposium (2016)

20. Lipp, M., et al.: Meltdown: reading kernel memory from user space. In: USENIX Security Symposium (2018)

21. Liu, F., Yarom, Y., Ge, Q., Heiser, G., Lee, R.B.: Last-level cache side-channel attacks are practical. In: S&P (2015)

22. Lou, X., Zhang, T., Jiang, J., Zhang, Y.: A survey of microarchitectural side-channel vulnerabilities, attacks, and defenses in cryptography. In: ACM CSUR (2021)

23. Loughlin, K., et al.: DOLMA: securing speculation with the principle of transient non-observability. In: USENIX Security Symposium (2021)

24. Maisuradze, G., Rossow, C.: ret2spec: speculative execution using return stack buffers. In: CCS (2018)

25. Maurice, C., Neumann, C., Heen, O., Francillon, A.: C5: cross-cores cache covert channel. In: DIMVA (2015)

26. Maurice, C., et al.: Hello from the other side: SSH over robust cache covert channels in the cloud. In: NDSS (2017)

27. Osvik, D.A., Shamir, A., Tromer, E.: Cache attacks and countermeasures: the case of AES. In: CT-RSA (2006)
28. Schwarz, M., Maurice, C., Gruss, D., Mangard, S.: Fantastic timers and where to find them: high-resolution microarchitectural attacks in javascript. In: FC (2017)
29. Schwarz, M., Schwarzl, M., Lipp, M., Gruss, D.: NetSpectre: read arbitrary memory over network. In: ESORICS (2019)
30. Schwarz, M., Weiser, S., Gruss, D., Maurice, C., Mangard, S.: Malware guard extension: using SGX to conceal cache attacks. In: DIMVA (2017)
31. Schwarzl, M., et al.: Dynamic process isolation. arXiv:2110.04751 (2021)
32. Shah, A.: Apple is beginning to undo decades of Intel, x86 dominance in PC market. The Register (2021). https://www.theregister.com/2021/11/12/apple_arm_m1_intel_x86_market/
33. Singh, A.: Mac OS X Internals: A Systems Approach: A Systems Approach. Addison-Wesley, Boston (2016)
34. Turner, P.: Retpoline: a software construct for preventing branch-target-injection (2018). https://support.google.com/faqs/answer/7625886
35. Vila, P., Köpf, B., Morales, J.: Theory and practice of finding eviction sets. In: S&P (2019)
36. Weber, D., Ibrahim, A., Nemati, H., Schwarz, M., Rossow, C.: Osiris: automated discovery of microarchitectural side channels. In: USENIX Security (2021)
37. Wu, Z., Xu, Z., Wang, H.: Whispers in the hyper-space: high-bandwidth and reliable covert channel attacks inside the cloud. ACM Trans. Netw. **23**, 603–615 (2014)
38. Yarom, Y., Falkner, K.: Flush+reload: a high resolution, low noise, L3 cache side-channel attack. In: USENIX Security Symposium (2014)

MPKAlloc: Efficient Heap Meta-data Integrity Through Hardware Memory Protection Keys

William Blair[1]([✉]), William Robertson[2], and Manuel Egele[1]

[1] Boston University, 111 Cummington Mall, Boston, MA 02215, USA
{wdblair,megele}@bu.edu
[2] Northeastern University, 360 Huntington Ave, Boston, MA 02115, USA
wkr@ccs.neu.edu

Abstract. Memory corruption exploits continue to plague high profile applications such as web browsers, high performance servers, and mobile devices. Modern defenses for these targets have rendered classic attack vectors that execute shellcode directly on the stack impotent and obsolete. Instead, modern exploits frequently corrupt the data structures found in a program's memory allocator in order to take control of running processes. These attacks against the heap are much harder to defend against versus classic stack-based buffer overflows because they often rely on an allocator acting on corrupted data in order to take control of a process. In this work, we introduce MPKAlloc, a memory allocator that utilizes memory protection keys (MPKs) found in recent Intel CPUs to effectively isolate heap meta-data from adversaries. We present our prototype implementation of MPKAlloc which hardens the `tcmalloc` and `PartitionAlloc` memory allocators used by the popular Chrome web browser. MPKAlloc protects each page containing heap meta-data with a key that provides an allocator exclusive access to the page. Effectively, MPKAlloc thwarts an adversary's ability to access or corrupt heap meta-data at the hardware level. We embed the MPKAlloc defense in the open-source Chromium web browser, and demonstrate MPKAlloc stopping realistic attack vectors. Furthermore, we evaluate the performance overhead of Chromium configured with MPKAlloc on the top 50 web sites contained in the Alexa site ranking. Our evaluation shows that MPKAlloc introduces a geometric mean of 1.71% performance overhead (2.44% on average) when browsing the most popular web sites, in exchange for a significant increase in security against heap meta-data exploitation.

Keywords: Memory protection keys · Hardened memory allocators · Hardware security

1 Introduction

The turn of the 21st century saw the explosive growth of the World Wide Web and with it the rapid adoption of web browsers as a means to consum-

L. Cavallaro et al. (Eds.): DIMVA 2022, LNCS 13358, pp. 136–155, 2022.
https://doi.org/10.1007/978-3-031-09484-2_8

ing entertainment, conducting business, and social networking. As the world flocked to the Web and began rapidly creating and sharing content within web browsers, the problem of securing individual computers from malicious content quickly emerged. In 2001, the classic unlink exploit became known on the popular Netscape browser using a seemingly harmless JPEG image [33]. This exploit only required a user to visit a web site hosting the hostile image in order to allow an adversary to hijack the browser process. The exploit itself took advantage of how Netscape's memory allocator failed to sufficiently validate pointers held in a memory chunk's meta-data. If an adversary could corrupt this meta-data, they could fool the allocator into writing into an arbitrary address once the allocator freed the corrupted chunk. In this case, a malicious JPEG file could trick the image processing module in the browser to corrupt a chunk of memory, free it later on, and take control of the Netscape process. In the decades since the disclosure of this exploit, heap exploitation has grown into a sophisticated craft that continues to evade the defenses found within modern memory allocators [6]. Memory allocators protect the integrity of meta-data with cookies [31], use advanced hardware features to check the integrity of pointers throughout program execution [18], or explicitly track pointers to prevent the exploitation of temporal memory errors [8]. Such defenses may come with non-trivial performance overhead in both execution time and memory usage. For example, the recent MarkUS allocator [8] can efficiently track dangling pointers throughout program execution. However, it does so at the cost of a worst-case 2X performance penalty and one-third memory overhead. Making a memory allocator more secure by adding additional checks to detect tampering with internal data structures creates tension with the allocator's intended purpose: efficiently providing memory chunks of arbitrary size to a program whilst minimizing fragmentation. Furthermore, recent work has begun automating the discovery of novel heap exploitation techniques [20,35,37] in the spirit of automated exploit generation (AEG) [10]. This automation complicates the task of reliably ensuring heap integrity. For these reasons, any proposed security improvement to a production-quality allocator requires significant evidence that the change will not negatively impact performance in the allocator's intended use cases.

In light of this tension, we propose MPKAlloc, a technique for hardening memory allocators that isolates heap meta-data by leveraging hardware memory protection keys (MPKs) available on recent CPU architectures. Unlike software-based integrity checks, MPKs immediately detect any attempt to read from or tamper with heap meta-data. In addition, MPKs incur no significant performance overhead and no memory footprint. Memory protection keys can also be found in ARM processors in the upcoming memory tagging extensions (MTE) [5] as well as IBM's AIX operating system as "storage protect keys" [3] for Power systems [21]. MPKs divide the pages that make up a process' address space into individual protection domains and allow each thread of execution to operate within one or more domains. MPKAlloc uses this functionality to confine a memory allocator to operate within its own (privileged) domain when reading from and writing to heap meta-data. MPKAlloc assigns regular (i.e., non meta-data) heap memory chunks a label with another (unprivileged) domain. Later on, if an adversary exploits a bug in the running program, any attempt to read or corrupt heap meta-data is prevented by the hardware and, by default, the OS terminates the offending process. This simple defense effectively neutralizes the entire class of heap meta-data corruption attacks that evolved from the classic unlink attack. Isolating heap meta-data from program components using memory protection keys can be accomplished with a compact implementation given sufficient domain knowledge of the memory allocators used by an application. We present a prototype implementation of MPKAlloc based on the popular `tcmalloc` and `PartitionAlloc` memory allocators and Intel MPK. We evaluate MPKAlloc on the SPEC CPU2006 benchmarks and show that MPKs introduce only marginal overheads. To evaluate MPKAlloc's defensive capabilities on real software, we embedded MPKAlloc within multiple allocators in the Chromium web-browser. Browsers based off of Chromium enjoy 63.59% of the worldwide browser market share as of 2021. We found that in a realistic scenario, where an adversary achieves an arbitrary write primitive by corrupting meta-data, MPKAlloc intercepts the adversary before the corruption and terminates the compromised Chromium process in response. We measure the performance impact of MPKAlloc when visiting the top 50 most popular web sites contained in the Alexa ranking. Our results show that MPKAlloc can protect widely used programs like the Chromium web browser from real attacks while introducing little performance overhead on average. Prior systems have focused on developing secure intra-process isolation schemes within specialized high-performance servers [19,34] or making MPKs a virtualized resource [28]. In contrast, MPKAlloc uses MPKs to ensure the security of sensitive data within widespread consumer software. In the interest of open science, the source code for MPKAlloc can be found online[1].

In summary, we make the following contributions in this paper.

- We recognize that heap meta-data and regular data allocated in the heap can be completely partitioned.
- We introduce MPKAlloc, a generic technique for hardening memory allocators that leverages memory protection keys to enforce these partitions. This implements intra-process code partitioning and provides an allocator exclusive access to its meta-data (see Sect. 3.2).
- We design and implement a prototype that applies the MPKAlloc technique by hardening Google's popular `tcmalloc` and `PartitionAlloc` allocators using Intel's memory protection keys.
- Our security evaluation shows that MPKAlloc prevents exploits that corrupt heap meta-data in the Chromium web browser.
- Finally, our performance evaluation demonstrates that MPKAlloc introduces little performance overhead as measured over the SPEC CPU2006 benchmarks (0.8% on average) and on page load times in Chromium (2.44% on average).

---

[1] https://github.com/BUseclab/mpkalloc.

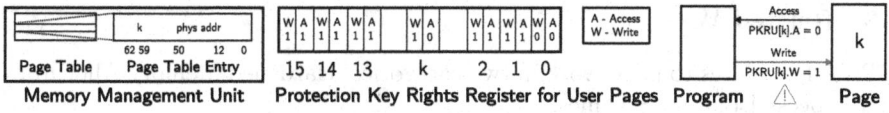

Fig. 1. Memory protection keys on intel CPUs.

2 Background and Threat Model

In this section, we provide a brief overview of memory protection keys, works related to MPKAlloc, and the threat model we assume in this work.

2.1 Memory Protection Keys

Recent Intel CPUs feature memory protection keys (MPKs) for partitioning memory pages into multiple intra-process domains. Figure 1 visualizes MPKs protecting a page associated with a key k. The memory management unit (MMU) within these CPUs maintains a page table which represents a mapping of virtual pages held by userspace processes to the physical pages located in hardware. Each page table entry (PTE) maps a single virtual page to a corresponding physical page and holds additional information, such as whether or not the page is dirty. On Intel, the PTE also includes an additional 4-bit value located at bits 59–62 that denotes the page's protection key. Intuitively, a page marked with key k can only be accessed or written to by properly configured threads. Since altering the page table requires executing privileged instructions on x86, the operating system kernel must provide a system call for programs to assign protection keys to individual pages. Note that, MPK currently only supports associating an individual page with a single key from the 16 available keys. By default, all pages are assigned the protection key $k = 0$.

During program execution, each CPU thread maintains its own protection key rights register for user pages (PKRU) that restricts the thread's access to individual protection key domains. Upon every memory load or store instruction, the MMU compares the protection key given in the accessed PTE to the permissions given in the current thread's PKRU register. If the PKRU register permits the operation, then the CPU carries out the instruction. Otherwise, the hardware will raise an error by notifying the operating system that a segmentation violation has occurred. An operation on a page with key k is permitted if the operation's bit is 0 at the relevant position in k's entry within the PKRU register. For the PKRU register given in Fig. 1, the access to the page with key k succeeds, while the write fails. An operator may therefore disallow either writes or all access to pages associated with k by setting the appropriate bit in the PKRU register. The CPU provides instructions available to userspace programs to fetch and alter an individual thread's PKRU register. By default, the PKRU register begins with a value of 0 which effectively disables MPKs. Note that, programs may not restrict access to $k = 0$ on current hardware. More details on the system calls and instructions required to use MPKs can be found in Sect. 4.

2.2   Related Work

MPKAlloc relates to prior work in two categories: Hardened Memory Allocators and Process Isolation Schemes.

Hardened Memory Allocators. Memory allocators often set aside a region of memory called the heap to store chunks needed by a program. Allocators must maintain data structures (heap meta-data) so that a program can efficiently obtain memory (heap chunks) of arbitrary size on demand. Isolating heap meta-data from adversaries is an important security goal since meta-data corruption can violate the integrity or confidentiality of a program. Numerous changes have been made over the last two decades to balance memory allocator performance requirements with the need to secure their data structures from corruption. As an example, the classic unlink [9,33] attack allows an adversary to write arbitrary data into any location in memory by overwriting pointers that refer to the next and previous chunks in the allocator's doubly-linked list. When the allocator attempts to free, or unlink, the corrupted chunk, the allocator instead writes an attacker-controlled value at an arbitrary address specified by the attacker which can have serious security consequences [11,32]. While the classic unlink attack has been mitigated for some time, this simple attack has spawned numerous variants that exploit binary programs through corrupting heap data structures [6]. For this reason, any defense that ensures the integrity of heap data structures without adversely affecting the performance of an allocator can provide significant security value, as it renders the entire class of heap meta-data corruption attacks moot [31]. MPKAlloc uses MPKs to isolate meta-data without requiring instrumentation or extensive changes to the allocator. This improves the allocator's security posture and enables easier adoption. That is, applications are typically implemented against a generic allocator interface, and so could easily be configured to use MPKAlloc instead of a default allocator. In some cases, MPKs can be easily added to an allocators like the big bag of pages (BiBoP) allocators found in some BSD derived operating systems [27] which store meta-data and allocated chunks on separate pages. Contrast this approach to one that requires explicitly changing the layout of memory within an allocator to accommodate MPKs [24]. Recent allocator fuzzing techniques like the Uninitialized module found in the HardsHeap [36] framework permit efficiently testing for the co-location of meta-data and allocated chunks without requiring extensive manual analysis. Furthermore, more offensive analysis could automatically discover novel exploits against allocators that fail to properly separate meta-data from allocated chunks [35]. In order to harden a given memory allocator using MPKs, developers could combine these two approaches in order to detect critical security flaws during development. This task may be difficult for glibc's ptmalloc [2], where meta-data immediately precedes allocated chunks in memory, but simpler for Firefox's jemalloc [1], where meta-data and allocated chunks are stored separately but still share pages in memory.

Process Isolation. Memory can also be partitioned using secure memory views (SMV) which permit operating system threads and their children access to memory associated with individual domains. Recent systems like ERIM [34] and Hodor [19] employ MPKs to isolate both individual workloads [34] and shared libraries [25] within the same process. More restrictive sandboxes can also be defined by embedding instruction monitoring directly into the hardware [16]. These works demonstrate MPKs preventing a compromised thread running within one protection domain from executing code in another domain. This builds upon widely used defenses such as data execution prevention (DEP) and $W \oplus X$. In contrast to these approaches, code domain partitioning uses MPKs to ensure the security of a library's sensitive memory pages, as opposed to developing general purpose intra-process sandboxes. Therefore, our defense complements prior work on intra-process sandboxes. The interface that allows programs to obtain and use MPKs can easily cause security problems and improvements have been proposed to make MPKs a proper virtualized resource [28]. NOJITSU [29] uses MPKs to ensure a Just in Time (JIT) compiler in web browsers has exclusive access to internal data structures and employs dynamic and static analysis that limits the performance overhead introduced by MPKs. In contrast, MPKAlloc establishes a memory allocator as a trusted component for managing sensitive meta-data. In both NOJITSU and MPKAlloc, MPKs enforce a security policy that provides a principal exclusive access to private resources. Prior works have also demonstrated the benefit of using hardware protection mechanisms to protect allocator meta-data [12,17,23]. However, these works primarily demonstrate the performance benefits of using hardware features. They do not investigate the security benefits of using MPKs beyond preventing simple heap overflows. In this work, we introduce an indirect meta-data attack vector (see Sect. 3.1) and show how MPKs prevent such attacks in a commodity web browser.

2.3   Design Assumptions and Threat Model

In this work, we assume that the protected program utilizes a memory allocator to dynamically allocate memory chunks. Meta-data documents the structure of the heap and allows an allocator to quickly meet the running program's memory demands. A memory chunk is a contiguous span of memory held by an allocator. In this work, we consider an allocator as a trusted component that stores heap meta-data and chunks on separate memory pages. Requiring meta-data and chunks to reside on separate pages is an inherent requirement when using existing Intel MPK technologies. If the program were to access memory chunks lying on the allocator's pages, MPKAlloc would trigger a segmentation fault upon every access. This implies that allocators that co-locate meta-data with allocated chunks, such as `ptmalloc` and `jemalloc`, cannot protect meta-data using Intel MPKs by default. The high performance allocators found within the Google Chromium web browser store meta-data and allocated chunks on separate pages, and therefore provide natural targets for prototyping MPKAlloc (see Sect. 4).

In this work, we assume the following threat model.

- The adversary's primary goal is to corrupt heap meta-data in order to achieve a malicious goal. One such goal would be to obtain a write primitive in a victim program. With the ability to write data anywhere in the process, an adversary can achieve more powerful capabilities such as escalating privileges or executing arbitrary code. We stress this represents just one example of what an adversary may achieve by corrupting meta-data.
- To this end, the adversary can inspect the protected program and all of its library dependencies.
- The adversary can further influence the input to the program (e.g., standard input, a remote socket, a file read by the program, or through specific command line arguments).
- Finally, the adversary has access to a vulnerability in the program or any of its libraries (with the exception of the memory allocator itself) that allow him to access the heap's meta-data and achieve his primary goal.

In this work, we assume an adversary does not begin with the ability to execute arbitrary code either explicitly or through code reuse attacks. Such an adversary has no motivation to corrupt heap meta-data since he can trivially take over a process or disclose any information reachable from the process. For this reason, we also assume the protected program does not utilize control flow integrity (CFI) [7] since the adversary specified by our threat model has no ability to alter the program's flow of execution or alter threads' protection domains. This is just an assumption made for our threat model, and in a deployed setting CFI could easily run alongside MPKAlloc to further protect a workload. The principal goal of MPKAlloc is to prevent adversaries from breaking the security of a running process by corrupting internal memory allocator data structures, not to design a general purpose intra-process isolation scheme that is resilient to compromised threads. At the time of writing, a secure intra-process isolation scheme using MPKs is still an active research topic [15]. As a concrete step under this broad objective, MPKAlloc uses memory protection keys to prevent adversaries from corrupting internal memory allocator data structures. At the same time, we acknowledge that MPKAlloc does not prevent issues caused directly by memory allocators, such as double-free corruptions.

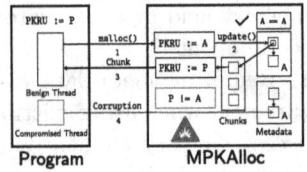

Fig. 2. Architectural overview of MPKAlloc.

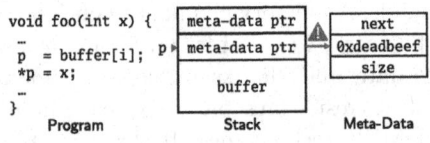

Fig. 3. MPKAlloc blocking a corruption performed by writing to a meta-data pointer obtained from an out-of-bounds read from the stack.

3   System Overview

In this section, we provide a high level overview of MPKAlloc. We show how MPKAlloc successfully detects and thwarts an adversarial attempt to transform a simple heap corruption into a powerful exploit. An adversary could easily use corrupted meta-data to place a ROP chain somewhere in the process, cause the program to jump to the chain, and connect to a remote command and control (C&C) server and install malware. We describe code domain partitioning, a technique that isolates memory allocator meta-data from the rest of the program, as a mechanism for isolating heap meta-data. Finally, we show that memory protection keys available in recent Intel CPUs provide an efficient implementation of code domain partitioning. Figure 2 shows the architectural overview of MPKAlloc and how it protects a memory allocator's meta-data from a vulnerable program. The key invariant MPKAlloc preserves is that any access made to a meta-data page must come from a privileged domain. By default, all threads in a running program run in an unprivileged domain. Upon invoking the memory allocator, MPKAlloc switches the thread to the privileged domain so that the allocator may access its internal meta-data. Note that this happens completely transparently to the running program. This allows MPKAlloc to be deployed by exclusively modifying the program's memory allocator. Later on, when a malicious or compromised thread attempts to access this internal data from an unprivileged domain, the hardware observes that the thread's protection key register disallows access to the domain's data. Upon receiving an exception from the hardware, the OS responds by terminating the program before any information is disclosed or corrupted. This prevents the malicious thread from successfully exploiting the heap. This is the default response, and, depending on the use-case, less drastic measures may be taken, such as alerting an administrator or raising a visual warning within the browser to alert a user of a possible exploit.

3.1   Indirect Meta-data Corruption

In allocators like `tcmalloc` and `PartitionAlloc`, chunk meta-data resides on separate pages which makes it difficult to successfully achieve the classic unlink attack given in Sect. 2. Fortunately, browsers like Chromium also place guard pages beneath meta-data pages which makes it impossible to corrupt pages via a direct overflow. Figure 3 shows an alternative attack vector where an adversary indirectly corrupts meta-data by writing to a pointer stored on the stack. At the beginning of the function `foo`, the adversary can influence the value of x and the index i used to read an element from `buffer`. In this attack, an adversary uses this capability in order to read past the boundary of `buffer` and obtain a pointer p that refers to meta-data. When the program writes to p, an adversary can then influence the contents of meta-data. In this case, if the target meta-data page contains a free list entry, then an adversary can replace a `prev` pointer with an address of their choice. Later, when the allocator frees the corrupted chunk, the allocator will inadvertently write to an attacker controlled address (`0xdeadbeef`). Targeting allocator meta-data on the stack has the advantage of corrupting a heavily used data-structure without requiring intricate knowledge of a victim application. That is, if an adversary is familiar with the memory allocator used by a victim application, and the application heavily relies on heap memory, then the adversary could attempt to spray attacker controlled values using meta-data pointers located on the stack. MPKAlloc prevents such an attack from achieving an arbitrary write primitive by detecting any successful meta-data corruption. Note that this is a two-stage attack, an adversary must first obtain a buffer over read to obtain a meta-data pointer, and then successfully dereference the obtained pointer. We also assume that no attacker controlled values are reachable on the stack, since an adversary could trivially obtain a write primitive by obtaining those values as opposed to meta-data. In the past, remote attackers have been able to achieve the first stage of our attack by exploiting an out-of-bounds read on the stack within libevent, a library used by the Chromium web browser [4]. In Sect. 5, we demonstrate our hypothetical attack vector in Chromium.

3.2   Code Domain Partitioning

Code domain partitioning allows a developer to grant regions of a program's code segment exclusive access to memory pages associated with a specific domain. MPKAlloc utilizes two domains and divides the heap into the allocator domain A and the program domain P. Pages in A belong exclusively to the memory allocator and pages in P belong to the program. To ensure the memory allocator has exclusive access to A, we alter the memory allocator to assign PKRU the appropriate domain A before entering every allocator routine. When the allocator obtains new pages for meta-data from the operating system, the allocator associates each page with the domain A using a variant of the mprotect system call that assigns pages to protection key domains. We do not need to explicitly assign other pages to the domain P since by default every page is assigned the MPK domain 0 by the hardware. In this case, any thread in the process is allowed to access pages in domain P subject to the "classic" read, write, and execute permission bits. Upon exiting any allocator routine, we remove the domain A from the PKRU register so that any attempt to alter a page in A yields a segmentation violation.

3.3   Detecting Domain Violations

Code domain partitioning delegates the task of detecting accesses made across domain boundaries to the CPU. Once an allocator's internal source has been altered to switch domains at the appropriate points, the hardware will detect any unprivileged accesses or writes made outside the allocator. For example, an adversary may attempt to corrupt a meta-data page by indirectly writing to a meta-data pointer as shown in Fig. 3. At this point, an adversary can take advantage of an indirect write to corrupt heap meta-data (e.g., overwrite pointers contained therein) in an attempt to exploit the program. The code causing the corruption is outside the memory allocator itself and the protection domain of the current thread belongs to P which differs from the domain A assigned to the victim meta-data page. As soon as the adversary in domain P issues a store instruction into a meta-data page associated with domain A, the hardware observes that the thread P cannot access the meta-data in domain A. This causes the hardware to notify the OS of the violation, and the OS terminates the process in response. This is the default response after detecting an MPK violation, and therefore we utilize it in MPKAlloc. This simple example shows how assigning meta-data pages their own protection domain A can prevent adversaries from corrupting heap meta-data. Section 4 provides an overview of the various data structures that `tcmalloc` and `PartitionAlloc` use as meta-data in order to implement a performant heap. Furthermore, the trend of automated heap exploitation suggests that anticipating all possible attack patterns facing a given memory allocator may become impractical. Storing meta-data within its own protection domain A successfully stops any attempt to access or alter meta-data. MPKAlloc thus defangs all attacks that rely on corrupting heap meta-data.

4   Implementation

In this section we describe our prototype implementation of MPKAlloc on the Intel x86-64 architecture. This allows us to apply code domain partitioning using the memory protection keys (MPKs) available on recent Intel CPUs. We choose to embed the MPKAlloc technique within the `tcmalloc` and `PartitionAlloc` allocators in our prototype. This implementation consists of 160 SLOC. This includes the implementation embedded within both `tcmalloc` contained in gperftools-v2.7 and `PartitionAlloc` included in Chrome version 84.0.4108.0. While the amount of code needed to implement MPKAlloc is small, understanding the structure and layout of two different high performance memory allocators and carefully adjusting their design to protect meta-data requires both significant domain knowledge and careful experimentation. The latest Intel CPUs provide a thread-specific register, `PKRU`, that defines each thread of execution's permissions for each memory protection domain. MPKAlloc uses the new instructions that alter this register to implement a security policy for an allocator's meta-data; accesses made by the program are forbidden, but those made by the allocator are allowed. We use functionality provided by the GNU/Linux kernel and glibc to label every page allocated for meta-data the domain A. Every time control transitions the boundary between the allocator and the rest of the program, MPKAlloc must switch between the two domains. The boundary between the domain of the program P and the domain of the allocator A consists of the Standard C Library functions that allocate and deallocate memory (e.g., `malloc`, `realloc`, `free`, etc.), and the C++ operators that allow programs to create and destroy objects (e.g., `new` and `delete`). In our implementation of MPKAlloc, we initialize the `PKRU` register with a specific domain assigned to the program P. As the pages backing the allocator's meta-data belong to domain A, any access made by P to these pages will generate a segmentation violation

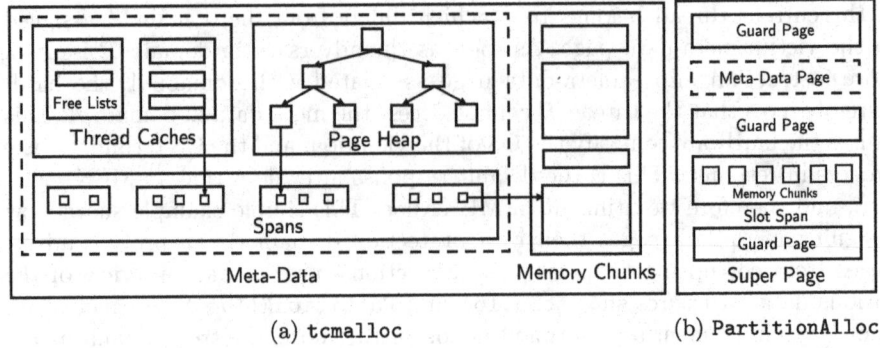

(a) `tcmalloc`   (b) `PartitionAlloc`

Fig. 4. Memory allocators protected by MPKAlloc.

before any meta-data can be disclosed or corrupted. Since both `tcmalloc` and `PartitionAlloc` store meta-data and allocated chunks on separate pages, our defense allows a program to read, write, or even execute allocated memory in P without requiring any modifications or instrumentation to the program itself.

4.1   Meta-data in `tcmalloc` and `PartitionAlloc`

The `tcmalloc` and `PartitionAlloc` allocators are high performance memory allocators found within the Chromium web browser. In `tcmalloc`, every allocated chunk is backed by one or more span objects that may extend across multiple pages in virtual memory. A single span is simply a collection of one or more pages in virtual memory. Figure 4a shows the layout of the various data structures that define `tcmalloc`'s meta-data. Within `tcmalloc`'s implementation, a special MetaDataAllocator class is responsible for allocating the pages that hold these internal data structures such as thread caches, free lists, a central page heap, and individual spans. Thread caches provide an efficient way for threads to allocate memory using free lists without having to consult the larger page heap that is shared across all threads. The page heap is a trie data structure that allows `tcmalloc` to quickly obtain the span object associated with a given pointer. In `PartitionAlloc`, the unit of allocation is a super page that records the set of memory chunks that reside across a series of allocated pages. Figure 4b visualizes the data structures that make up each super page. Each allocated page is referred to by an individual slot span located in the super page. At the top of the super page lies a meta-data page surrounded by guard pages that prevent linear overflows from corrupting the data structures that document the super page's contents. Upon allocation of every super page, MPKAlloc assigns the meta-data page with the domain A to ensure that the allocator retains exclusive access to its meta-data during run-time. In this design, we assign all the instructions found within the `tcmalloc` and `PartitionAlloc` allocators the domain A, and the rest of the process' code to the domain P.

4.2   Code Domain Partitioning

Both `tcmalloc` and `PartitionAlloc` rely on the `mmap` system call to obtain pages from the operating system upon which they build a heap. In `tcmalloc` we implement code domain partitioning by altering the MetaDataAllocator class to tag every page allocated by `mmap` with the appropriate protection key and permissions. Before the program allocates any memory, we must allocate a protection key for the domain A within `tcmalloc`'s initialization routine. This involves simply calling the `pkey_alloc` function with our desired permissions (e.g., to disable access and write operations). Whenever a MetaDataAllocator obtains new pages, MPKAlloc calls `pkey_mprotect` on a pointer to the new pages with the allocated protection key. This assigns the pages to the protection domain A and prevents threads outside of A from accessing the pages. Likewise, every time `PartitionAlloc` allocates a super page, MPKAlloc associates the corresponding meta-data page with the domain A. This implements a form of code domain partitioning that divides the pages in the virtual address space into two domains, the domain A reserved for memory allocators, and the domain P for memory allocated in the heap. Furthermore, this approach allows us to initialize MPKAlloc's context without modifying the running program. Later on, if a thread does not hold the proper permission in the `PKRU` register while reading from or writing to one of the key's pages, the hardware will raise an exception and prevent the memory access from succeeding. The OS will then send a SIGSEGV signal to the offending process and, by default, terminate it. Since both allocators reside in Chromium's source tree, they can easily share A's protection key. Once we obtain a protection key from the operating system, we store the key in a static variable which makes the key available throughout both `tcmalloc` and `PartitionAlloc`. Under our threat model, disclosing the protection key does not help an adversary corrupt meta-data, but in a production deployment it would be wise to obscure the protection key's location by storing it outside the allocator's structures.

In order for an allocator to access internal meta-data pages, MPKAlloc must perform a domain switch whenever the program manipulates the heap using one of the allocator's public APIs. This is accomplished by simply writing the appropriate value to the `PKRU` register as specified by the Intel Architecture Software Developer Manual [22]. That is, MPKAlloc zeros the bits reserved for the allocated key in the `PKRU` register which permits full access to A's pages. The `wrpkru` instruction allows MPKAlloc to alter the contents of the `PKRU` register in order to perform this privilege escalation. When the memory allocator runs in domain A, the hardware will see A's entry in `PKRU` is zero, which permits full access to all pages associated with A. Once an allocation or deallocation routine returns, the allocator no longer needs to alter heap meta-data. At this point, MPKAlloc switches the thread's domain by setting the write and access bits at A's offset in the `PKRU` register, which causes any future attempt to read from or write to A's pages to fail. After the context switch completes, the function returns to the code that invoked the allocator. The high performance memory allocators given in our evaluation often do not have a clear boundary between entering and leaving the memory allocator. This can lead to redundant writes to the PKRU register when performing a context switch. Writing to the PKRU register incurs more clock cycles than reading its contents. For this reason, we follow the example set by prior work [29] by checking the contents of the PKRU register before altering it whenever we enable or disable our defense. In our evaluation, we saw this straightforward optimization reduce the average performance overhead from 5.4% to 2.4% when loading the top 50 websites in the Alexa ranking (see Sect. 5.6).

4.3 Detecting Corruptions

Protecting meta-data from adversaries can be accomplished by switching a thread's protection domain to A whenever a program enters an allocator's public function. This ensures that whenever an allocator alters its internal data structures, the calling thread has the proper protection domain to pass the protection key check performed by the CPU on all pages holding heap meta-data. Furthermore, once a thread leaves an allocator's functions, MPKAlloc transitions to the protection domain reserved for the program P. Any attempt made by an adversary to access or alter the allocator's meta-data while the program is in this unprivileged domain will fail. Note that each thread has its own value for the PKRU register which obviates any synchronization between different threads and similarly forestalls race conditions that could occur while switching domains.

5 Evaluation

In this section, we evaluate both the performance overhead and security benefits provided by MPKAlloc. First, we embed MPKAlloc within the stock tcmalloc allocator, and measure the performance overhead induced by MPKAlloc over the SPEC CPU2006 benchmarks. We compare this overhead to the runtime we observe when using a stock tcmalloc allocator in the benchmarks (see Sect. 5.2). Next, we evaluate the feasibility of embedding MPKAlloc into two memory allocators found within the Chromium web browser (see Sect. 5.3). Once we confirmed that Chromium can benefit from MPKAlloc, we evaluate the feasibility of our PoC attack that indirectly corrupts meta-data. This involves writing directly through pointers that refer to meta-data. In Sect. 5.4 we confirm that meta-data pointers occur frequently in Chromium's process address space. We use this information to construct a PoC that corrupts meta-data by writing through such a pointer, and show how MPKAlloc prevents the corruption from occurring (see Sect. 5.5). Finally, we measure the performance impact a user may experience when using Chromium hardened with MPKAlloc (see Sect. 5.6).

5.1 Experimental Set Up

We evaluated MPKAlloc on an Ubuntu 20.04 LTS server with 96 Intel Xeon Platinum 8000 CPUs and 192 GB of RAM. The initial experiments for evaluating MPKAlloc over the SPEC CPU2006 benchmarks used tcmalloc available in

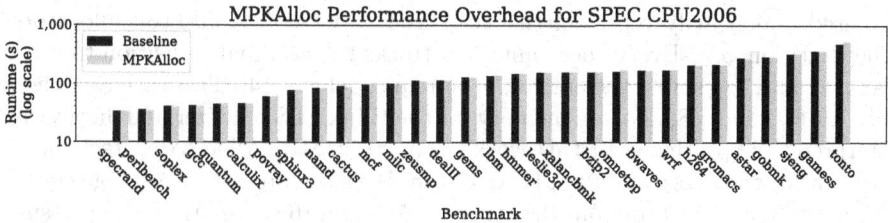

Fig. 5. Measuring MPKAlloc's performance overhead (+0.8% on average) using an unmodified `tcmalloc` as a baseline.

gperftools version 2.7. The browser experiments were conducted using `tcmalloc` and `PartitionAlloc` found in version 84.0.4108.0 of Chromium. We built and evaluated Chromium within a container running the Ubuntu 16.04 LTS distribution as recommended by the browser's documentation for developers.

5.2   SPEC CPU2006 Benchmarks

Figure 5 summarizes the performance overhead of running the SPEC CPU2006 benchmarks with MPKAlloc compared to using an unmodified `tcmalloc` allocator as a baseline. In this evaluation, each benchmark is ran three times with each allocator. The main source of performance overhead introduced by MPKAlloc comes from issuing the relatively expensive `wrpkru` instruction when switching between protection domains. On average, we observed low performance overhead across all the SPEC CPU2006 benchmarks (+0.8%). Based on this result, we argue that MPKAlloc could be applied to production programs without substantially affecting their performance.

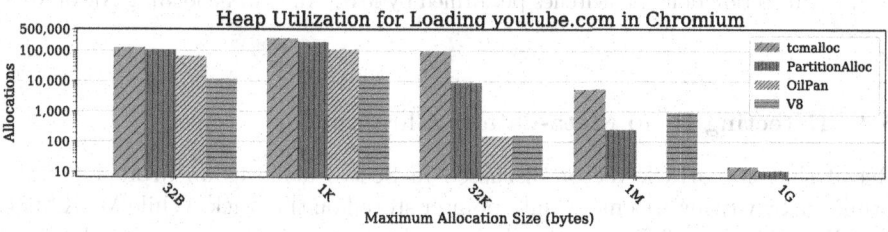

Fig. 6. Measuring each memory allocator's activity inside Chromium while loading youtube.com. Each allocation fits within a bin given on the x-axis.

5.3   Hardening Chromium with MPKAlloc

The positive result obtained from the SPEC CPU2006 benchmarks makes MPKAlloc a natural candidate to protect the Chromium web browser. Chromium is an open source browser upon which the Google Chrome browser is based and heavily relies on the `tcmalloc` and `PartitionAlloc` allocators. The PartitionAlloc-Everywhere initiative tracks the eventual transition to using `PartitionAlloc` across the entire Chromium codebase [14]. Two garbage collectors, OilPan and V8, allocate memory for the Blink CSS renderer and Javascript interpreter, respectively. In this work, we restrict MPKAlloc to protect meta-data within `tcmalloc` and `PartitionAlloc`. We leave protecting garbage collectors' meta-data in Chromium to future work. Figure 6 summarizes the pressure placed on each memory allocator while Chromium renders youtube.com, a widely viewed media heavy web site. For every chunk allocated by a heap, we place the chunk in the smallest bin that will hold it. For example, the largest bin of size 1 GB holds all chunks that cannot fit in the bin of size 1 MB. Even though all allocators are utilized while rendering youtube.com, we observed that Chromium utilized `tcmalloc` and `PartitionAlloc` the most, measured by the total number of chunks allocated. To ensure that different web sites stress MPKAlloc, we counted the number of protection domain context switches performed by MPKAlloc while rendering the top 50 web sites contained in the Alexa ranking. Figure 7 visualizes the number of protection domain context switches observed and shows popular web sites utilize MPKAlloc by placing significant pressure on the protected allocators.

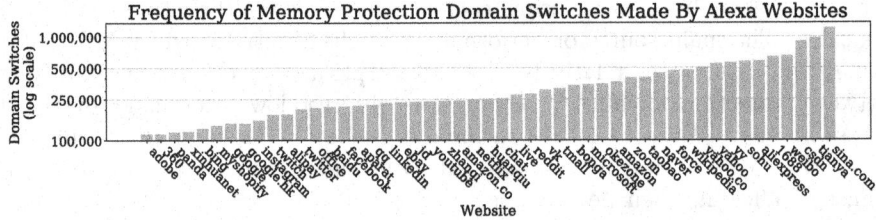

Fig. 7. Protection domain switches performed by MPKAlloc while loading Alexa websites.

5.4   Detecting Heap Meta-data in Chromium

Recall that the attack vector discussed in Sect. 3 achieves an arbitrary write primitive by writing to a meta-data pointer stored on the stack. While MPKAlloc is oblivious to an adversary's goals beyond compromising heap meta-data, an adversary can easily use a write primitive to corrupt arbitrary data and escalate privileges, disclose sensitive information, or execute arbitrary code. In order to understand the practicality of this attack vector within the Chromium web browser, we altered `tcmalloc` and `PartitionAlloc` to record every memory region allocated for heap meta-data while loading Google's home page. As the most popular website on Alexa's ranking, Google's home page can provide a good reference as to whether an adversary can reach heap meta-data from the stack through a buffer over read.

Detecting Meta-data Pointers. In order to determine whether such a scenario is possible, we implemented a meta-data memory scanner that attaches itself to each process in Chromium's process tree using the `ptrace` API. The scanner starts with the set of memory pages allocated as meta-data by Chromium. The scanner then examines every readable memory region mapped into the process. The scanner enumerates each region 8 bytes at a time in order to detect any pointers that refer to a meta-data page. This initial scan revealed that heap meta-data pointers frequently appear on the stack. In order to be useful to an adversary, the pointers themselves must be located at a memory address higher than a given function's stack frame so an adversary may reach the pointer through a buffer over read. The current stack can be obtained through the `RSP` register which represents the top of the stack in the x86-64 architecture. To measure how often heap meta-data appears at memory addresses higher than a given stack frame, we implemented a PINtool using the Intel PIN framework [26] that scans a fixed amount of memory located higher than `RSP` (256 bytes) upon every function return. This allows the PINtool to scan memory on the stack for pointers to meta-data pages throughout Chromium's execution. We limited our scan to 256 bytes in order to quickly see whether meta-data was located close to the stack pointer. In addition to trapping on every function return, the PINtool traps on every call to functions that allocate heap meta-data which identifies the location of meta-data pages in virtual memory. The previous scanner provided evidence that heap meta-data occurs at the high addresses reserved for the stack. This second scanner confirms all the opportunities an adversary may have to reach meta-data during execution. We observed that the browser appears to start with a fixed set of meta-data pages which are referred to throughout browsing. This suggests the meta-data pointers we observed remain valid throughout our scan. Our second scan which tracks meta-data in real-time revealed that simply loading `google.com` causes heap meta-data to be within reach in over 52,000 distinct methods in the Chromium source tree. This implies that if an adversary can write to a pointer stored somewhere on the stack in any one of these methods, they can successfully corrupt a heap meta-data pointer, and achieve an arbitrary write primitive. For example, functions in the `blink` module may be of interest since the Blink renderer parses cascading style sheet (CSS) files downloaded from the Internet. In this setting, adversaries may craft CSS files that exploit a bug in the renderer's implementation. This more detailed scan also revealed meta-data is reachable in modules that parse URLs, handle network traffic, and interact with the domain object model (DOM). All of these modules are viable targets for an attacker looking to exploit a web browser. One explanation for meta-data pointers' frequent appearance on the stack is Chromium methods reusing stack frames belonging to internal allocator routines that store meta-data pointers on the stack while accessing data structures. For example, suppose a routine that parses CSS files calls a routine to allocate a chunk of memory. After these functions return, a CSS rendering routine is called, and a meta-data pointer may remain on the stack in place of an uninitialized variable at an address higher than the stack frame of a method vulnerable to the hypothetical attack described in Sect. 3.1. An adversary could take advantage of this layout by obtaining the meta-data pointer, corrupting meta-data, and achieving an arbitrary write primitive.

5.5   Corrupting Meta-data in Chromium

In order to demonstrate the security benefit of MPKAlloc we follow the approach taken by recent work that protects components in Mozilla's SpiderMonkey Javascript JIT compiler [29] using MPKs. Instead of developing a full exploit to test the defense, the authors introduced a bug into the code base and showed how their defense stopped the bug's exploitation. In this work, we select one of the Chromium functions that can reach heap meta-data located on the stack. We then show how MPKAlloc prevents an adversary from corrupting meta-data by exploiting this bug. Note that, while our presented attack is artificial, it shows the security consequences of an out-of-bounds stack read which has been seen in the past in Chromium's library dependencies [4] when an additional dereference is present. Within the Blink renderer a function called `ConsumeShorthandGreedilyViaLonghands` populates a shorthand representation of multiple CSS properties using longhand declarations. This Blink function holds an array of pointers within its stack frame in order to update CSS data structures. This function is interesting for two reasons. First, our PIN-tool observed heap meta-data pointers lying at addresses located higher than a function's stack pointer. Second, the function writes to pointers stored on the stack. This implies that if an adversary could trick the function into fetching an element beyond the boundary of the array located on the stack, the function would fetch and write to a heap meta-data pointer. This could give an adversary the opportunity to corrupt meta-data by authoring malicious CSS snippets. To demonstrate MPKAlloc stopping this attack, we altered the vulnerable method to search upwards in memory starting from the stack buffer containing pointers until it detected a meta-data pointer. After writing to the meta-data pointer, we observed MPKAlloc terminate the browser with a segmentation violation.

5.6   Impact on Page Load Times

In order to evaluate the performance impact MPKAlloc has on web browsing, we compared the page load times, defined as the amount of time needed to render a web page and all its dependencies, with an unmodified Chromium browser and with one protected by MPKAlloc. We evaluate MPKAlloc in this way for the top 50 websites given in the Alexa ranking. In order to prevent network latency from skewing our measurements, we utilize the Web Page Replay tool provided by prior work [30] in the Catapult framework [13]. The Web Page Replay tool records the traffic generated when visiting a website, and allows us to replay this traffic while recording measurements in our evaluation. For every website included in our evaluation, we load the website one hundred times and record the amount of time required to load the website and all its external dependencies, such as CSS, Javascript, and image data. We repeat this both with

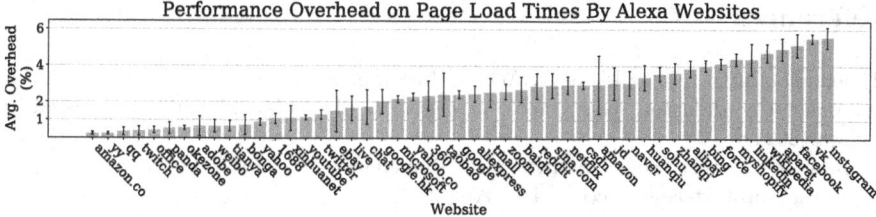

Fig. 8. Average performance overhead incurred by MPKAlloc with standard error while loading Alexa websites.

MPKAlloc enabled in Chromium and with an unmodified Chromium browser with identical versions. After running this experiment, we have one hundred load times from an unmodified Chromium instance and one hundred produced by Chromium protected with MPKAlloc. Overall, the overhead for all websites in our evaluation stayed below 5.58%. While this is the worst case overhead we observed for a single website, MPKAlloc caused 2.44% overhead on average with a geometric mean of 1.71%. Figure 8 summarizes the average performance impact MPKAlloc has on page load times for the top 50 websites given in the Alexa ranking. The main source of overhead introduced by MPKAlloc comes from switching between protection domains which requires issuing the wrpkru instruction. It has been observed that the worst case execution time for this instruction is 260 cycles [34]. In our evaluation, we observed that loading a website can incur at most 1.5 million domain switches, which puts a theoretical maximum overhead of a naive implementation of our defense at 130 ms when running on a 3 GHz processor. Many of the web pages in our evaluation take multiple seconds to complete loading, and so this theoretical worst case may not hinder MPKAlloc's use. In addition to page load times, we evaluated MPKAlloc on several Javascript benchmarks in order to understand the impact of MPKs on interpreting Javascript programs, which utilize the browser's general purpose allocators in addition to the V8 garbage collector. We observed MPKAlloc introduce a small amount of overhead on three Javascript benchmarks, Speedometer (0.95%), Octane (0.57%), and Sunspider (0.73%).

6   Conclusion

In this paper, we presented MPKAlloc, a defense that isolates heap meta-data via in-process memory protection domains made possible by recent Intel CPUs. Our prototype implementation of MPKAlloc protects heap meta-data used by the tcmalloc and PartitionAlloc memory allocators. We evaluated MPKAlloc on the SPEC CPU2006 benchmarks and showed that it induces merely 0.8% performance overhead on average. Furthermore, when used in Chromium, MPKAlloc detects and prevents potential exploits. Finally, MPKAlloc protects Chromium while introducing a geometric mean of 1.71% performance overhead (2.44% on average) on page load times.

References

1. jemalloc. http://jemalloc.net/. Accessed 31 Mar 2021
2. A memory allocator. http://gee.cs.oswego.edu/dl/html/malloc.html. Accessed 31 Mar 2021
3. Storage protect keys. https://www.ibm.com/docs/en/aix/7.2?topic=concepts-storage-protect-keys. Accessed 16 Aug 2021
4. CVE-2016-10195 (2016). https://cve.mitre.org/cgi-bin/cvename.cgi?name=CVE-2016-10195. Accessed 04 May 2022
5. Memory tagging extension: Enhancing memory safety through architecture (2019). https://community.arm.com/arm-community-blogs/b/architectures-and-processors-blog/posts/enhancing-memory-safety. Accessed 27 Feb 2022
6. Educational heap exploitation (2021). https://github.com/shellphish/how2heap. Accessed 31 Mar 2021
7. Abadi, M., Budiu, M., Erlingsson, U., Ligatti, J.: Control-flow integrity principles, implementations, and applications. ACM Trans. Inf. Syst. Secur. **13**(1), 1–40 (2009)
8. Ainsworth, S., Jones, T.M.: MarkUs: drop-in use-after-free prevention for low-level languages. In: IEEE Symposium on Security and Privacy (2020)
9. Anonymous: Once upon a free(). http://phrack.org/issues/57/9.html. Accessed 14 Mar 2021
10. Avgerinos, T., Cha, S.K., Rebert, A., Schwartz, E.J., Woo, M., Brumley, D.: Automatic exploit generation. Commun. ACM **57**(2), 74–84 (2014)
11. Bletsch, T., Jiang, X., Freeh, V.W., Liang, Z.: Jump-oriented programming: a new class of code-reuse attack. In: ACM ASIA Conference on Computer and Communications Security (2011)
12. Cha, M.H., Lee, S.M., An, B.S., Kim, H.Y., Kim, K.H.: Fast and secure global-heap for memory-centric computing. J. Supercomputing **77**, 13262–13291 (2021). https://doi.org/10.1007/s11227-021-03806-4
13. Chromium authors: Catapult. https://chromium.googlesource.com/catapult. Accessed 12 Oct 2021
14. Chromium Authors: Deploy PartitionAlloc-Everywhere. https://bugs.chromium.org/p/chromium/issues/detail?id=1121427. Accessed 12 Oct 2021
15. Connor, R.J., McDaniel, T., Smith, J.M., Schuchard, M.: PKU pitfalls: attacks on PKU-based memory isolation systems. In: USENIX Security Symposium (2020)
16. Delshadtehrani, L., Canakci, S., Blair, W., Egele, M., Joshi, A.: FlexFilt: towards flexible instruction filtering for security. In: Annual Computer Security Applications Conference (2021)
17. Demeri, A., Kim, W.H., Krishnan, R.M., Kim, J., Ismail, M., Min, C.: POSEIDON: safe, fast and scalable persistent memory allocator. In: International Middleware Conference (2020)
18. Farkhani, R.M., Ahmadi, M., Lu, L.: PTAuth: temporal memory safety via robust points-to authentication. In: USENIX Security Symposium (2021)
19. Hedayati, M., et al.: Hodor: intra-process isolation for high-throughput data plane libraries. In: USENIX Security Symposium (2019)
20. Heelan, S., Melham, T., Kroening, D.: Automatic heap layout manipulation for exploitation. In: USENIX Security Symposium (2018)
21. IBM Corporation: Power ISA version 3.0b (2017)
22. Intel Corporation: Intel 64 and IA-32 Architectures Software Developer's Manual: Volume 3 (2016)

23. Kim, Y., Lee, J., Kim, H.: Hardware-based always-on heap memory safety. In: IEEE/ACM International Symposium on Microarchitecture (2020)
24. Kirth, P., et al.: PKRU-safe: automatically locking down the heap between safe and unsafe languages. In: European Conference on Computer Systems (2022)
25. Koning, K., Chen, X., Bos, H., Giuffrida, C., Athanasopoulos, E.: No need to hide: protecting safe regions on commodity hardware. In: European Conference on Computer systems (2017)
26. Luk, C.K., et al.: Pin: building customized program analysis tools with dynamic instrumentation. ACM SIGPLAN Not. **40**(6), 190–200 (2005)
27. Otto Moerbeek: A new malloc(3) for openBSD. http://www.openbsd.nl/papers/eurobsdcon2009/otto-malloc.pdf. Accessed 23 Mar 2021
28. Park, S., Lee, S., Xu, W., Moon, H., Kim, T.: libmpk: Software abstraction for intel memory protection keys (intel MPK). In: USENIX Annual Technical Conference (2019)
29. Park, T., Dhondt, K., Gens, D., Na, Y., Volckaert, S., Franz, M.: NOJITSU: locking down javascript engines. In: Network and Distributed System Security Symposium (2020)
30. Reis, C., Moshchuk, A., Oskov, N.: Site isolation: process separation for web sites within the browser. In: USENIX Security Symposium (2019)
31. Robertson, W.K., Kruegel, C., Mutz, D., Valeur, F.: Run-time detection of heap-based overflows. In: Conference on Systems Administration (2003)
32. Shacham, H.: The geometry of innocent flesh on the bone: Return-into-libc without function calls (on the ×86). In: ACM Conference on Computer and Communications Security (2007)
33. Solar Designer: JPEG COM Marker Processing Vulnerability. https://www.openwall.com/articles/JPEG-COM-Marker-Vulnerability. Accessed 23 Mar 2021
34. Vahldiek-Oberwagner, A., Elnikety, E., Duarte, N.O., Sammler, M., Druschel, P., Garg, D.: ERIM: secure, efficient in-process isolation with protection keys (MPK). In: USENIX Security Symposium (2019)
35. Yun, I., Kapil, D., Kim, T.: Automatic techniques to systematically discover new heap exploitation primitives. In: USENIX Security Symposium (2020)
36. Yun, I., Song, W., Min, S., Kim, T.: HardsHeap: a universal and extensible framework for evaluating secure allocators. In: ACM Conference on Computer and Communications Security (2021)
37. Zhao, Z., Wang, Y., Gong, X.: HAEPG: an automatic multi-hop exploitation generation framework. In: Maurice, C., Bilge, L., Stringhini, G., Neves, N. (eds.) DIMVA 2020. LNCS, vol. 12223, pp. 89–109. Springer, Cham (2020). https://doi.org/10.1007/978-3-030-52683-2_5

A Human in Every APE: Delineating and Evaluating the Human Analysis Systems of Anti-Phishing Entities

Bhupendra Acharya and Phani Vadrevu[✉]

University of New Orleans, New Orleans, LA 70148, USA
bacharya@uno.edu, phani@cs.uno.edu

Abstract. We conducted a large-scale evaluation of some popular Anti-Phishing Entities (APEs). As part of this, we submitted arrays of CAPTCHA challenge-laden honey sites to 7 APEs. An analysis of the "click-through rates" during the visits from the APEs showed strong evidence for the presence of formidable human analysis systems in conjunction with automated crawler systems. In summary, we estimate that as many as 10% to 24% of URLs submitted to each of 4 APEs (Google Safe Browsing, Microsoft SmartScreen, Bitdefender and Netcraft) were likely visited by human analysts. In contrast to prior works, these measurements present a very optimistic picture for web security as, for the first time, they show presence of expansive human analysis systems to tackle suspicious URLs that might otherwise be challenging for automated crawlers to analyze.

This finding allowed us an opportunity to conduct the first systematic study of the robustness of the human analysis systems of APEs which revealed some glaring weaknesses in them. We saw that all the APEs we studied fall prey to issues such as lack of geolocation and client device diversity exposing their human systems to targeted evasive attacks. Apart from this we also found a specific weakness across the entire APE ecosystem that enables creation of long-lasting phishing pages targeted exclusively against Android/Chrome devices by capitalizing on discrepancies in web sensor API outputs. We demonstrate this with the help of 10 artificial phishing sites that survived indefinitely despite repeated reporting to all APEs. We suggest mitigations for all these issues. We also conduct an elaborate disclosure process with all affected APEs in an attempt to persuade them to pursue these mitigations.

1 Introduction

As web-based social engineering attacks continue to rise in number and variety, it has become imperative for security organizations to invest in systems that inspect web sites for signs of maliciousness. Such systems are commonly referred to as **Anti-Phishing Entities (APEs)** and play a critical and omnipresent role in preventing web users from visiting harmful websites. For example, the Google Safe Browsing (GSB) service is a popular APE that receives URL reports from

© The Author(s), under exclusive license to Springer Nature Switzerland AG 2022
L. Cavallaro et al. (Eds.): DIMVA 2022, LNCS 13358, pp. 156–177, 2022.
https://doi.org/10.1007/978-3-031-09484-2_9

users around the world and verifies them. After verification, GSB sends malicious URLs to URL blocklists that are currently deployed in about 4 billion devices of users around the world [20]. It is to be noted that despite the name, APEs are not only meant for thwarting phishing attacks and have the responsibility of identifying and blocking all kinds of malicious web content.

Given the scale of the web, it is reasonable to expect that a large proportion of visits from these APEs are from fully automated **web security crawler bots** which would likely be using machine learning techniques or carefully crafted heuristics to detect whether or not a given candidate page is malicious. In order to foil such attempts of these bots, attackers have begun to design and use phishing pages that are fitted with CAPTCHAs in the initial landing pages [14, 23]. Since CAPTCHAs are inherently designed to prevent bots from bypassing them, they can be used effectively as a cloaking vector against APEs. Thus, it has now become imperative for APEs to augment security crawler bots with **human analysis systems** where human security analysts manually inspect (a subset of) web sites reported to them. Another important reason we expect APEs to have human analysis subsystems is for evaluating the potential false positive and false negative cases that might inevitably result from the bot-based automated analysis systems. Thus, these human analysis systems are vital for functioning of APEs. In addition to such importance, human analysis systems are by nature very expensive to maintain due to high labor costs. Given this, it is crucial for organizations to maintain robustness of these expensive human analysis systems to make sure they are not subject to targeted evasion attacks. To the best of our knowledge, there has been no study to date that focuses on evaluating the robustness of these human analysis subsystems of APEs.

In this paper, we attempt to fill this knowledge gap. We conduct the largest study thus far on delineating the human-based visits made by APEs. The most closely related work to ours is [13] which conducted a small scale study to detect the capability of APEs to overcome CAPTCHA-based blockages. The study limited each one of 7 popular APEs to 6 test phishing sites fitted with a CAPTCHA. However, unfortunately, quite contrary to our expectations laid out above, this study has found that none of the studied APEs were capable of clicking through CAPTCHAs in potential phishing pages. For this paper, we attempted to repeat this experiment albeit on a much larger scale. For this, we leveraged a scalable APE evaluation design methodology recently proposed in [10]. This allowed us to submit multiple test site sets of 100 sites each with different CAPTCHAs to each of 7 popular APEs. We also utilized this opportunity to also collect a wider range of data that captures the dynamic behavior of APEs when visiting websites. This data included all mouse, touch and key press events as well as events garnered from other advanced web sensor APIs such as Gyrometer, Accelerometer etc. To the best of our knowledge, this is the first work to collect and analyze such biometric data from APEs. With a similar setup, we also performed a user study involving 433 users in order to contrast this biometric data with that of regular users in order to gauge the existence of anomalies that can be abused by attackers for evasion attacks in the future.

In complete contrast to the results from [13], our study showed the existence of a vibrant and powerful ecosystem of human analysts being employed by at least 4 of the 7 popular APEs that we studied. These are Microsoft SmartScreen, Google Safe Browsing (GSB), Bitdefender and Netcraft. Our conservative estimates based on CAPTCHA-solving rates show that these APEs are capable of arranging as many as 10–24% of submitted URLs to be visited manually by a human analysts. Thus, our such high numbers show present-day APEs in a very positive light for the first time in terms of their efforts to support formidable manual analysis systems. These measurements present a very optimistic picture for web security as, for the first time, they show presence of expansive human analysis systems to tackle suspicious URLs that might otherwise be challenging for automated crawlers to analyze.

These new findings thus also allowed us to perform the first systematic study of the robustness of these human analysis systems which revealed some glaring weaknesses in them. We saw that all the APEs we studied fall prey to the same issues such as lack of geolocation and client device diversity that exposes their human systems to targeted evasive attacks. Significantly, our analysis reveals that even cumulatively, the APEs are being affected by these issues. While prior works such as [17] have helped improve network and device diversity [10], we find that these changes have not carried over to the human analyst subsystems. For instance, while some APEs are using more than 40 different countries as sources for their bot visits, all of them seem to be using only one or two countries for sourcing traffic from human analysts. Similarly, we observed that large APEs such as GSB and Outlook were only using APE-specific browsers (such as ChromeOS and Microsoft Edge respectively) for their human analysts despite them lacking in general popularity. Also, none of the APEs are using mobile user agents for human vetting thus exposing users to potential "mobile-only" malicious web pages that completely avoid human analyst systems. In the case of Google Safe Browsing, we also saw evidence for some timing-based blind spots as no human analyst visits have occurred during the weekends.

Interestingly, we also found that most of these problems are generally not associated with the automated bot systems of these APEs. This indicates that these issues can likely be fixed easily for the expensive human inspection systems as well. However, as an exception to this, we found one issue that is currently affecting all APE systems purported to be visiting from Android/Chrome devices. Namely, we found that none of these visits were giving away web sensor API data upon page load in sharp contrast to most real Android/Chrome devices that do so in their default configuration (as per our user study). We show that this discrepancy can be leveraged to create long-lasting phishing pages tailored towards this very popular platform. We suggest mitigations for all these issues. We conducted an elaborate disclosure process with all APEs in an attempt to persuade APEs to pursue these mitigations and help make a practical impact in improving the security posture of all APEs.

In summary, our contributions with this paper are as follows:

1. Delineation: With the help of a large-scale study, we demonstrate for the first time, evidence for industry-wide use of elaborate human analysis systems by APEs.
2. Evaluation: We conduct the first systematic evaluation of the robustness of these human systems and find multiple serious issues across different APEs that expose them to targeted evasive attacks.
3. Impact: We suggest practical mitigations to resolve these issues and conduct an elaborate disclosure process with the affected APEs.

2 System Description

2.1 System Overview

The predominant goal of our project was to measure the prevalence of any human analysis systems being deployed by popular APEs. If we found the presence of any such human analysis systems, we had also planned to conduct forensic analysis on such systems in an effort to evaluate their robustness to evasion attacks. In order to support these goals, we built a measurement and data collection system for APEs. An overview of this system is presented in Fig. 1.

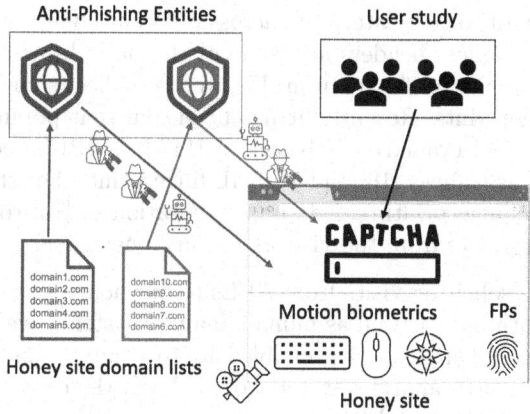

Fig. 1. System overview

The main component of our system is the honey server that is capable of serving several identical honey sites that are designed for the measurements in this project. Each honey site is fitted with a CAPTCHA in order to help us determine if the visitor is human. The ethical considerations behind this design are discussed in Sect. 5. We relied upon the APE evaluation approach proposed in [10] in order to make our system scalable. Concretely, we registered multiple domain names and made them all point to the same honey server. We then separated these domain names into disjoint sets and submitted them to various APEs. These submissions thus elicited visits from both the bot and human subsystems of these APEs. For each visit, we leveraged the event knowledge of whether a relevant CAPTCHA challenge has been solved or not as a data point to infer whether that visitor is human or bot.

Besides deploying CAPTCHA challenges, we also equipped each honey site with two kinds of forensic recording capabilities as discussed below.

1. Motion biometrics. We embedded JavaScript code in our honey sites to listen and record multiple Web API events generated from UI devices such as mouse events (e.g. `click`, `mousemove` etc.), keyboard events (e.g. `keyup`, `keydown` etc.), and Touch events (e.g. `touchstart`, `touchmove`). Furthermore, upon page load, we register event listeners for Web Sensor APIs to record data from common mobile-specific devices such as gyroscope, accelerometer, magnetometer and light sensors. As some of this data (such as movement data) is continuously generated as long as visitors are on the honey site, we added the ability to offload the collected data to our server every 500 ms in order to minimize the risk of losing data due to unexpected network issues. We later analyze this collected data to reveal some interesting insights.

2. Browser fingerprints. We also fitted each of the honey sites with capabilities to collect different valuable browser fingerprints from the visitors. Our plan was to utilize this data to correlate visits across different honey sites. Source IP address and HTTP request headers are some of the basic browser fingerprints that we collect from a visitor. Apart from this, we also collect some other sophisticated browser fingerprints. Recently, it has be shown that popular APEs can be easily identified (and evaded) [10] based on HTML5 API-based fingerprinting techniques such as Canvas [16] and WebGL fingerprints. For this reason, we utilized the browser fingerprinting code implementation in [10] to collect these two additional data points from the visitors to our honey sites.

User Study. While soliciting visits from APEs to our honey sites allowed us to collect data from both bots as well as human analysis systems, we also collected similar data from real humans. This enabled us to compare and contrast the set up used by the human analysis systems of APEs in the context of how well they blend in with systems used by regular humans. For this, we set up a user study in which we requested each participant to solve the CAPTCHA challenges presented to them. More details about this are described later in this section.

2.2   CAPTCHAs for Honey Sites

As mentioned previously, we wanted to use the ability of the visitors to solve CAPTCHA challenges as a key data point to positively identify human visitors from APEs to our honey sites. However, depending on only a single type of challenge to differentiate between humans and bots is risky as APEs might utilize sophisticated bots or other specialized solutions that might break such a challenge. Hence, instead of relying on just a single challenge, we use an array of 7 CAPTCHAs ranging from those that are easily by-passable to commercial as well as custom-built variants. We describe them below along with our rationale for choosing them.

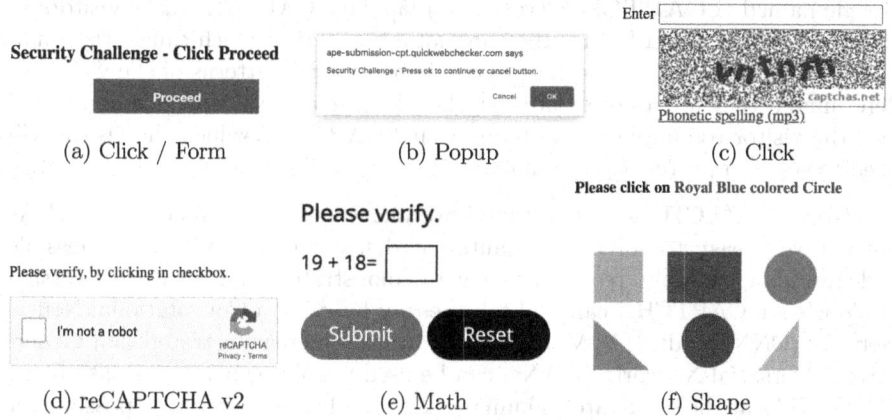

Fig. 2. Various CAPTCHAs deployed in honey sites used for studying APEs.

Easy CAPTCHAs. We crafted three CAPTCHAs which can potentially be easily circumvented by a bot. These CAPTCHAs require the user to simply click on a regular HTML clickable button or a form element or a JavaScript `confirm()` dialog box. We refer to these as **Click**, **Form** and **Popup** CAPTCHAs respectively. Click and Form challenges have to be solved by clicking on an element. They visually look alike and are shown in Fig. 2a. These can be brute-forced easily by any web crawling that uses an automated browsing tool (for example, Selenium [6] or Puppeteer [4]) to click on all "clickable" elements in a page. When implementing these two CAPTCHAs, we used a JavaScript function as the `onclick` event handler for the buttons to record CAPTCHA success. However, these functions can also be called directly giving the appearance of a successful button click to our backend server. Thus, this provides for another simple bypass mechanism for bots which might be configured to blindly call event handler functions even without making any clicks whatsoever. The Popup challenge pages trigger a function on page load which a `Window.confirm()` DOM API call. If this call returns `true`, then passes a success indicator to our backend server. For this to happen, the browsing agent needs to click on (or presses `return` key) on the "OK" button on the JavaScript dialog that pops up (Fig. 2b). However, we point that some previous security crawler setups have managed to automate JS dialogs interactions with the help of in-browser code changes [21] or browser extensions [15] which can be some potential ways to bypass this CAPTCHA in an automated fashion.

Commercial CAPTCHAs. As the CAPTCHAs above can potentially be brute-forced or bypassed by an automated agent, these are not sufficient to confidently separate humans from bots being used by APEs. Hence, we also used two CAPTCHAs that are much more sophisticated and similar to the ones used in real websites. The first one we used is a **text** CAPTCHA service provided by captchas.net [1] (Fig. 2c). The second is a "behavioral" CAPTCHA from Google named **reCAPTCHA** (version-2) [5]. This CAPTCHA asks visitors to click on a button to verify that they are not a bot during which time a risk analysis engine checks static as well as dynamic behavioral patterns of the visitor to determine if they are a bot or not (Fig. 2c). In case of suspicion, the engine will lead the visitor to an image-grid based visual CAPTCHA which the visitor will need to solve to prove they are human [5].

Custom CAPTCHAs. While the above mentioned commercial CAPTCHAs are not very easy to solve in an automated fashion, it is not an impossible endeavor. For example, researchers have demonstrated that an earlier version of Google's reCAPTCHA can be broken easily by using a Convolutional Neural Network (CNN) model [12]. More recently, it has been demonstrated that Generative Adversarial Networks (GANs) can be used to solve generic versions of text CAPTCHAs at the same rate as humans [22]. Furthermore, it is also possible for APEs to seek cooperation from CAPTCHA providers in order to bypass them. This is especially possible if the APE as well as the CAPTCHA provider are from the same organization. For example, Google's Safe Browsing service can potentially have an internal arrangement with Google's reCAPTCHA service so as to allow their crawlers to automatically bypass all their requests. In order to account for such potential automated bypasses, we crafted two custom in-house variants of CAPTCHAs: Math and Shape CAPTCHA.

The **Math** CAPTCHA asks the visitor to give the output of a simple arithmetic operation. It is to be noted that our intention here was to keep this CAPTCHA's functionality similar to existing Math CAPTCHAs such as [3] while at the same time using our own code for implementation. In addition, we also built a new custom CAPTCHA named **Shape** CAPTCHA. It simply asks the visitor to click on a random geometric shape made of a random color (Fig. 2f).

Thus, we design our CAPTCHA challenges above and separate them into 3 categories with an expectation that they are going to be increasingly difficult to be solved by an automated bot. However, we clarify that our goal with these challenges is not to create any CAPTCHA that is impossible for bots to solve. We concede that even our custom challenges can be tackled successfully by APEs if they tailor their bots after analyzing some samples of our challenges. Instead, our goal here is simply to utilize multiple CAPTCHAs so as to enable collection of data on click-through rates from multiple vantage points and then correlate this information with other forensic data from these visits in order to estimate the extent of human analysis components being deployed by present-day APEs.

2.3   Experimental Setup

We will now describe the experimental setup we used for the measurements and analysis we performed for this paper.

Anti-phishing Entities. We tried to cast a wide net in terms of the anti-phishing entities we consider for this work in order to ensure our results are generalizable across the spectrum of APE providers. The prior work [13] which first attempted to study the human analysis systems of APEs focused on 6 providers in their main analysis. Out of these 6, PhishTank has disabled new user registrations to their web portal for submitting URL reports and was hence left out of consideration for this paper. We included the remaining 5 providers in our analysis: Google Safe Browsing (GSB), Microsoft SmartScreen, APWG, Netcraft and OpenPhish. Further, we also added two other APEs in our analysis: Bitdefender and ZeroCert. As in [10], using Python and Selenium-based browser automation, we created a system to be able to send URL reports containing links to our honey sites to the web portals of these 7 providers at a preset frequency.

Honey Sites. For each of the 7 APEs and 7 CAPTCHAs we considered, we created 100 honey sites. Thus, throughout our experimentation period, we submitted 700 honey sites to each of the 7 APEs. We utilized a distinct and new domain name for each honey site but due to financial restrictions we could only register 10 new second-level domain names (TLD+1) for this entire experiment. We created unique TLD+2 domains for the honey sites uniformly under these 10 TLD+1 domains. These domains were registered under the popular .com TLD as well as other extensions often abused by phishing actors such as .xyz, .site and .club. We relied on wildcard DNS records and .htacess rewrite rules in the web server to support these TLD+2 domains for all the 4900 sites utilized in our study. We note that this practice of relying upon a handful of TLD+1 domain names to conduct a large-scale analysis of APEs has been demonstrated to be a viable method in [10]. We avoid discussing this design rationale here for brevity but instead refer interested readers to [10] for detailed arguments as well as experimental results supporting this approach.

We spread out these 700 URL submissions to each APE over a five week period in March and April 2021 averaging about 20 per day.

User Study. For our user study, we first sought an IRB exemption from our university and then used Amazon's Mechanical Turk (MTurk) platform to recruit participants for clicking through the CAPTCHAs on our honey sites. For this, we created a dedicated honey site with 7 different web pages for each of the 7 CAPTCHA challenges. As explained before, these pages are identical to the pages on honey sites distributed to the APEs. We set up this study as 7 different user surveys on MTurk in order to ensure that no same participant visits a particular challenge page more than once. We conducted this study over a one week period in the first week of April 2021. Overall, each of our 7 web pages were visited 210 times thus generating a total of 1470 visits in the user study. Based on data provided by MTurk and IP address information, we were able to attribute these visits to 433 unique participants from about 26 different countries all over the world.

3   Delineation of Human Analysis Systems

The experiment described previously yielded data about the click-through rates of APEs for various CAPTCHAs as shown in Table 1. In the table, the first "Visits" sub-rows for all APEs show information about the number of visits (i.e. HTTP sessions) that were made to the honey sites of different categories that we submitted. Specifically, the first sub-columns (marked by ♟) show the number of visits in which the given category's CAPTCHA challenge was solved successfully and is hence indicative of a human visit. The second "All" sub-columns represent the total number of visits made for each of the 100 sites submitted in a given category irrespective of whether the challenge was solved. It is to be noted how many of these numbers are more than 100 as APEs often make repeated visits to a submitted site. The next "Sites" sub-row for each APE shows these same counts at a "site-level" i.e. the number of unique sites whose CAPTCHA pages were clicked-through or visited by APEs out of a maximum of 100 for each category. Analysis of the number of unique sites visited shows that our submission module has successfully solicited requests from APEs in most cases. Except for Bitdefender, most other APEs have visited most of the sites we submitted to them. APWG, Netcraft, OpenPhish and ZeroCert in particular, have visited all 700 sites that we submitted to them at least once. Across all APEs, we can infer that many sites are visited multiple times by the large amount of visits for each category of submitted sites. These results indicating very high scan-back rates and repeated visits agree with prior recent results from [10].

One key thing to observe from Table 1 is that 4 APEs, namely, Bitdefender, GSB, SmartScreen and Netcraft, have had significant and consistent success in clicking through the entire spectrum of our challenges including customized CAPTCHA challenges. This indicates high likelihood of a human analysis component in their systems. These 4 APEs are highlighted in blue color in the table and we focus most of our attention on these in the rest of this paper. Other than a couple of exceptions, these 4 APEs have been able to click-through at least 10% of the submitted sites across all challenges. This result indicates a stark contrast from the results presented in [13] which showed that practically none of the APEs studied were able to solve the CAPTCHAs presented to them. While we cannot ascertain the reason for this difference, we surmise that this could either be due to the small scale of their experiments which occluded these insights or the early timeline of their experiments at which time APEs have potentially not yet deployed the human analysis systems.

Table 1. APE/CAPTCHA success rates; The ♯ column columns shows information about successful click-through visits while "All" column shows all visits. "Visits" sub-rows show # of HTTP Sessions while "Sites" sub-rows show the # of unique sites visited. APEs that can be deduced to have significant human analysis components are highlighted in blue . Gray cells indicate cases where APEs are successfully using some automated solutions to solve CAPTCHAs. We accounted for these cases and deducted the numbers with the help of a clustering process as described in Sect. 3

CAPTCHA / APE		Easy — Click ♯	Click All	Form ♯	Form All	Popup ♯	Popup All	Commercial — Text ♯	Text All	reCAPTCHA ♯	reCAPTCHA All	Custom — Math ♯	Math All	Shape ♯	Shape All	Summary ♯	Summary All
APWG	Visits	0	455	0	471	0	2575	0	466	0	466	0	471	0	473	0	5377
	Sites	0	100	0	100	0	100	0	100	0	100	0	100	0	100	0/700 (0%)	700/700 (100%)
Bitdefender	Visits	19	610	19	713	~~71~~ 32	735	14	754	11	740	20	509	14	447	129	4508
	Sites	15	38	17	33	~~28~~ 27	38	14	46	11	44	16	34	12	37	112/700 (16%)	270/700 (39%)
GSB	Visits	37	236	36	243	~~192~~ 8	226	23	238	28	228	32	238	26	249	190	1658
	Sites	29	98	31	97	~~92~~ 5	92	23	97	27	96	27	97	26	99	168/700 (24%)	676/700 (97%)
SmartScreen	Visits	27	156	30	90	44	86	12	96	18	87	18	89	11	90	160	694
	Sites	22	84	29	84	44	83	12	86	18	79	18	88	11	85	154/700 (22%)	589/700 (84%)
Netcraft	Visits	~~111~~ 12	902	~~116~~ 16	899	0	1306	15	813	1	571	11	929	15	837	70	6257
	Sites	~~99~~ 12	100	~~100~~ 16	100	0	100	15	100	1	100	11	100	15	100	70/700 (10%)	700/700 (100%)
OpenPhish	Visits	0	588	0	579	0	583	4	47366	0	584	0	586	1	577	5	50863
	Sites	0	100	0	100	0	100	3	100	0	100	0	100	1	100	4/700 (0.5%)	700/700 (100%)
ZeroCERT	Visits	0	208	0	204	~~57~~ 0	186	0	134	0	130	0	155	0	154	0	1171
	Sites	0	100	0	100	~~57~~ 0	100	0	100	0	100	0	100	0	100	0/700 (0%)	700/700 (100%)

When looking at the success rates of submitted sites, 5 CAPTCHA/APE combinations (highlighted in gray) stand out in terms of anomalously high click-through rates in comparison to other numbers in the same rows[1]. For example, GSB made 192 successful visits to Popup challenge pages while the number of successful visits to all other challenges were only around 30. Similarly, Bitdefender visited 71 Popup pages successfully while the rest of the pages had a maximum of 20 visits. Netcraft made 111 and 116 successful visits to Click and Form challenge pages while the remaining categories solicited only about 15 successful visits. Finally, ZeroCERT was only successful in solving Popup challenges. It is to be noted that all these 5 cases involve Easy category CAPTCHAs which as we mentioned previously can easily be tackled by automated crawler setups. We suspected that this is the case with these pages and conducted a clustering analysis that helped us identify such cases in a generic, non-heuristic manner. We discuss this below.

3.1   Filtering Automated Crawler Visits

As discussed in the previous section, our honey sites collected the Canvas and WebGL browser fingerprint information as well as motion biometrics data from all the visits. For each of the APEs, we leveraged this information to cluster all the successful CAPTCHA solving visits that were made to our sites. The results of this clustering process were very insightful. We noticed that across multiple APEs, there were a few clusters where all of the component visits had no motion biometric data whatsoever (i.e. keyboard, mouse or touch data) despite solving the challenge each time. Since it is not possible for a human analyst to solve these challenges without such movement we consider these as actions of automated analysis systems. Interestingly, for each APE, all these "no-motion" clusters corresponded with the 5 APE/CAPTCHA combinations (the gray cells in the table) which we already suspected. As a result, we decided to discount all the visits that were parts of these clusters from the human analysis components of our study. The resulting numbers after these deductions are shown in the table itself.

It is to be noted how these deductions greatly decreased the numbers in the suspected cases and made the human visit counts for all 4 APEs ultimately much more uniform across different challenges. These deductions show that GSB, Bitdefender and ZeroCERT used bots to solve Popup CAPTCHA challenges and that Netcraft used bots for solving large numbers of Click and Form CAPTCHA. This is likely using the mechanisms we already discussed in Sect. 2.2. Interestingly, after these deductions we can see that Netcraft has a 1 to 1 correspondence for sites and visits from human systems for all challenges. This means that with Netcraft, human analysts typically do not revisit a visited site unlike in the case of the other APEs. Another interesting thing to note in is the absence of any evidence for bot-assisted challenge solving for GSB's reCAPTCHA

---

[1] Please refer to the numbers that were struck through in the gray cells in Table 1.

challenges despite both GSB and reCAPTCHA services belonging to Google. GSB's automation seemed to only be limited to Popup challenges.

3.2   Human Systems' Impact Analysis

The last column of Table 1 indicating the summary statistics of human visits for each APE paints a very optimistic picture. In summary, the 4 APEs were able to visit between 10% and 24% of the submitted sites. These are very impressive numbers given that APEs such as Google Safe Browsing receive billions of URL reports everyday [2]. This shows that current APEs have likely invested large amounts of financial resources towards building these expansive human analysis systems. Assuming that each APE has an independent mechanism for deciding if a submitted site will be viewed by human analyst, we can also compute the probability for a candidate site that is submitted to all the APEs to be inspected by a human. Concretely, let p_i denote this probability for each APE. Then, the summary probability can be computed by $1 - \prod_{i=1}^{4} (1 - p_i)$ which gives a formidable probability value of 43% for human analysis of a candidate site. In addition, it should also be noted that we only made a single submission of report to APEs for each honey site from a single end point. In the real world, large-scale social engineering attacks will often trigger repeated reporting of the complicit URLs from diverse sources. In such a case, it is possible for this manual analysis probability to be even more than computed here.

4   Evaluation of Human Analysis Systems

The previous section demonstrated that multiple APEs built elaborate human analysis systems which are arguably much more expensive to maintain and scale than their bot counterparts. Given this, it is very important to ensure that these systems are robust and do not carry any undue weaknesses. In this section, we focus on studying the prevalence of any such issues which can potentially enable targeted cloaking attacks against human analysis systems in the future.

4.1   Geolocation-Based Evasion Attacks

Prior works have advocated the use of diverse geolocations for APEs when visiting candidate phishing sites in order to thwart geolocation-based cloaking techniques used by attackers [17]. More recent work has shown that many APEs have in fact heeded this recommendation and heavily diversified the network infrastructure used for visits to the candidate sites [10]. We now investigate if the diversification has also made its way to the human analysis systems used by APEs. For this, we compare the network diversity of visits coming from human analysts with the overall network diversity of the visits. These results can be seen in Table 2 which shows the distinct number of IP addresses (IP) as well as countries associated with these IP addresses in the two sets of data for each APE. We also repeat the numbers about site visit counts for the two sets in order to present a context for this comparison.

Table 2. Table demonstrating the lack of diversity of geolocation in requests made by the human analysis systems across different APEs.

APE	Sites		IP		Country	
	⚑	All	⚑	All	⚑	All
APWG	-	700	-	3793	-	14
Bitdefender	112	270	37	940	1 (Romania)	40
GSB	168	676	85	843	1 (India)	2
SmartScreen	154	589	100	326	1 (India)	13
Netcraft	70	700	14	1633	2 (UK: 97%)	49
OpenPhish	4	700	-	4452	-	63
ZeroCERT	-	700	-	3	-	1

Firstly, we can see that the data in the "All" column are mostly in agreement with prior results in [10] and show that APEs are persisting to invest in diversification of the network infrastructure used for vetting websites. For instance, OpenPhish used 4452 IP addresses and APWG used 3793 IP addresses to visit the 700 sites we submitted to them. Similarly Netcraft used 1633 addresses for crawling the 700 sites submitted to them. However, their human analysis system, on the other hand, visited 70 sites using only 14 different IP addresses showing a vast difference in the ratio of IP addresses used to the number of sites visited between the two cases (2.33 for all vs. 0.2 for the human system). Same is the case for IP addresses of other APEs as well. These differences become even more stark when we consider the country associated with these IP addresses. While Bitdefender uses 40 different countries all over the world for visiting candidate phishing sites, their human analysis system uses only IP addresses belonging to Romania for this purpose. Similarly, 97% of Netcraft's human system visits (68/70 visits) are from UK, although overall, they use IP addresses from 49 different countries. It is to be noted here that Bitdefender is head quartered in Romania while Netcraft is headquartered in UK which likely explains why these countries were chosen by them for hosting their human analysis systems. On a similar note, GSB and Microsoft SmartScreen are only using IP addresses from India for all their human analysis system visits. Thus, even though all of these are global companies with users all over the world, an attacker can easily avoid their elaborate human analysis systems by simply ignoring potential victims from a handful of countries. Concretely, if an attacker can set up an evasive malicious site that specifically serves benign content to India, Romania and UK, our results show that majority of human analysis visits can be evaded.

Mitigations. We strongly recommend APEs to adopt network request diversification infrastructure for their human analysis systems to avoid geolocation-based evasion attacks discussed above. This can be easily achieved with the help of solutions such as commercial VPNs which can provide support for switching between multiple IP addresses globally. Our results above which indicate the general visits of APEs coming from a large number of geolocations already points to the fact that APEs are already potentially using such mechanisms for their bot analysis systems. Upon further analysis of the data pertaining to visits from diverse geolocations, we found an interesting case study regarding Bitdefender. We noticed that 54 honey sites submitted to Bitdefender had HTTP sessions in which each session involved HTTP requests from IP addresses in 2–5 different countries all over the world. Collectively, we noticed that IP addresses from 13 different countries were used for this. While switching IP addresses mid-session might unfortunately make these mechanisms conspicuous and thus make the IP addresses fingerprintable by attackers, nevertheless, this is still a step in the right direction. Proper implementation of such IP address switching mechanisms (without any side channels such as session cookie sharing) in human analysis systems can make them thwart geolocation-based evasion attempts by attackers. We thus recommend APEs to pursue such tactics.

4.2   User Agents

Another important issue pointed out in [17] was the effectiveness of certain "device-type" based cloaking attacks on APEs. For example, their research showed that a phishing website set to distribute malicious content only to mobile (Android/iOS) user-agents tends to be very resistant to blocklisting. As a result, APEs have evolved tremendously to improve user agent diversity as was evidenced in [10]. We also attempted to measure this with our data. Table 3 demonstrates this. The second column in the table shows the popularity of OS/Browser combinations as per our user study. While the source of our user study participants (Amazon MTurk), might have biased the data towards more desktop users than normal, we believe that the proportion of users using various platforms in desktop and mobile platforms is still a good indicator of the popularity of user agents as it falls in line with results from larger studies [7]. The "All Requests" part of the table shows the probability that a domain visited by any of the APEs will be done so with a particular User-Agent header as per our data. We marked any probability value less than 0.1 in red and any value more than 0.5 in green to highlight good and bad values. Note that these values often sum up to more than 1 as the same domain submitted to an APE is often visited from multiple platforms. For the "Combined" column, we treat these individual probabilities as being related to a random event and obtain the combined probability for a domain that is submitted to all APEs to be visited by a particular user agent. To clarify, assume p_i is the probability for a user agent to be visited by an APE i. We compute the combined probability for a visit from the same user agent by computing $1 - \prod_{i=1}^{n}(1 - p_i)$. The results confirm those in [10] that APEs have largely evolved to improve diversity in the user agents they use to vet candidate phishing pages. We can see that even the lowest combined probability is about 0.25 for Windows/Opera thus showing that all popular user agents are adequately represented (cumulatively) by the APEs. Of particular note is Bitdefender and OpenPhish both of which have a significant amount of visitors from a diverse set of user agents.

Table 3. Lack of diversity in the browsing agents used for human analysis systems of APEs. The numbers in the cells indicate the probability that a given APE will visit a submitted site with a given `User-Agent` header. Values above 0.5 are in green and below 0.1 are in red.

OS/Browser	User Study	All Requests								Human System				
		APWG	Bitdefender	GSB	SmartScreen	Netcraft	OpenPhish	ZeroCERT	Combined	Bitdefender	GSB	SmartScreen	Netcraft	Combined
Windows/ Chrome	279/433 (0.64)	0.51	0.74	1.00	0.10	0.95	1.00	0.00	1.00	0.82	0.00	0.18	0.14	0.87
Windows/ Firefox	32/433 (0.07)	0.82	0.32	0.00	0.00	0.46	0.14	0.00	0.94	0.12	0.00	0.00	0.01	0.14
Windows/ Edge	18/433 (0.04)	0.14	0.07	0.08	0.91	0.00	0.14	0.00	0.94	0.02	0.00	0.82	0.00	0.83
Windows/ Opera	6/433 (0.01)	0.00	0.14	0.00	0.00	0.00	0.12	0.00	0.25	0.00	0.00	0.00	0.00	0.00
Android/*	40/433 (0.09)	0.04	0.14	0.00	0.00	0.69	0.14	0.00	0.78	0.00	0.00	0.00	0.00	0.00
macOS/*	33/433 (0.08)	0.00	0.16	0.00	0.00	0.26	1.00	0.00	1.00	0.00	0.00	0.00	0.00	0.00
ChromeOS/*	13/433 (0.03)	0.00	0.00	0.38	0.00	0.00	0.00	0.00	0.38	0.00	1.00	0.00	0.00	1.00
Linux/*	7/433 (0.02)	0.01	0.28	0.00	0.00	0.34	0.17	0.43	0.78	0.05	0.00	0.00	0.84	0.85
iOS/*	5/433 (0.01)	1.00	0.18	0.00	0.00	0.97	0.15	0.00	1.00	0.00	0.00	0.00	0.00	0.00

The corresponding probability that a human analyst will use a particular user agent is on the last section of the table. We only consider the 4 main APEs which had human visitors for this. These probabilities are also combined similar to the other section and are in great contrast with the other one. In particular, we can see that there is not a single human request from Android, iOS, macOS, Windows/Opera user agents from even a single APE. This leaves all these popular platforms exposed to targeted evasion attacks that completely avoid human analysis. Note that as this includes both Android and iOS, this finding means that all mobile users can be exposed to targeted phishing attack pages that can evade all human analysis. It is also interesting to see the user agent diversities for human analysis systems of individual APEs. We note that all GSB systems simply use Google's own Chrome OS based systems for all of their human analysis despite them being not very popular in the wild. Similarly, SmartScreen's human analysis systems are predominantly using the Microsoft's own Edge browsers for this. Both of these APEs are thus largely using uncommon browsing agents leading to potential cloaking attacks. It is also interesting to see how Bitdefender also has a great lack in diversity in their human systems (compared to their general requests) although they fare better than Google and Microsoft by atleast using the most popular "Windows/Chrome" user agent for all their visits thus protecting at least a majority of users from targeted evasion attacks.

Mitigations. We strongly recommend APEs to improve user agent diversity for their human analysis systems. However, this is arguably a complicated problem. While simple measures such as adopting user-agent changing extensions [8, 9] might seem to solve this problem on the surface, APEs will face a risk of creating new browser anomalies which miscreants can abuse to fingerprint or evade analysis systems [10]. Another more viable solution is to truly improve diversity in the systems used by human analysts by adopting diverse browser/OS platforms for their systems. At the very least, all popular desktop and mobile platforms used by majority of users should be covered by these analysis systems.

4.3   Timing Blind Spots

We next measured the time it takes for human analysts of different APEs to first visit a submitted site. The median times for different APEs varied with Bitdefender and SmartScreen being the fastest APEs with less than 4 h of human response time. GSB was the slowest with a median turnaround time of about 30 h. This is very slow compared to GSB's overall median response time of only about 34 min; but this is understandable as this figure includes automated crawlers which are expected to be more responsive. However, we were still intrigued by this relatively low response time of GSB's human analysis system in comparison to other APEs and investigated this further. For this, we mapped the time of visits from human analysts into Indian Standard Time (IST) as we saw previously that all GSB human visits were from IP addresses in India. The graph depicting the day of these visits in Fig. 3 shows that none of the 190 visits from GSB happened over the weekends (per IST). This is likely because the human analyst system was being run in a typical office like setup that does not operate over the weekends. However, this can be abuse by attackers. For example, a social engineering attacker who starts a campaign on Friday night can effectively have two full days before the attack is analyzed by a human from GSB. This leaves a sufficiently large time gap for a large-scale campaign.

Mitigations. Such timings blind spots need to be plugged by APEs by promoting capabilities for human analysis at least on a daily basis. If such changes are infeasible due to financial restrictions, then another potential approach could be to share candidate phishing URL data with other APEs that have complementary human analysis capabilities.

4.4   Sensor API-based Mobile Evasion Attacks

As described in Sect. 2, one of the novelties of our experimental setup was the collection of biometric data from APEs such as information about keyboard, mouse events as well as other events from sensor devices. Therefore, we explored the possibility of developing evasive attacks against APEs by using this data. Interestingly, while human visits from APEs did result in keyboard and mouse data, we were unable to collect any sensor data from any of the APEs we studied. Note that none of the APE visits had any web sensor data even when they

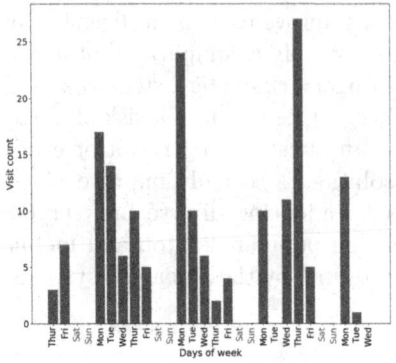

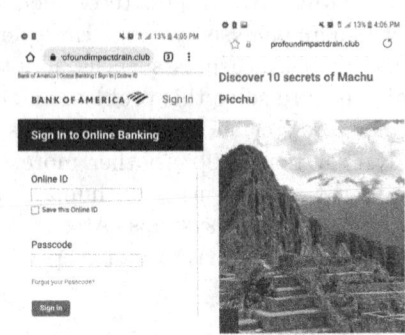

Fig. 3. Daily visits of GSB analysts

Fig. 4. Uncloaked and cloaked sensor API-based phishing pages

proclaimed to be coming from mobile user agents. This is anomalous as our tests with multiple Android/Chrome devices showed that they all emit sensor data from the `Accelerometer` as well as `deviceMotion` web APIs in their default settings. In order to remove personal bias, we also performed the same analysis on 35 users in our MTurk study and found that all of them were also emitting data from the `accelerometer` API and `deviceMotion` APIs thus showing that many users do not change the default settings on these devices. Our data analysis also showed that all the affected Android/Chrome devices emit the first movement data with in the first few seconds (median time = 2.5 s). On the other hand, all the user agents for whom the `accelerometer`/`deviceMotion` web APIs are inaccessible due to user permission issues or lack of support (such as in the case of APEs) throw an error message during page load itself. We thus concluded that it will be possible to create effective phishing sites capitalize on these anomalies to target Android/Chrome users. Given that Android/Chrome is one of the most popular mobile user agents (35/45 mobile users in our study), this attack can leave a lot of users exposed to pages that conduct targeted social engineering attacks with impunity.

Evaluation. We implemented the cloaking logic in JavaScript and PHP and registered 10 new domain names to host 10 evasive phishing sites for evaluation. All of these sites show a "Bank of America" phishing page for any Android/Chrome user agent that emits `accelerometer` and `deviceMotion` data. On the other hand, if there is any error in accessing these web APIs or if there is a 10 s timeout without any such data emissions, we display a cloaked page to the user as in Fig. 4. As baseline, we also created 5 phishing sites that show the same phishing page without any cloaking logic. We started the evaluation in July 2021 when we reported all 15 sites to the 7 APEs we considered in this paper. On the very first day of this experiment, after our reporting, all 5 baseline sites got blocked in all major web browsers with GSB blocklisting them in as little as 2.5 h. This figure is in line with prior studies [10,17] and shows that the phishing pages we created are considered as malicious by APEs. Upon noticing that none of the 10 evasive sites got blocked, we continued to report these 10 sites daily over the next two weeks to all 7 APEs. Despite this, all of these 10 sites remained unblocked indefinitely until now spanning a period of more than seven months.

Mitigations. We showed that it is possible to create evasive phishing attacks against Android/Chrome platform due to two main reasons: (1) None of the APEs' human analysis systems perform testing using Android/Chrome devices. (2) None of the APE's general visitors that purport to use Android/Chrome user agents (likely bots) emit web sensor API data similar to how the real devices behave. Solving either of the problems will help thwart this attack vector. As already discussed earlier, the mitigation for (1) is to simply support more diversity in the devices used by human analysis systems of APEs. To handle (2), one potential solution is to improve the automated crawler technology used by the APEs emit fake web sensor data similar to real devices. We already saw similar methods being used by Netcraft in a lot of their failed visits to our CAPTCHA pages where the visitors were inputting random repeated textual content into text boxes. APEs should adopt similar approaches for the web sensor APIs as well. A much simpler and complementary approach to eliminate this entire attack surface is for Android or Chrome developers to disable this default configuration of allowing websites access to these sensor APIs. This action which will be in line with other mobile OSs (such as iOS) and browsers (such as Firefox) will also have the added benefit of improving user privacy as prior research has shown that these APIs can be used for fingerprinting attacks [11].

Other Attacks. While most of the above evasive attacks were mainly focused on the human analysis systems, our data analysis also revealed some weaknesses in what are most likely the automated crawler systems being used by APEs. For example, all of GSB's visits that were solving Popup challenges from non-India IP addresses were solving the challenges in less than a second. This is in sharp contrast to the solution times for GSB's human analysts as well as our user study participants that took at least 10 s. Such timing discrepancies can easily be utilized to identify APE bot IP addresses and them to a blocklists in phishing kits as is often done in the wild [18]. Similarly, we notice that all of the APEs ecosystems (human+bot) continue to lack heavily in diversity of browser fingerprints which keeps them prone to evasive attacks as proposed in [10]. We avoid discussing this in detail here as similar issues that affect all APE ecosystems have been tackled in earlier works. Instead, we chose to only focus on those issues that largely affect the human analysis systems of APEs in this paper.

5   Discussion

Conservative Estimates. In this paper, we primarily relied upon the event of whether a visitor is solving a particular CAPTCHA challenge in order to deduce if that visitor is human. However, there might be human analysts who do not solve some CAPTCHA challenges as a result of a notion that our pages are not suspicious enough to warrant inspection. We thus concede here that the numbers presented in Sect. 3 might be a lower-bound on the actual size of human analyst systems being used by APEs. This only means that the APEs are spending even more resources to host such analysis systems than what was implied earlier and is hence even more important to take measures to protect them form evasion attacks.

Further, since the cases in which analysts are solving CAPTCHA challenges can be considered a random subset of all cases of human visits, we expect the same outcomes as in Sect. 4 when analyzing the set of all human visits as well. In order to demonstrated this, we used GSB as a case study. We repeated the browser fingerprint-based clustering we described earlier for all visits from GSB irrespective of whether the visit resulted in a CAPTCHA solution. 3 of the 4 clusters that we determined in Sect. 3 to be coming from humans have now "expanded" on their size and included several visits where the challenges were not solved but shared the same fingerprints. In total, these clusters were covering 258 distinct sites (in 295 visits) instead of the 168 distinct sites where challenges were solved thus indicating an even healthier human-analysis rate of 37%. However, as expected, all the weaknesses remain the same with this expanded dataset of probable human visits as well. For example, all the 295 visits were from Indian IP addresses with Chrome OS user agents none of which have happened over the weekends.

Industry Disclosure. We have conducted an elaborate industry disclosure process with all four affected APEs. As part of this, we have disclosed all of our findings in the form of detailed reports describing our experimental procedures and the weaknesses we discovered in their human analysis systems. In the case of Google, we have also disclosed information about the evasive phishing attacks we were able to launch against the Android/Chrome ecosystems which can easily be addressed by turning off the default emission of web sensor API data similar to other platforms. The response from APEs has been positive with one APE mentioning that multiple internal bug reports have been filed as a result of our disclosures.

Ethical Considerations. Our APE evaluation setup involved sending honey site URLs to APEs. We limited these submissions to only about 20 per day which is much smaller in comparison to the large number of suspicious URLs vetted by these APEs everyday. Further, based on our server logs, we estimate that the total time spent by the human analysts of all the APEs vetting our CAPTCHA-laden honey pages is only about 1.2 h. We thus argue that the small temporary overhead experienced by the APEs during our experimental period far outweighs the security benefits gained by the insights we present in this study. Our setup is also similar to prior studies on APEs such as [10,17,19] all of which involved submitting similar honey URLs to APEs. Similar to these prior works, we made the phishing pages described in Sect. 4.4 non-functional in order to prevent accidental sensitive information input from random visitors. Finally, our user study received exemption from the university IRB board and we also sought prior approval from the participants describing all the data collection methodologies before directing them to the CAPTCHA challenge pages.

6 Related Work

As discussed in Sect. 1, despite phishing being an old problem, only recently has the research community begun to focus its attention on studying the robustness of APEs with studies such as [10,13,17,19,23]. Among these, only [13] (and a small part of [23]) have tried to focus on the ability of APEs to overcome CAPTCHA-based cloaking challenges. However, they have concluded that APEs were largely incapable of solving such challenges. In sharp contrast to this, our study showed strong evidence that multiple APEs do in fact have ability to solve a large portion of such challenges there by indicating presence of elaborate human analysis systems complementing their automated crawler infrastructure. We attribute this difference to either the gap in the timelines of these studies during which time APEs could have potentially improved or the larger scale of our evaluation experiments. We relied on a recently proposed APE evaluation methodology [10] for achieving this scale. Our discovery of human analysis systems in the APEs thus allowed us an opportunity to conduct the first systematic study of the robustness of the human analysis systems of APEs which revealed several weaknesses in these systems as presented in Sect. 4.

7 Conclusion

We conducted a large-scale study that tests the ability of 7 popular APEs to overcome CAPTCHA-based challenges. Through this, we provide strong evidence for the presence of an elaborate human analysis system in 4 of the 7 APEs we studied. These are: GSB, SmartScreen, Bitdefender and Netcraft. While this measurement bodes well for the web security community, unfortunately, our study went on to show some grave weaknesses which can be abused by future attackers to launch evasive attacks against these elaborate human analysis systems. Interestingly, many of these weaknesses can be easily mitigated and are already being done so in most of the automated crawler systems of these APEs. We thus provided recommendations to APEs for doing the same with the expensive and vital human analysis systems as well. Our work in this paper is therefore crucial to help improve the current security posture of Anti Phishing Entities (APEs).

Acknowledgements. This work was inspired by a comment from an anonymous reviewer at IEEE SSP 2021 where we submitted our prior work [10]. We thank Wingate Jones for help in exploring AI-based techniques to evade APEs. We also thank all the anonymous reviewers for their very helpful feedback. This work was partly supported by the National Science Foundation (NSF) under grant CNS-2126655.

References

1. Free CAPTCHA-Service. http://captchas.net/
2. Google transparency report. https://transparencyreport.google.com/safe-browsing/search. Accessed 13 Jan 2022
3. Math Captcha. https://www.jotform.com/widgets/math-captcha
4. Puppeteer. https://github.com/puppeteer/puppeteer. Accessed 13 Jan 2022
5. ReCAPTCHA demo. https://www.google.com/recaptcha/api2/demo
6. Selenium. https://www.selenium.dev/. Accessed 13 Jan 2022
7. Statscounter: Browser market share. https://gs.statcounter.com/browser-market-share
8. User-agent switcher and manager. https://chrome.google.com/webstore/detail/user-agent-switcher-for-c/djflhoibgkdhkhhcedjiklpkjnoahfmg
9. User-agent switcher and manager. https://addons.mozilla.org/en-US/firefox/addon/user-agent-string-switcher/
10. Acharya, B., Vadrevu, P.: PhishPrint: evading phishing detection crawlers by prior profiling. In: 30th USENIX Security Symposium, USENIX Security 2021, 11–13 August 2021, pp. 3775–3792. USENIX Association (2021)
11. Das, A., Borisov, N., Caesar, M.: Tracking mobile web users through motion sensors: attacks and defenses. In: NDSS (2016)
12. Goodfellow, I.J., Bulatov, Y., Ibarz, J., Arnoud, S., Shet, V.D.: Multi-digit number recognition from street view imagery using deep convolutional neural networks. In: 2nd International Conference on Learning Representations, ICLR 2014, Banff, 14–16 April 2014, Conference Track Proceedings (2014)
13. Maroofi, S., Korczynski, M., Duda, A.: Are you human?: resilience of phishing detection to evasion techniques based on human verification. In: IMC 2020: ACM Internet Measurement Conference, Virtual Event, USA, 27–29 October 2020, pp. 78–86. ACM (2020)
14. Maroofi, S., Korczyński, M., Hesselman, C., Ampeau, B., Duda, A.: COMAR: classification of compromised versus maliciously registered domains. In: 2020 IEEE European Symposium on Security and Privacy (EuroS&P), pp. 607–623. IEEE (2020)
15. Miramirkhani, N., Starov, O., Nikiforakis, N.: Dial one for scam: analyzing and detecting technical support scams. In: 22nd Annual Network and Distributed System Security Symposium NDSS, vol. 16 (2016)
16. Mowery, K., Shacham, H.: Pixel perfect: fingerprinting canvas in HTML5. In: Proceedings of W2SP 2012 (2012)
17. Oest, A., Safaei, Y., Doupé, A., Ahn, G.J., Wardman, B., Tyers, K.: PhishFarm: a scalable framework for measuring the effectiveness of evasion techniques against browser phishing blacklists. In: 2019 IEEE Symposium on Security and Privacy (SP) (2019)
18. Oest, A., Safei, Y., Doupé, A., Ahn, G.J., Wardman, B., Warner, G.: Inside a phisher's mind: understanding the anti-phishing ecosystem through phishing kit analysis. In: 2018 APWG Symposium on Electronic Crime Research (eCrime), pp. 1–12. IEEE (2018)
19. Peng, P., Yang, L., Song, L., Wang, G.: Opening the blackbox of VirusTotal: analyzing online phishing scan engines. In: Proceedings of the Internet Measurement Conference, pp. 478–485 (2019)
20. Roy-Chowdhury, R.: Google: How we keep you safe online every day (2020). https://blog.google/technology/safety-security/how-we-keep-you-safe-online-every-day/

21. Vadrevu, P., Perdisci, R.: What you see is not what you get: discovering and tracking social engineering attack campaigns. In: Proceedings of the Internet Measurement Conference, pp. 308–321 (2019)
22. Ye, G., et al.: Yet another text captcha solver: a generative adversarial network based approach. In: Proceedings of the 2018 ACM SIGSAC Conference on Computer and Communications Security, CCS 2018, Toronto, 15–19 October 2018, pp. 332–348. ACM (2018)
23. Zhang, P., et al.: CrawlPhish: large-scale analysis of client-side cloaking techniques in phishing. In: 2021 IEEE Symposium on Security and Privacy (SP) (2021)

Amplification Chamber: Dissecting the Attack Infrastructure of Memcached DRDoS Attacks

Mizuki Kondo[1], Rui Tanabe[1(✉)] [iD], Natsuo Shintani[1], Daisuke Makita[1,2], Katsunari Yoshioka[1], and Tsutomu Matsumoto[1]

[1] Yokohama National University, YNU, Yokohama, Japan
{tanabe-rui-xj,yoshioka,tsutomu}@ynu.ac.jp
[2] National Institute of Information and Communications Technology, NICT, Tokyo, Japan
d.makita@nict.go.jp

Abstract. Distributed and reflective denial-of-service (DRDoS) attacks have been one of the most devastating and harmful threats on the Internet. By abusing open Internet services such as DNS and NTP, attackers can boost traffics without revealing their IP addresses. In the case of Memcached DRDoS attacks, adversaries often set large caches on amplifiers using TCP requests before launching the attack, which gives us hints on the IP addresses of the attack infrastructure. In this paper, we trace back the anonymous attack to their origins and investigate their attack infrastructure. During the 15 months of monitoring (September 2018 to November 2019) via eleven honeypots, we observed 820,729 Memcached DRDoS attacks. Out of them, 370,795 attacks were associated with TCP set requests, and 127,771 attacks were associated with UDP set requests. We found 199 unique IP addresses in 54 ASes used to set the large caches for these attacks and that attackers keep using the same large caches or even borrow the cache set by someone else. This implies a relatively small number of threat actors compared to the vast number of attacks. In the case of hotspots where setters are concentrated, the attack infrastructures had functionalities such as scanners to find amplifiers, setters to prepare the attacks, and launchers to generate the DDoS traffic. By conducting a TTL-based trilateration analysis, we found that 7,407 attacks originated from the setters, indicating 16.6% of the setters also worked as launchers.

Finally, we confirmed that there were still over 15,000 amplifiers in the wild scattering over 1,000 ASes. This result suggests that the threats of Memcached DRDoS attacks will continue to exist, and our analysis of the attack infrastructures could provide helpful information to take practical actions such as takedowns. We have provided the obtained results on the attack infrastructures to our national CERT.

Keywords: Memcached DRDoS attack · Amplifier

M. Kondo and N. Shintani—This work was done while researching at the University.

L. Cavallaro et al. (Eds.): DIMVA 2022, LNCS 13358, pp. 178–196, 2022.
https://doi.org/10.1007/978-3-031-09484-2_10

1   Introduction

Distributed and reflective denial-of-service (DRDoS) attacks, in which an attacker aims to consume the bandwidth of a victim, have long been a significant threat on the Internet. In the DRDoS attacks, adversaries abuse the fact that public servers of UDP-based network protocols respond to requests without further validating the sender's identity (i.e., the IP address). They can multiply their attack bandwidth by simply sending packets with their source IP addresses spoofed as targets' to the public servers (i.e., the amplifiers).

The adversaries are continuously finding new attack vectors. One protocol that suits the desired attack features is Memcached, whose amplification factor* can be extremely high. Memcached [4] is a high-performance distributed memory cache system used to speed up dynamic web applications. It is widely used by companies such as Facebook, YouTube, Twitter, GitHub, and so on [27]. However, attackers have misused open Memcached servers as powerful amplifiers to launch extremely high-volume DRDoS attacks [24]. In February 2018, the repository hosting service GitHub was flooded with 1.35 Tbps peak incoming traffic [6]. Just a few months after, Arbor Networks observed another attack with a strength of 1.7 Tbps [25]. Therefore, in 2018, the UDP protocol (port 11211/UDP) was disabled by default in Memcached version 1.5.6 [3].

While the overwhelming attack continues, prior works have revealed some essential aspects of the Memcached DRDoS attack. First, by using *"add"* or *"set"* commands to put chunks of data into the server, adversaries can quickly load up large values and use them as responses [17]. Second, more than one thousand Memcached servers were found from IXP traffic along with details of how high their amplification factors can be [11]. Another study also shows that more than fifty thousand Memcached servers were found from Internet-wide scans [26]. Third, most of the Memcached servers being abused for the attack are hosted at VPS hosting services and other small hosting providers [19]. These works provide interesting insights on misused Memcached servers but still lack the picture of the whole attack infrastructure. The fact that TCP packets are used to load a large cache into the amplification chamber indicates that the source IP addresses of the attack infrastructure are not spoofed. Besides, IP traceback aims to identify the origin of spoofed packets. Moreover, more recent work proposed a method to correlate the scans for amplifiers with the observed attacks [14]. Both previous works need a prior arrangement for traceback, while the setting of a large cache by TCP can be observed without any initial arrangement except running the honeypot itself. This is an essential fact for observing Memcached attacks.

In this paper, we conduct a long-term observation of the attack infrastructure and trace back the anonymous attack to their origins. We first utilize high-interaction Memcached honeypots to investigate how attackers set cache data into the server's response. We then used a TTL-based trilateration method [14]

---

* The term amplification factor stands for the number of UDP payload bytes that an amplifier sends to answer a request, compared to the number of UDP payload bytes of the request [10].

to see if the hosts that prepared the attack were topologically close to those actually launched the attacks. By looking into the darknet data, we also reveal the IP addresses of hosts that were scanning the Internet to search for Memcached servers as possible reflectors. We compare these hosts by dividing their functionalities into *Scanners* that find amplifiers, *Setters* that prepare the attacks, and *Launchers* that generate the DDoS traffic and reveal how Memcached DRDoS attacks are conducted. Finally, we utilize Internet-wide scan results to show that the issue of open Memcached servers still exists with more recent data.

During the 15 months of monitoring (September 2018 to November 2019) via eleven honeypots, we observed 820,729 Memcached DRDoS attacks. Before observing the attacks, we saw various request packets to set cache data into the honeypots. Namely, 370,795 attacks (45.2%) were associated with TCP set requests, and 127,771 attacks (15.6%) with UDP set requests. We found 199 unique IP addresses in 54 ASes used to set the large caches for these attacks. Compared to the number of TCP packets that aim to set the cache data, the number of attack packets that request the cache data was much higher. This means that attackers keep using the same large caches or even borrowing the cache set by someone else instead of setting it by themselves. On the other hand, the number of UDP packets that aim to set the cache data were nearly the same as those of the attack packets.

In the case of hotspots where setters were concentrated, each hotspot had multiple functionalities such as scanning, setting, and launching attacks. The set events and the attack event almost always appeared together, indicating that the caches were abused for attacks immediately after being set.

With a TTL-based trilateration analysis, we determined that 7,407 attacks were launched from the setters, indicating 16.6%(33/199 IP addresses) of the setters worked as launchers as well. In fact, many attacks were launched from the same setter.

Furthermore, we found that 18.6% of the setters were used as scanners to find new amplifiers. On the other hand, we found little evidence that front-end booter websites were hosted on the setters.

Finally, we demonstrate that the issue of open Memcached servers still exists by investigating the number of amplifiers in the wild using the Internet-wide scan results from Censys [2] every week from January 2020 to October 2020. We found that many network operators have eliminated open Memcached servers but there are 15,000 constant amplifiers scattering over 1,000 ASes. This result suggests that the problem of Memcached DRDoS attacks would continue and our analysis could provide useful information to take practical actions such as takedowns. In fact, we have provided the result of our analysis on the attack infrastructures to our national CERT. The honeypot dataset will also be available and can be requested via our website [1] by interested researchers.

The remainder of this paper is structured as follows. In Sect. 2, we explain the threat model of the Memcached DRDoS attack. In Sect. 3, we show our real-world observation result via eleven honeypots. In Sect. 4, we analyze the attack infrastructure by examining the relationship between the IP address of the

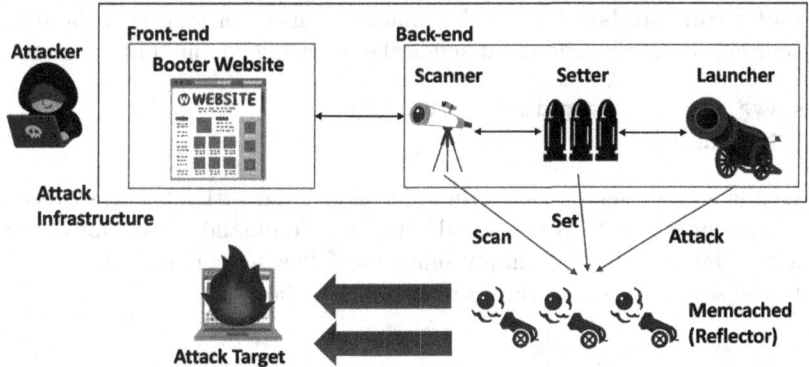

Fig. 1. Overview of Memcached DRDoS attack infrastructure.

attacking source, the cache data sent from that address, and scanners searching for Memcached servers. In Sect. 5, we discuss limitations and ethics. In Sect. 6, we explain related works. Finally, we conclude in Sect. 7.

2   Threat Model

Typically in a DRDoS attack, the attacker does not directly send traffic to the victim but instead sends IP spoofed packets to open servers and reflect the attack traffic to the target. Moreover, adversaries abuse the fact that public servers amplify the traffic (henceforth, amplifiers), and thus, the target faces massive attack traffic. Internet-facing services, such as DNS and NTP servers, have long been misused as powerful amplifiers [10,11]. New amplifiers are continuously explored, and Memcached servers have become one of the prime targets recently [24].

Memcached is a high-performance, distributed memory object caching system [4]. By default, the Memcached server listens on ports 11211/TCP and 11211/UDP. In the case of TCP connections, after the client connects and sends a command to the Memcached server, it reads the response and finally disconnects. It is also possible to send and receive commands in UDP. Several commands are prepared for enhancing the use of Memcached servers. The following describes typical commands used in Memcached DRDoS attacks.

Stats Command: The *"stats"* command is used to obtain statistical information and other internal data managed by the Memcached server. Attackers can send a request packet with the command with the spoofed IP address (i.e., victim's IP address). The response to the commands can be over 1,500 bytes, and therefore, the amplification factor can be 300 or more.

```
stats\r\n
```

Set/Get Commands: The *"set"* command is used for storing cache data on the Memcached server. The client sends the following command to the server.

```
set <key> <flags> <exptime> <bytes> \r\n
<value> \r\n
```

The Memcached server caches the value associated with a key when receiving the set command. On the other hand, the *"get"* command is used for obtaining the cached data. The client simply sends the following command with a list of keys to the server to obtain the corresponding caches.

```
get <key>*\r\n
```

Using these basic commands, an attacker can set a sufficiently large cache data and then reflect the cached data to the victim's IP address. By default, the maximum size for cache data is about 1 MB. When an adversary sets 1 MB cache associated with a single character key *"a"*, a 5-byte get request *"get a"* generates 1 MB response. The attackers can use TCP or UDP to set caches. However, if they want to set a large cache, TCP requests are required or otherwise use the *"append"* command to add many small caches to the same key using UDP. As we show in the following sections, while many attackers set caches by themselves, some attackers exploit caches that were set by someone else.

Therefore, our threat model is that the attackers first send packets to search for Memcached servers (henceforth, scanners), then send packets to set cache data into the server's response (henceforth, setter), and finally send IP-spoofed packets to launch the attack (henceforth, launcher). Such open Memcached servers receive the TCP or URP request without user authentication and attackers can misuse the services without restriction. Figure 1 shows the overview of Memcached DRDoS attack infrastructure based on our observation. We suppose that the infrastructure consists of visible front-end and hidden back-end parts. The front-end is typically a booter Website that interacts with the customers of the DDoS-as-a-Service. The back-end components are scanners that conduct Internet-wide scanning, setters that load caches into the chamber, and launchers that generate amplification DDoS attack traffics. In this work, we seek to understand how attackers conduct the Memcached DRDoS attack by tracing back the anonymous attacks to their origins.

3   Real-World Observations

As a first step to trace back the anonymous attacks to their origins, we monitor attack traffic by setting decoy servers, namely a DRDoS honeypot on the Internet, and investigate how attackers abuse them.

3.1   Observing Memcached DRDoS Attacks

We used a real Memcached service for high-interaction honeypots placed at several ISPs in a country. We limit outgoing packets from the honeypots to

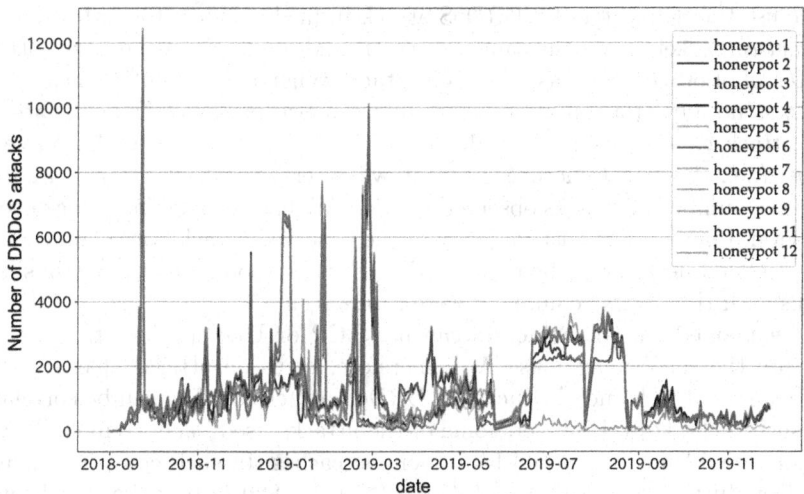

Fig. 2. The number of Observed DRDoS attacks per honeypot (honeypot data).

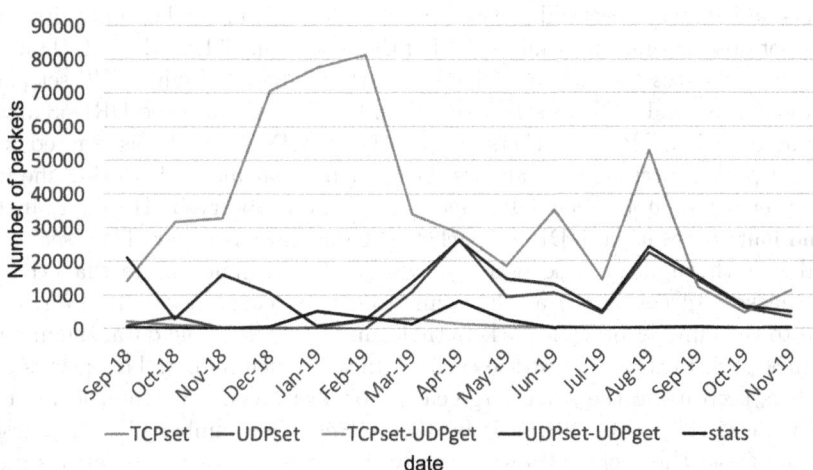

Fig. 3. The number of observed Memcached DRDoS attacks associated with TCP/UDP packets that set cache data into the server's response (honeypot data). (Color figure online)

three packets per hour for each source IP address. Moreover, we deleted cached data once a minute to prevent attackers from misusing the honeypots. We first started our observation with a single Memcached honeypot in June 2018 and expanded it to eleven in August 2018. We used Memcached version 1.4 which was running on Ubuntu Server 16.04. The settings of the Memcached system were by default listening on 11211/TCP and 11211/UDP. For further analysis, we use the data obtained from the eleven honeypots from September 2018 to November 2019.

We use the definition of a DRDoS attack from the paper [18] and count 100 *consecutive* packets from the same source IP address to the same port without an interval of 60 s or more as a DRDoS attack. Whereas consecutive means that there was no gap of a minute or more between two packets. We aggregate the same attack events observed by different honeypots based on their source IP address (i.e., the attack victim). In total, we observed 820,729 attacks. Figure 2 shows the number of attacks observed per day. We can see ongoing attack events with several peaks. The vast majority of the observed attacks were launched by UDP *"get"* requests with their source IP addresses spoofed as the victims' and attacks with the *"stats"* command were rarely seen.

As explained earlier, attackers can use TCP or UDP packets to set cache data into the server's response. We, therefore, focus on attacks that used the *"get"* command to launch Memcached DRDoS attacks as they can be correlated with such cache keys. However, some of the attacks used *"get"* commands with keys that could not be related to any of the caches. In such cases, we exclude them from further analysis. About 45.2% (370,795/820,729) of the attacks were associated with TCP set requests, and about 15.6% (127,771/820,729) of the attacks were associated with UDP set requests. Figure 3 shows the number of set packets and attacks observed per month. At this stage, instead of analyzing each honeypot observation, we combined all of them into one. The red label "TCPset-UDPget" indicates a Memcached DRDoS attack associated with TCP set packets, and the blue label "UDPset-UDPget" indicates a Memcached DRDoS attack associated with UDP set packets. Memcached DRDoS attacks associated with TCP set packets were almost always the most popular method. During the first half observation, not much UDP set packets were observed. However, in the second half observation, UDP set packets became more popular. The *"set"* command sent through TCP sessions (yellow label) was much more than that of UDP packets (green label) as they can store large cache data. However, compared to the number of TCP packets that aim to set the cache data, the number of attack packets that request the cache data was much higher. This means that attackers keep using the same large caches or even borrowing the cache set by someone else instead of setting it by themselves. The number of UDP packets that aim to set the cache data were nearly the same as those of the attack packets. Although we leave the further analysis for future works, we presume that the attackers send UDP set packets just before conducting the attack. We also show the number of attacks with the *"stats"* command in black labels, which were rarely seen.

3.2   Amplification Request and Factor

We now look into the features of the TCP/UDP set packets. In total, we observed TCP set packets from 199 IP addresses of 54 ASes. We used GeoIP2 datadase [22] to identify AS numbers. We then categorize the request into seven patterns by seeing the key strings, value strings, and cache size (i.e., payload length when launching DDoS attacks). Table 1 shows the number of attacks for each pattern. Pattern A always uses a fixed key "Vco0W" with corresponding caches of random

Table 1. Number of attacks per request pattern (honeypot data).

Protocol	Pattern	\<Key\> of set command	\<Value\> of set command	Cache size	# Setter IPs (# setter ASes)	# Attacks associated to set requests
TCP	A	"VcoOW"	Random#1 (Example:lLcs6p0igLrXwYUKt...)	Variety	16(7)	351,608(94.8%)
	B	"aa"	"aaaaaaaaaaaa..."	Fixed (1.04 MB)	5(4)	428(0.1%)
	C	"hh2"	Random#2 (Example:\ x98.:+\ x94\ xd8\ xeb...)	Fixed (1.0 MB)	11(7)	2,487(0.6%)
	D	MD5hash	Random#2 (Example:\ x98.:+\ x94\ xd8 \ xeb...)	Fixed (1.0 MB)	125(46)	12,765(3.4%)
	Others	Variety			21(15)	3,507(0.9%)
UDP	U	"dc"	"Atatata taata taatatata..."	Fixed (1.27 KB)	–	106,846(83.6%)
	Others	Variety			–	20,925(16.4%)

character strings in various sizes. It is the most common pattern observed among 94.8% of the attacks associated with TCP set requests. Pattern B always uses key "aa" with a fixed cache size. Pattern C always uses key "hh2" with a random payload and fixed cache size. Payload D uses an MD5-like key with a random payload and fixed cache size. It was observed from 125 different IP addresses of 46 ASes. These four patterns filled 99% of the attacks associated with TCP set requests. Finally, other payloads did not match any of the four patterns. We labeled them as others, but they were observed rarely, and their amplification rate was low. In the case of UDP packets, there were 730,928 set requests. Pattern U always uses key "dc" with a fixed cache size. For others, we labeled them as others. We note that their payload length was not as high as the previous TCP set requests.

To estimate the impact of the attack, we used the definition of BAF (Bandwidth Amplification Factor) from the paper [10] rather than using AAF(Attack Amplification Factor) from the paper [28] that aims to estimate the amount of bandwidth generated by the intermediary systems. We calculated the amplification factor as below. We note that a single request packet may trigger multiple response packets if the requested payload does not fit in a single packet. In such cases, we sum up all payloads from the response packets triggered by the request.

$$Amplification\ Factor = \frac{\sum_{responses} Payload\ size}{Payload\ size\ of\ request}$$

Figure 4 shows the transition of the amplification factor for each pattern. The x-axis is the observed date, and the y-axis is the amplification factor. Pattern A is depicted with a red plot, and we can see that its amplification factors were scattered in a wide range from 40,000 to 110,000. This may be because multiple attackers sent different payloads of the keys. Pattern B had the highest amplification factor, as high as 140,000. Pattern C also had a high amplification factor close to 130,000. Payload D had amplification factors close to 30,000. Compared to existing attacks, these patterns achieve enormous amplification factors. Finally, the amplification factor of UDP (pattern U) was low compared to those of TCP.

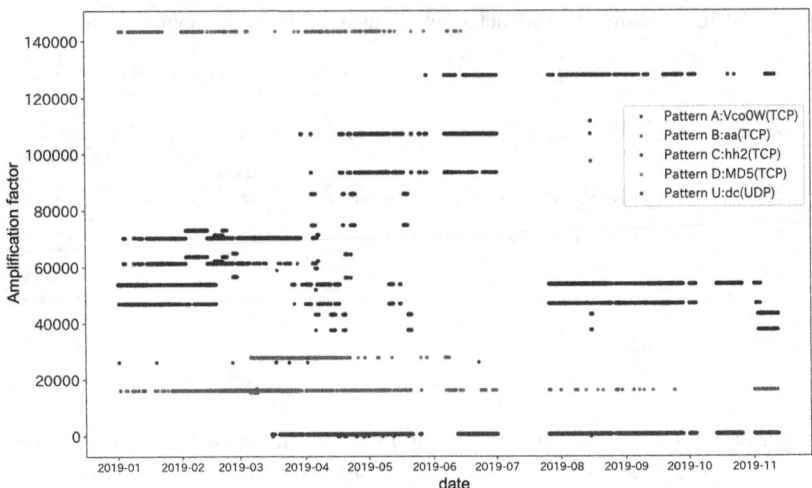

Fig. 4. The transition of the amplification factor per request pattern (honeypot data).

4 Attack Infrastructure Analysis

To further understand how Memcached DRDoS attacks are conducted, we analyze the back-end of the attack infrastructure. We also examine the relationship between the front-end and the back-end. We then investigate hotspots where many setters are concentrated. Finally, we analyze Internet-wide scan results and analyze whether open Memcached services would continue to exist.

4.1 Back-End of Attack Infrastructure

Seeing the previous observation results, the fact that TCP packets were used to set cache data indicates that the source IP addresses of the setters are not spoofed. With this idea, we attribute setters to their sources identifying 199 IP addresses in 54 ASes as setters. Most of these ASes provide web hosting services and cloud services. Furthermore, we used a TTL-based trilateration method [14] to see if actual DRDoS attack packets are likely from one of the setters.

The basic idea of TTL-based trilateration is to verify if packets observed at multiple vantage points (i.e. honeypots) are from the same origin by comparing the TTL differences (i.e. hops) between the origin and the vantage points. In our case, we verify if the TCP setter of a cache key is indeed the origin of the Memcached DRDoS attacks. Therefore, we compare the TTL values of set requests with those of the get requests observed by honeypots. Note that we can compare the TTL values only when both set and get requests with the same cache key are observed by the same honeypot. Moreover, we compare each attack traffic with all TCP set requests observed within the 24-hour-window around the attacks to ensure high relevance between them. In order to derive the threshold

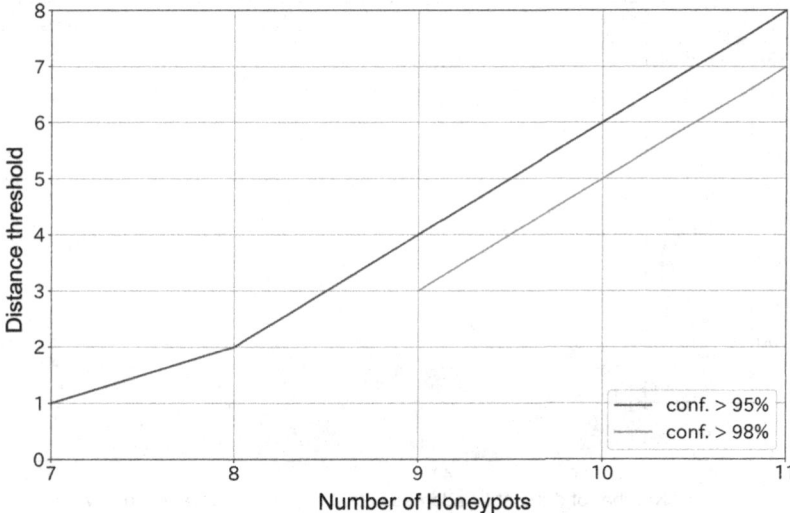

Fig. 5. TTL distance thresholds (y-axis) depend on the receiver set sizes (x-axis).

for deciding if the packets are indeed from the same origin, we conducted several probes using widely distributed sensors of the Atlas project by RIPE [5]. We used the resulting measurement as the ground truth. Figure 5 shows the thresholds obtained from the Atlas probe for each size of available vantage points with a confidence level of 95% and 98%. Due to the biased distribution of the honeypots, more vantage points were required than that of the related paper [14]. The way the threshold for TTL-based trilateration analysis is calculated prevents us from misidentifying the origin of the packets even if honeypot distribution is biased. However, it would increase unidentifiable cases.

Out of the Memcached DRDoS attacks associated with TCP set requests, 141,464 attacks had duplicate keys with set packets sent within 24 h before the attack. Among these attacks, 62.6%(88,590/141,464) were observed by at least six honeypots, which is the minimum number of honeypots we need to conduct TTL-based trilateration analysis. As a result, 8.3%(7,407/88,590) of the attacks were determined to be launched from the setters with 95% confidence. On the other hand, 16.6%(33/199 IP addresses) of the setters were determined to be the origin of DRDoS attacks at least once.

To shed light on the scanning functionalities, we investigated the hosts that scanned ports 11211/TCP and 11211/UDP on our darknet (i.e., unused IPv4 addresses). We analyze the traffic of a /24 * 2 darknet (i.e. 512 unused IP addresses) placed at an academic network from September 2018 to November 2019. Figure 6 shows the distribution of the number of packets sent from each host per day. The y-axis (logarithmic scale) is the number of hosts that sent packets to the darknet, and the x-axis is the number of darknet IP addresses that received a packet in a day. As the figure shows, 97% of visiting hosts do not

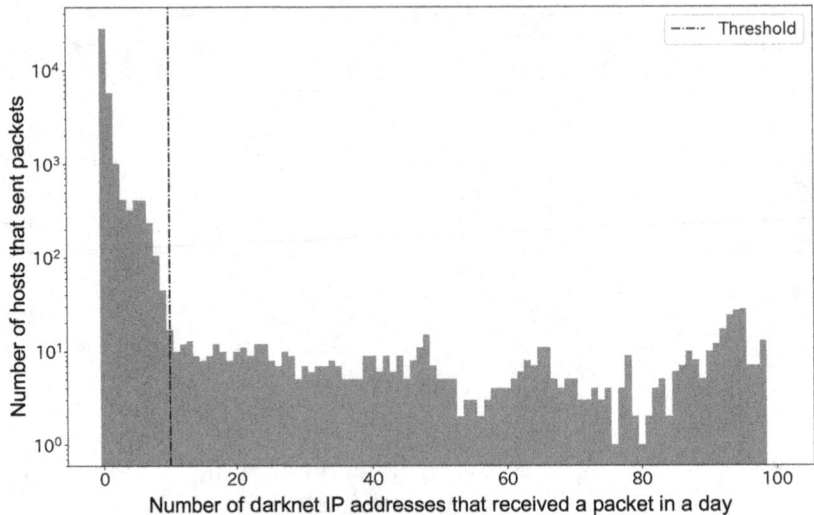

Fig. 6. Distribution of visiting hosts in terms of the scan coverage (darknet data).

cover more than 10% of our darknet per day. Hereafter, we consider a host is a scanner if it covers more than 10% of our darknet in a day. In total, we identified 1,384 IP addresses as scanners. Among the scanners, 18.6%(37/1,384) were also observed as setters. The overlap indicates that attackers utilize the same host as a setter and a scanner.

4.2   Front-End of Attack Infrastructure

In order to examine the relationship between the front-end booter services and the attack infrastructures, we investigate what kind of domains were associated with them. We used DNSDB [29], the passive DNS database, to obtain the domains associated with the IP addresses. We consider a domain is associated with an IP address when the following inequality holds: where *"Time-first-resolved"* and *"Time-last-resolved"* means the first and last time when the domain was resolved to the IP address. Also, *"Time-first-set"* is the first time the IP address was used to set a cache to one of our honeypots.

```
Time-first-resolved <= Time-first-set
<= Time-last-resolved
```

Among the 199 setter IP addresses, 32 IP addresses were associated with 141 domains. Likewise, among the 1,384 scanner IP addresses, 510 IP addresses were associated with 1,175 domains. We first checked if these domains contain strings like *"booter"*, *"stresser"*, or *"ddos"*. As a result, we found three domains "ddos[dot]5z4[dot]cn[dot]", "17ddos[dot]com[dot]", and "100gddos[dot]com[dot]" Among them, we found only one domain "ddos[dot]5z4[dot]cn[dot]" that had been resolved 1,503 times during the observation period, implying the host had provided the DDoS service to a certain degree. However, the other two were resolved only around 100 times.

We then checked if domains from the known booter website list [15] were resolved to any of the IP addresses of the attack infrastructures. The list contains 713 domains of the known booters, and 498 of them were still active, and frequently resolved during the honeypot observation. The 498 domains were not resolved to any setter or scanner IP addresses, indicating the low relevance between booter websites and the back-end infrastructure. However, we used only a small portion of known booters, and we leave this analysis for future works.

Table 2. Number of the observed attacks per hotspots (honeypot data).

AS	# Setter IPs	# Set requests	# Attacks linked to setter by cache keys
208217	30	5,258	148,607
12876	22	1,591	3,349
9009	8	627	587
46573	8	185	65,934
21409	6	956	184
45102	6	519	82,172
134520	1	54	60,837

4.3 Infrastructure Hotspots

Among the setters, only a few of them were continuously used. For further analysis, we will call an AS a "hotspot" if it satisfies at least one of the three conditions: 1) the number of setters' IP addresses is five or more 2) the number of set events is 500 or more 3) the number of DRDoS attacks associated with the set activities is 50,000 or more. Table 2 lists up all seven hotspots where setters are concentrated. In total, 81 IP addresses are included.

We then investigated if setters in hotspots are also conducting Memcached DRDoS attacks (launchers) and even work as scanners. Figure 7 shows the activity of all 81 setters in 7 hotspots observed from January 2019 to November 2019. We use different plot colours depending on activity type, namely "scan (blue)", "set (orange)", "attacks (red)" and "attack origin (black)", where attack indicates an attack event whose cache is set by the setter, and attack origin suggests that the setter is also the origin that launched the DRDoS attack determined by the TTL-based trilateration analysis. We also use different shapes for set and attack depending on the payload patterns defined in Sect. 3. The y-axis represents the setter sorted by their AS number, and the x-axis is the observed date. We separate each ASes with horizontal lines.

Seeing the result, each hotspot had multiple functionalities such as scanning, setting, and launching attacks. The set events and the attack event almost

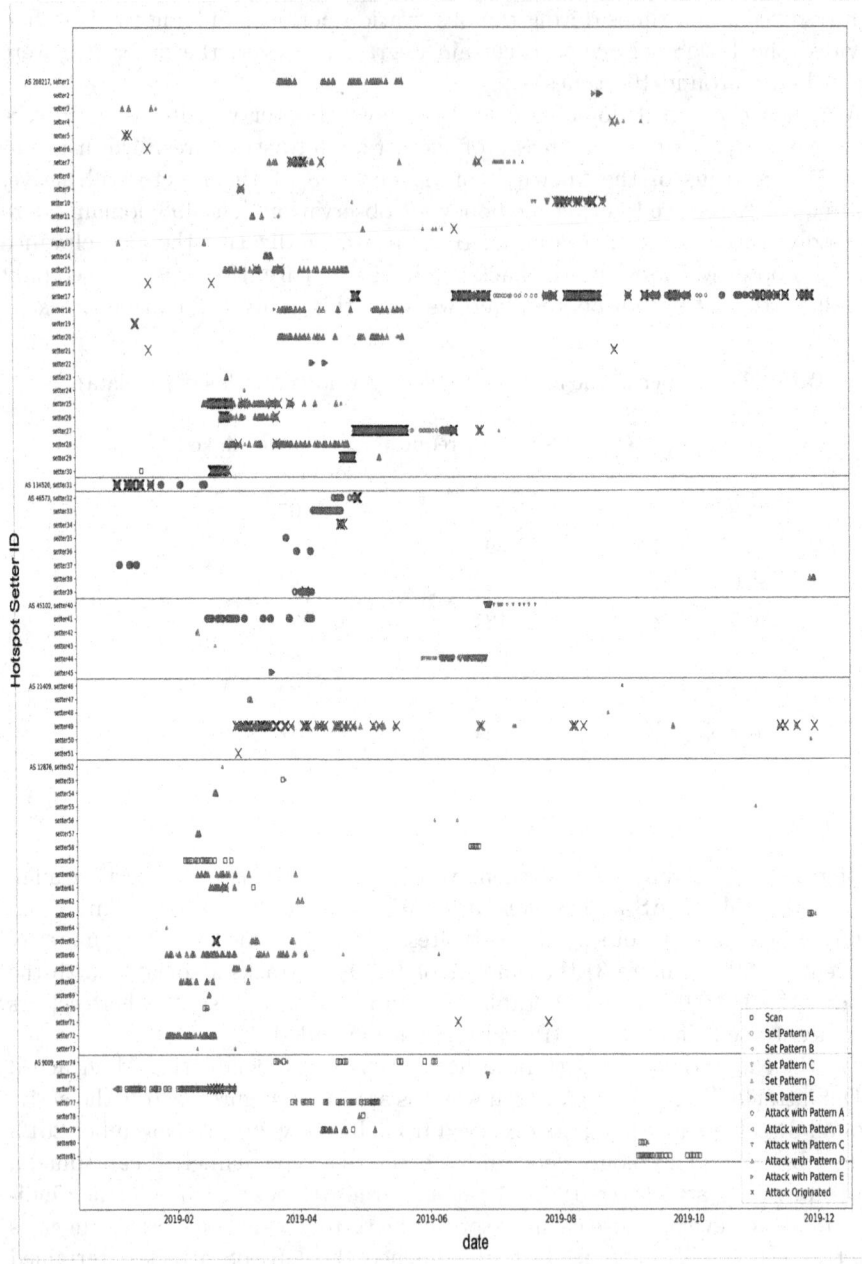

Fig. 7. Mapping scanners, setters, and launchers in hotspots. The blue plot indicates scan events, the orange plot indicates set events, and the red or black plot indicates attack events. The square shapes indicate scan events, the circle or triangle shapes indicate set events with different patterns, the circle or triangle shapes indicate attack events with different patterns, and the cross shape indicates originated attacks. (Color figure online)

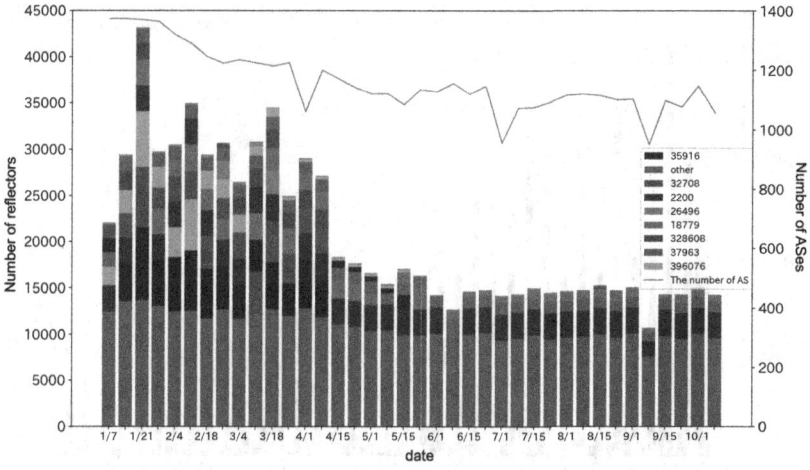

Fig. 8. Number of Memcached servers and their ASes (Internet-wide scan data)

always appeared together, indicating that the caches were abused for attacks immediately after being set. Moreover, many attacks were launched from the same setter and six out of the seven hotspots had setters that also launched the DRDoS attack. In the case of scans, only a few setters were used as scanners, and the scan activities were seen for a brief period. As for individual hotspots, AS 208217 was the most active as it conducted many set activities and launched attacks during the entire observation period. Not all but almost all IP addresses of the setters had the same first to third octet that, we suppose that they were controlled by the same attacker. We can also see that other hotspots became less active in the second half observation period. On the other hand, setters in AS 208217 seldom scan for amplifiers, while others in AS 12876 and 9009 frequently scan to update the amplifier list. As for AS 9009, many scans were seen just before set or attack started. Therefore, it seems that some hotspots have all-in-one attack infrastructure that conduct scan, set, and launch attacks.

4.4 Memcached Servers in the Wild

As we have shown important pieces of information about the attack infrastructure, we further focus on dissecting the surface of amplifiers. We investigate the number of servers in the wild and then dig into their lifespan. We analyzed 10-month historical data (January 2020 to October 2020) of Censys data [2], which logs the results of ongoing ZMap scans. Figure 8 shows the number of Memcached servers and ASes in the wild. We note that we only count hosts running services on both 11211/TCP and 11211/UDP. In the figure, ASes that contained 1,000 or more servers are color-coded. After April 15, 2020, the number of servers in several ASes drastically decreased. We suppose that some coordinated actions were taken in these hosting and cloud services. On the other hand, after April 2020, the number of servers became stable at around 15,000. The figure also shows the number of ASes in the line graph. Similar to Memcached servers, the number

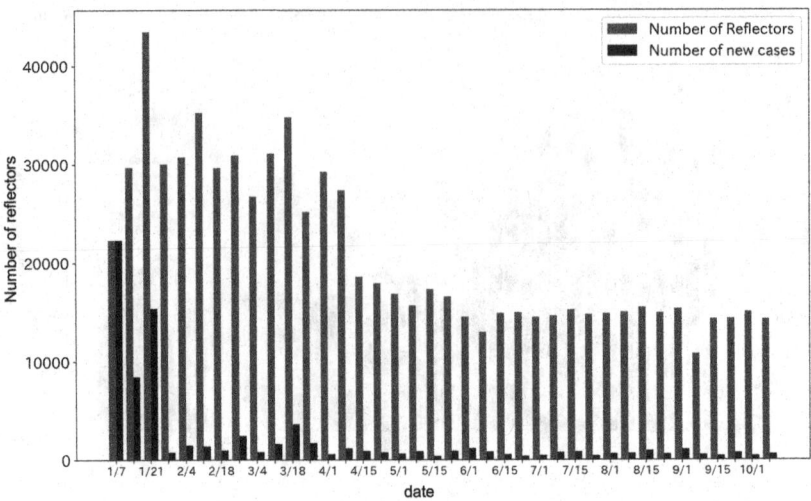

Fig. 9. Number of Memcached servers vs newly found servers (Internet-wide scan data)

decreased initially but became stable above 1,000. As the remaining servers are scattered over different ASes, more significant efforts or practical actions would be required to eliminate them.

To understand the lifespan of the servers we calculated the unique number of IP addresses of these servers. Figure 9 shows the number of newly found IP addresses. The figure shows that the number of new IP addresses becomes low after a few Censys scans, which implies that the IP addresses of these servers are mostly static. This suggests that Internet-wide scans can provide meaningful information to take effective actions such as takedowns.

5   Discussion

5.1   Ethical Consideration

With the honeypot observation, we provide valuable insights into Memcached DRDoS attacks that otherwise could not be observed on such a large scale. Unfortunately, we face a dilemma, as these insights can only be revealed if our honeypot participates in the attacks to some extent. Kramer *et al.* chose to use a rate-limiting mechanism to mitigate the risk [18]. We follow this idea and apply a more strict limitation to the outgoing packets and delete cached data once a minute to prevent attackers from misusing the honeypots.

5.2   Limitations

Although we have included a rate-limiting mechanism to our honeypots still, this leaves a small number of attack packets, and this would enable attackers to trivially detect the amplifier as a monitoring system. Furthermore, protocols that have comparatively chatty responses, such as the *monlist* reply in the NTP protocol implementation, which consists of dozens of response packets will also fail. An alternative might be to include dynamic thresholds for rate-limiting, which vary depending on the response size and aggressiveness of the requests. Still there are some limitations, we observed an enormous amount of incoming traffic and gained insights into the attacks. As we have shown, some of the attackers exploit caches set by someone else. In this case, it would be difficult to reveal the attack infrastructure. Similarly, attackers who use the *stats* command and other commands are also difficult to trace back. The IP addresses of setters maybe those of compromised hosts, VPN exit nodes, Tor exit nodes, proxies, and others. We leave this analysis for future work.

5.3 Dataset

Our main goal is to analyze the attack infrastructures and gain insights into the attacks. We consider that it is important to make the dataset available to the research community hoping to provide helpful information to take practical actions such as takedowns. For this reason, the honeypot dataset will be available and can be requested via our website [1] by any interested researchers. Moreover, we have provided the analysis results on the attack infrastructures to our national CERT and asked for further coordination.

6 Related Work

It is known that botnets are one of the main generators of DDoS attacks. Therefore, a lot of research has been done to shed light on DDoS botnets. Welzel *et al.* tracked commands of two DDoS botnet families and monitored whether victims of DDoS botnets were affected by the attacks [7]. Similarly, Büscher and Holz monitored the C&C servers of DDoS botnets to analyze the attacks and their targets and documented TCP and HTTP-based attacks [8].

Research that focuses on analyzing DRDoS attacks has long been done. Paxon pointed out the concept of using reflectors for DDoS attacks [31]. They show that three types of reflectors pose particularly significant threats. Although, in the early stage of DDoS attacks, the idea of reflection attacks that use the spoofed address of the victim machine with multiple replies sent back to the victim had been discussed [12,13]. After more than ten years, Rossow revealed popular UDP-based protocols of network services, online games, P2P filesharing networks, and P2P botnets to assess their security against DRDoS abuse [10]. As a follow-up, Kührer *et al.* have shed light on the amplifiers' landscape, revealing their fingerprints and observing their lifetime [20]. Mishra *et al.* pointed out that some new attack vectors, such as Apple remote management services, Ubiquiti discovery protocol, Constrained Application Protocol, Web Services Dynamic Discovery, HTML5 hyperlink-auditing ping redirection, and Memcached are already used for DRDoS attacks [26]. Kopp *et al.* found new protocols that have received little to no attention in the literature so far to be observed in

Internet traffic including Ubiquiti Device Discovery, WS- Discovery, ARMS, and OpenVPN [11]. These works inspect concrete amplification vulnerabilities in protocols and propose defense mechanisms and survey amplifiers. Furthermore, techniques to mitigate DRDoS attacks have been proposed. Jonker *et al.* presented a longitudinal overview of operational deployment of blackholing during DoS attacks [21]. Giotsas *et al.* developed a methodology to automatically detect BGP (Border Gateway Protocol) blackholing activity in the wild [30].

While these works show various findings, only a few studies have particularly dissected Memcached DRDoS attacks. Kai described the principle of Memcache DRDoD attack and along with a solution such attackss [17]. Kulvinder *et al.* proposed prevention and practices to mitigate Memcached DDoS attacks [19]. Starting from updating and monitoring the server (firewalling or disabling the UDP port), deleting all cached data, not allowing execution of commands, patching vulnerabilities, checking the response size, and preventing IP spoofing. These works provide fascinating glimpses of misused Memcached servers but still lack the picture of the whole attack infrastructure. Kramer *et al.* implemented AmpPot, a characteristic monitoring system to trace amplification attacks [18]. Durumeric *et al.* have analyzed the darknet data to explore scanning behaviors [32]. Johannes *et al.* proposed a TTL-based trilateration method and investigated the attack infrastructure behind the DRDoS attack [14]. We were inspired by these works and revealed how Memcached DRDoS attacks are organized by combining honeypots and darknet data.

Besides these works, studies based on analyzing booters have also been done. Karami and McCoy were the first to monitor such booter services and observed booters that launch amplification attacks by studying the adversarial DDoS-As-a-Service [23]. Similarly, Santanna *et al.* analyzed the databases and payment of 15 booters [16]. On the other hand, countermeasures have been studied. Santanna *et al.* presented a rigorous methodology to identify a comprehensive set of existing booters and generate a blocklist by crawling suspect URLs [15]. Colleier *et al.* have measured the impact of police interventions against booter services and show that including arrests and website takedown have had a statistically significant impact on the number of attacks [9]. Kopp *et al.* investigated booter-based DDoS attacks in the wild and the impact of an FBI takedown targeting 15 booters from the perspective of a major IXP and two ISPs.

7   Conclusion

We utilized a high interaction honeypot for monitoring Memcached DRDoS attacks. Over the course of 15 months, we observed 820,729 attacks. We then analyzed the payloads of these attacks and found that 370,795 attacks were associated with TCP set requests, and 127,771 attacks with UDP set requests. We then focused on the fact that setting a large cache has to be done using TCP, and therefore, the IP addresses of attackers are not spoofed. As a result, we found that 199 IP addresses were responsible setters. In addition, we discovered that seven hotspots were responsible for most of the set and attack activities.

The TTL-based trilateration analysis revealed that the attack infrastructure in such hotspots could generate actual amplification DDoS attacks and scan for new amplifiers. In contrast, we see low relevance between front-end booter websites to the back-end infrastructure based on the analysis of related domains. Although the number of amplifiers has decreased, still 15,000 amplifiers are scattering over 1,000 ASes. As the setters are involved in many attacks, we not only reveal our dataset to researchers but have already provided the information on the attack infrastructures to our national CERT. We wish our results can be utilized for further actions such as takedowns of attack infrastructures.

Acknowledgements. A part of this research was conducted in "WarpDrive: Web-based Attack Response with Practical and Deployable Research Initiative" project, supported by the National Institute of Information and Communications Technology, Japan. A part of this research was conducted in "MITIGATE" project among "Research and Development for Expansion of Radio Wave Resources (JPJ000254)", supported by the Ministry of Internal Affairs and Communications, Japan. A part of this research was supported by JSPS KAKENHI Grant Numbers 21H03444.

References

1. Amppot: Honeypot for monitoring amplification ddos attacks — datasets. https://sec.ynu.codes/dos/datasets
2. Censys. https://censys.io/
3. Cve-2018-1000115 detail. https://nvd.nist.gov/vuln/detail/cve-2018-1000115
4. Memcached–a distributed memory object caching system. https://memcached.org/
5. Ripe atlas. https://atlas.ripe.net
6. Akamai SIRT Alerts. Memcached-fueled 1.3 tbps attacks. https://securityboulevard.com/2018/03/memcached-fueled-1-3-tbps-attacks/
7. Büscher, A., Holz, T.: Tracking DDoS attacks: insights into the business of disrupting the web. In: Proceedings of the 5th USENIX LEET, LEET 2012 (2012)
8. Welzel, A., Rossow, C., Bos, H.: On measuring the impact of DDoS botnets. In: Proceedings of the 7th European Workshop on Systems Security, EuroSec 2014 (2014)
9. Collier, B., Thomas, D.R., Clayton, R., Hutchings, A.: Booting the booters: evaluating the effects of police interventions in the market for denial-of-service attacks. In: Proceedings of the 2019 Internet Measurement Conference, IMC 2019 (2019)
10. Rossow, C.: Amplification hell: revisiting network protocols for DDoS abuse. In: Proceedings of the 2014 Network and Distributed System Security Symposium, NDSS 2014 (2014)
11. Kopp, D., Dietzel, C., Hohlfeld, O.: DDoS never dies? An IXP perspective on DDoS amplification attacks. In: Hohlfeld, O., Lutu, A., Levin, D. (eds.) PAM 2021. LNCS, vol. 12671, pp. 284–301. Springer, Cham (2021). https://doi.org/10.1007/978-3-030-72582-2_17
12. Mirkovic, J., Reiher, P.: A taxonomy of DDoS attack and DDoS defense mechanisms. ACM SIGCOMM Comput. Commun. **34**(2), 39–53 (2004)
13. Mirkovic, J., Dietrich, S., Dittrich, D., Reiher, P.: Internet denial of service: attack and defense mechanisms. In: Perlman, R. (ed.) Computer Networking and Security Book Series (2004)

14. Krupp, J., Backes, M., Rossow, C.: Identifying the scanners and attack infrastructure behind amplification DDoS attacks. In: Proceedings of the 23rd ACM Conference on Computer and Communications Security, CCS 2016 (2016)
15. Santanna, J.J., De Schmidt, R.O., Tuncer, D., De Vries, J., Granville, L.Z., Pras, A.: Booter blacklist: unveiling DDoS-for-hire websites. In: Proceedings of the 2016 12th International Conference on Network and Service Management, CNSM 2016 (2016)
16. Santanna, J.J., Durban, R., Sperotto, A., Pras, A.: Inside booters: an analysis on operational database. In: Proceedings of the IFIP/IEEE International Symposium on Integrated Network Management, IM 2015 (2015)
17. Bai, K.: Analysis and prevention of Memcache UDP reflection amplification attack. Int. J. Sci. 5(3), 297–302 (2018)
18. Kramer, L., et al.: Amppot: honeypot for monitoring amplification DDoS attack. In: Proceedings of the 18th International Symposium on Research in Attacks, Intrusions and Defenses, RAID 2015 (2015)
19. Singh, K., Singh, A.: Memcached DDoS exploits: operations, vulnerabilities, preventions and mitigations. In: Proceedings of the 2018 IEEE 3rd International Conference on Computing, Communication and Security, ICCCS 2018 (2018)
20. Kührer, M., Hupperich, T., Rossow, C., Holz, T.: Exit from hell? Reducing the impact of amplification DDoS attack. In: Proceedings of the 23rd USENIX Security Symposium, USENIX 2014 (2014)
21. Jonker, M., Pras, A., Dainotti, A., Sperotto, A.: A first joint look at DoS attacks and BGP blackholing in the wild. In: Proceedings of the 2018 Internet Measurement Conference, IMC 2018 (2018)
22. MaxMind: GeoIP2 database. https://www.maxmind.com/
23. Karami, M., McCoy, D.: Understanding the emerging threat of DDoS-as-a-service. In: Presented as part of the 6th USENIX Work- shop on Large-Scale Exploits and Emergent Threats (2013)
24. Morales, C.: 1 Terabit DDoS attacks become a reality; reflecting on five years of reflections. https://www.netscout.com/blog/asert/1-terabit-ddos-attacks-become-reality-reflecting-five-years
25. Morales, C.: Netscout arbor confirms 1.7 Tbps DDoS attack; the terabit attack era is upon us. https://www.netscout.com/blog/asert/netscout-arbor-confirms-17-tbps-ddos-attack-terabit-attack-era
26. Nivedita, M., et al.: Memcached: an experimental study of DDoS attacks for the wellbeing of IoT applications. Sensors (Basel) 21(23), 8071 (2021)
27. Nishtala, R., et al.: Scaling Memcache at Facebook. In: Proceedings of the 10th USENIX Symposium on Networked Systems Design and Implementation, NSDI 2013 (2013)
28. Kumar, S.: Smurf-based distributed denial of service (DDoS) attack amplification. In: Proceedings of the of the Second International Conference on Internet Monitoring and Protection (ICIMP 2007) (2007)
29. Farsight Security: Dnsdb. https://www.dnsdb.info/
30. Giotsas, V., Smaragdakis, G., Dietzel, C., Richter, P., Feldmann, A., Berger, A.: Inferring BGP blackholing activity in the internet. In: Proceedings of the 2017 Internet Measurement Conference, IMC 2017 (2017)
31. Paxson, V.: An analysis of using reflectors for distributed denial-of-service attacks. ACM SIGCOMM Comput. Commun. 31(3), 38–47 (2001)
32. Durumeric, Z., Bailey, M., Halderman, J.A.: An internet-wide view of internet-wide scanning. In: Proceedings of the of the 23rd USENIX Security Symposium, USENIX 2014 (2014)

Consistency is All I Ask: Attacks and Countermeasures on the Network Context of Distributed Honeypots

Songsong Liu[1]([✉]), Pengbin Feng[1], Jiahao Cao[2], Xu He[1], Tommy Chin[1], Kun Sun[1], and Qi Li[2]

[1] George Mason University, Fairfax, VA, USA
{sliu23,pfeng4,xhe6,tchin2,ksun3}@gmu.edu
[2] Tsinghua University, Beijing, China
qli01@tsinghua.edu.cn

Abstract. The honeypot technique has proved its value in system protection and attack analysis over the past 20 years. Distributed honeypot solutions emerge to solve the high cost and risk of maintaining a functional honeypot system. In this paper, we uncover that all existing distributed honeypot systems suffer from one type of anti-honeypot technique called network context cross-checking (NC3) which enables attackers to detect network context inconsistencies before and after breaking into a targeted system. We perform a systematic study of NC3 and identify nine types of network context artifacts that may be leveraged by attackers to identify distributed honeypot systems. As a countermeasure, we propose HoneyPortal, a stealthy traffic redirection framework to defend against the NC3 attack. The basic idea is to project a remote honeypot into the protected local network as a believable host machine. We conduct experiments in a real testbed, and the experimental results show that HoneyPortal can effectively defeat NC3 attacks with a low performance overhead.

Keywords: Distributed honeypot system · Anti-honeypot technique · Network context inconsistency · eXpress Data Path (XDP)

1 Introduction

Over the past 20 years, the honeypot technique has demonstrated its unique value in identifying unauthorized or illicit use of computer resources [26]. By monitoring and analyzing suspicious activities in honeypot systems, administrators have a better chance to detect and constrain attacks. To confront massive sophisticated attackers (e.g., APT attackers [5]), today's honeypot solutions pursue the scalability in the deployment and the capability to provide a detailed understanding of the attack. The local honeypot implementations are limited by their architecture and could achieve only one of the two.

© The Author(s), under exclusive license to Springer Nature Switzerland AG 2022
L. Cavallaro et al. (Eds.): DIMVA 2022, LNCS 13358, pp. 197–217, 2022.
https://doi.org/10.1007/978-3-031-09484-2_11

The typical goal of honeypot operators target detecting early reconnaissance and reducing the attacker's dwell time. The detection is necessary while reducing the attackers dwell time could cause the honeypot operators cannot identify all the tactics, techniques, and procedures (TTP) used in the sophisticated attack. It is not sufficient to simply eliminate APT threats. Therefore, in some cases, the honeypot operators need to increase the attackers dwell time in order to feed fake information to APT attackers and observe the complete sophisticated attack. The key point of increasing the attackers dwell time is to prevent the attacker from being aware of the honeypot environment.

Based on the distinct characteristics of each standalone honeypot, the attacker can leverage fingerprinting-based detection techniques [20,29] to identify the honeypots and avoid them. Besides, although the distributed honeypot systems can provide more flexible deployment and centralized management, they also introduce extra network context inconsistency between the front ends and the back ends, which could be exploited by attackers to identify the distributed architecture of the deployed honeypot system. For instance, the back-end network may have different network configurations (e.g., host number, IP address, services) and network traffic than the front-end network. Moreover, most distributed honeypot systems [1,4,14,24,28,30] allow the front end to reply to initial simple requests (e.g., ICMP) of the attacker and forward more sophisticated requests to the back-end honeypot; however, this division in the function may be exploited by an attacker, since those requests replied in the front end will not be logged in the access history of the back-end honeypot.

Since the fingerprinting of the standalone honeypot has been well studied in previous work [20,29], we focus on the inconsistent network context caused by the architecture of the distributed honeypot systems in this paper. We perform a systematic study on existing typical distributed honeypot systems to check if they are robust under a new anti-honeypot technique called *network consistency cross-checking attack* (NC3).

This attack consists of two stages, namely, *pre-exploitation reconnaissance* and *post-exploitation reconnaissance*. Before initiating an attack on a target machine, the attacker collects information (artifacts) related to the target machine during the pre-exploitation reconnaissance stage. The attacker may transition to the post-exploitation reconnaissance stage to retrieve a more comprehensive collection of artifacts on the target machine after successful exploitation efforts. We summarize nine types of network context artifacts that may be collected in the two aforementioned stages that attackers may leverage to identify distributed honeypot systems by means of inconsistencies in the data set. We study two types of attackers based on their locations, including an *insider* who resides in the same local subnetwork as the front end, and a *semi-insider* who is in the same local network but in a different subnetwork as the front end. Our theoretical analysis and experimental results show that they can utilize NC3 attacks to successfully identify all popular distributed honeypot systems.

To protect those distributed honeypots, whose goal is to increase the attackers dwell time, from the NC3 attack, we develop a countermeasure called Honey-

Portal to remove the network context inconsistency between the pre-exploitation and post-exploitation stages. Precisely, the overall approach projects the remote back-end honeypot into the front-end network using a transparent traffic redirection strategy, where the front end redirects all incoming traffic (i.e., layer 2 and above) to the back end and vice versa. A back-end controller is responsible for forwarding the packets between the front end and the back end by using the redirection channel. For instance, when attackers break into the back-end honeypot and generate network traffic (flows) between the attacker's host machine and the back-end honeypot, HoneyPortal redirects all the outbound traffic of the back-end honeypot back to the front end. The front end then forwards the traffic to the attacker's host machine and forwards the attacker's response traffic to the back-end honeypot. By integrating the front end and the back end as one logic honeypot, we can eliminate the network context inconsistency introduced by the distributed honeypot systems.

Since the attacker may compromise the back-end honeypot with the root privilege, it is critical to ensure that our countermeasure, particularly, the back-end controller, cannot be detected by the attacker. We propose to use XDP (eXpress Data Path) [11] to isolate the back-end controller from back-end honeypots as XDP can transparently intercept and redirect the traffic flow of honeypots without interference. When we implement the back-end honeypot using a virtual machine, the XDP program runs in its corresponding virtual NIC in the back-end controller. When we implement the back-end honeypot using a physical machine, the XDP program runs on its corresponding NIC in the back-end controller.

We implement a prototype of HoneyPortal that supports the running of the front end on a physical machine and the deployment of the back-end honeypot on the virtual machine. We build a testbed for evaluating the effectiveness and performance of our HoneyPortal system. The experimental results show that HoneyPortal can successfully defeat NC3 attacks with low overhead. When packet sending rates reach 700 kpps, the front end only costs less than 1% CPU utilization in our testbed. Our back-end controller costs about 8% CPU utilization.

In summary, we make the following contributions:

- We perform a systematic study on one anti-honeypot technique called the network context cross-checking (NC3) attack that exploits various network context information to detect distributed honeypots. We summarize nine types of artifacts that attackers could exploit to defeat all existing distributed honeypot systems.
- We propose a countermeasure to defeat NC3 attacks against the distributed honeypots. By projecting the remote back-end honeypot into the local network as a host machine, our defense can successfully remove the network context inconsistency introduced by the distributed honeypot systems.
- We implement a prototype of HoneyPortal. The experimental results in our testbed show that HoneyPortal can effectively defeat NC3 attack with low overhead.

2   Related Work

Distributed Honeypot. A distributed honeypot [3,7] typically consists of three parts, i.e., a front end, a back end, and a redirection channel. Its design aims to (1) combine the benefits of the lightweight low-interaction honeypots and the highly believable high-interaction honeypots and (2) achieve centralized management and control of the high-interaction honeypots. The front end is deployed in the protected network and may simulate several services and applications to directly respond to simple network reconnaissance requests. Meanwhile, more complex and suspicious network requests are redirected to a remote back-end network via the redirection channel. A back-end controller controls and logs network traffic between the front-end honeypot and the back-end honeypot. The back end is capable of generating more believable responses by running application services on a full-fledged operating system.

Bailey et al. [3] propose a globally distributed architecture, which deploys the low-interaction honeypot as the front end to redirect interesting attack traffic to the high-interaction honeypot for detailed attack information investigation. This architecture provides distributed deployment and centralized management. Jiang et al. [14] propose Collapsar, a distributed architecture to improve the coverage of the high-interaction honeypot using a number of redirectors in different production networks to tunnel attack traffic to the remote high-interaction honeypots. Potemkin [30] follows a similar architecture, exploiting late binding and aggressive memory sharing to accommodate more VM-based honeypots. Hyhoneydv6 [24] provides a distributed architecture in the IPv6 address space.

Emerging techniques such as software-defined networking (SDN) and moving target defense (MTD) have been integrated to extend the capability of hybrid honeypots. Fan et al. [9] propose an SDN-based distributed honeypot to support a transparent TCP connection hand-off mechanism. Honeyprox [15] enhances the current honeynet design via SDN to defer the internal propagation of attackers within the honeynet. HoneyDOC [8] leverages SDN to support all-around honeypot, which provides transparent traffic redirection and high-quality attack capture. Artail et al. [1] introduce an adaptable distributed honeypot dynamically changing with the organizational network. Sun et al. [28] propose a distributed decoy architecture that may dynamically shift the network attack surface. Chovancova et al. [4] propose an autonomous distributed honeypot that is capable of adapting to environmental changes in real-time.

Anti-honeypot Mechanism. As the weapon for attackers to identify honeypots, anti-honeypot mechanisms can be divided into three categories: *network-level fingerprinting, system-level fingerprinting*, and *operation-level fingerprinting* [20,29].

Network-level honeypot fingerprinting focuses on detecting the discrepancy in network activities and network latency. Since honeypot systems may provide only a limited number of services and/or have constrained interactions with other real hosts and the Internet, attackers may observe fewer network activities of honeypots compared to those of legitimate hosts [19,22]. When the honeypot system is deployed in a separate network, it may introduce higher network latency than other hosts in the protected local network, and attackers can compare the latency differences to detect honeypots [10,21]. System-level honeypot fingerprinting is based on the information collected from operating systems and applications. A honeypot and a real host may have different system artifacts [6,12,21], such as operating system flags, running processes, volatile user information, files, and installed programs. By analyzing this information, attackers can infer if a host is in a honeypot. Operation-level honeypot fingerprinting is to measure if attackers can use the victim host to communicate with other hosts [35]. Since most honeypot systems are located in a constrained environment to prevent compromised honeypots from attacking other real hosts, these operation limitations may be notable honeypot indicators.

3   Threat Model

In this paper, we assume that the attacker intends to compromise the legitimate hosts inside the intranet and maintains long-term access, while the honeypot operator intends to increase the attacker's dwell time as long as possible to observe all the TTP used in the attack. The attacker is able to conduct network reconnaissance to collect network and system artifacts after fully controlling a computer. Based on the location of the attacker, we classify them into three types, namely, *insider*, *semi-insider*, and *external attacker*.

The first type of attackers is the insiders located in the front-end network, the same subnetwork as the front-end honeypot. If there is an internal firewall in the subnetwork, we assume that the insider and the target host are in the same network segmentation. They are capable of scanning the hosts in this subnetwork or network segmentation. If the subnetwork is constructed with a hub, an insider can monitor all the network flows by setting the NIC into promiscuous mode. In practice, more and more networks are constructed with switches directly. In this case, the insider needs to conduct an ARP spoofing attack to redirect all the traffic to its own machine to monitor all the network flows. With the deployment of static ARP and PC firewall, the insiders may not always conduct the ARP spoofing attack successfully. Therefore, we assume the insider can only observe the network flows between itself and the target host.

The second type is the semi-insiders, who are located in the intranet but with different subnetworks or network segmentations as the front-end honeypot. Due to the security policies of the internal firewall, the semi-insiders may only scan partial hosts in the front-end network. Both insiders and semi-insiders could be disgruntled employees or attackers who have successfully broken into the intranet via social engineering or unfixed security vulnerabilities.

The third type is the external attackers who are located outside the intranet. Due to the strict firewall policy or DMZ configuration, the external attackers can only interact with the hosts open to the public and usually have quite limited knowledge about the intranet. They cannot conduct the network context cross-checking, thus we don't discuss the external attacker in this paper. However, in

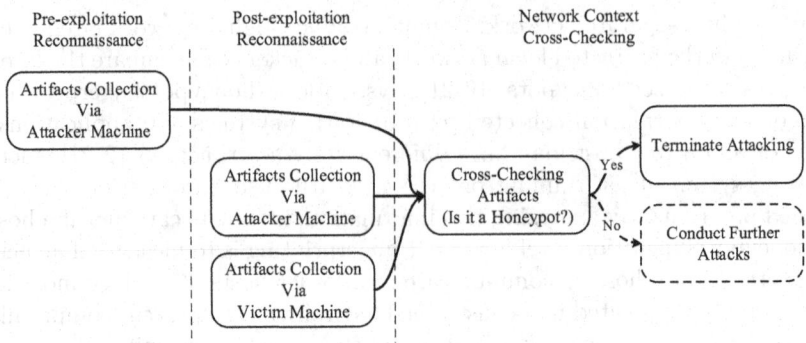

Fig. 1. The attack procedure of NC3

some specific cases [23], external attackers may collect partial information about the intranet across the gateway. In this paper, we treat this kind of external attacker as semi-insiders.

After breaking into the back-end honeypot, we assume that attackers may gain the root privilege. They can access the logs of network services, monitor the network flow in the honeypot, and conduct one more round of reconnaissance from the back-end honeypot. Then they perform a cross-checking with the scanning results before attacking the honeypot.

4   Network Context Cross-Checking Attacks

Figure 1 shows the entire attack procedure of NC3, which consists of three steps, namely, *pre-exploitation reconnaissance*, *post-exploitation reconnaissance*, and *network context cross-checking*. Before attacking the target machine (i.e., the front-end honeypot), the attacker may collect the artifacts related to the target machine via traditional network reconnaissance [25]. We call this stage of attack as *Pre-exploitation Reconnaissance*. After breaking into the target machine (or the honeypot), the attacker can reissue network reconnaissance from the compromised target machine to collect network and system artifacts. We call this stage of attack as *Post-exploitation Reconnaissance*. Meanwhile, the attacker can reissue the network reconnaissance from their host machine once more. Finally, the attacker will compare the three sets of artifacts collected in two stages and detect potential inconsistency to check if the target machine is a honeypot.

4.1   Pre-exploitation Reconnaissance

Suppose the attacker resides on a host machine and is interested in attacking the victim machine. By running network scanning tools (e.g., Nmap[1], Nessus[2]),

---

[1] https://nmap.org/.

[2] https://www.tenable.com/products/nessus.

the insider may first inquire about the total number of live hosts in the local network. The insider can collect the victim machine's network address (IP and MAC addresses), OS information (i.e., OS type and version), open network ports (i.e., TCP or UDP ports), and service information (i.e., application types and versions). Similarly, the insider may collect the artifacts of another legitimate machine in the same subnetwork. The insider can also use network diagnostic tools (e.g., Traceroute) to collect the routing information (i.e., the outermost router in the path) from its host to an external machine on the Internet. All the interactions between the insider and the victim machine are recorded as the access history (e.g., SSH, HTTP, FTP, etc.). The insider can obtain the access history manually by using the packet introspect tools (e.g., Wireshark[3], Tcpdump[4]) to record the timestamp and metadata of each packet. Also, the insider can measure the link latency between the host and the victim machine using the *ping* command.

Due to the security policies on the internal firewall, the semi-insider may only scan a small portion of hosts in the target subnetwork thereby retrieving fewer artifacts than an insider. Also, since the semi-insider locates in a different subnetwork, the routing information is unable considered as a criterion to perform the cross checking.

4.2   Post-exploitation Reconnaissance

In this stage, the attacker may collect artifacts from both the victim machine and the attacker's host machine respectively. From the victim machine, the insider can collect the number of hosts in the local network and its own network address, OS information, open ports, and service information. It can also collect another legitimate host's network addresses, OS information, open ports, and service information. Moreover, the insider can record the routing path to an external server. By filtering the log of network services, the insider may extract the past access history that should have happened in the pre-exploitation stage. Normally, legitimate hosts log their network activities for troubleshooting. The insider can expect to obtain these logs from a real host. The insider can measure the link latency from the victim node to its host machine. The insider can also generate network traffic (e.g., ARP, UDP, TCP, and ICMP flow) between its host machine and the victim machine and then observe the network flow on the victim machine. From the attacker's host machine, the insider has the ability to recollect similar artifacts as those in the pre-exploitation stage. Additionally, the insider can observe the network flow on its host machine. The insider can observe these packets on both the victim machine and its own machine with the packet introspect tools (e.g., Wireshark, Tcpdump) in real-time.

Similar to insiders, the semi-insiders can collect the artifacts from the victim machine, while quantifiable differences limit the collection to only the victim machine and other visible hosts in the pre-exploitation stage. Also, due to the

---

[3] https://www.wireshark.org/.
[4] http://www.tcpdump.org/.

internal firewalls, the traffic flow between the semi-insider and the victim may differ when observing from both sides. From the view of the victim machine, the insider can discover more hosts in the target subnetwork. However, for NC3 attack, the semi-insider only needs to collect the artifacts related to the victim machine and visible hosts in the pre-exploitation stage.

4.3   Artifacts Cross-Checking

In this stage, the attacker can cross-check the artifacts collected in the pre-exploitation stage and post-exploitation stage to check if the target machine is a honeypot. For the nine types of artifacts collected in three sets (i.e., pre-exploitation artifacts from the host machine, post-exploitation artifacts from the victim machine, and post-exploitation artifacts from the host machine), the attacker checks the consistency of artifacts in the same type of artifacts from different sets. As the insiders and semi-insiders have different capabilities and confidence in collecting reliable artifacts, they may adopt different decision policies on identifying potentially distributed honeypots.

Insider. The insider can directly interact with the victim machine, thus it can use all the nine artifacts to conduct NC3 attacks. Among these artifacts, the insider defines four types of consistency criteria. First, for the number of hosts, network addresses, open ports, services, routing information, and access history, consistency means the artifacts should be the same. Second, for the OS information, since the remotely obtained OS information may not be as accurate as the one collected on the local host, the consistency means that the artifacts obtained from the attacker's host machine should be the subset of the artifacts obtained from the local host. Third, for the link latency, considering the uncertainty of network transmission and request handling, the attacker can use T-test to compare them. If the *p-value* is greater than a given threshold (e.g., 0.05), the attacker can consider the link latency is consistent. Fourth, the network flows between the insider host machine and the victim machine are considered consistent when the network flows observed on the insider's host machine match the network flows observed on the victim machine.

Semi-insider. Due to the existence of internal firewalls, some network traffic may be filtered, and only partial live hosts are visible from the outside of the victim's subnetwork. Therefore, the semi-insider adopts a different decision policy. First, the number of hosts observed from the attacker machine stage should be less than or equal to the number of hosts observed from the victim machine. Second, for the network addresses and the access history of visible hosts, consistency means they should be the same. Third, the judgments for consistency on the link latency and OS information of visible hosts are the same as the insider's scenario. Fourth, some open ports and services are not visible from the attacker's machine. Therefore, those artifacts observed from the attacker's host machine are subsets of the artifacts observed from the victim machine. Similarly, considering some network traffic may not pass the internal firewall, the attacker cannot

Table 1. The effectiveness of NC3 attacks against distributed honeypot systems

Distributed Honeypot System		Network Context Consistency															
	Number of Hosts		Network Address		OS Information		Open Ports		Services		Route		Access History		Link Latency		Network Flow
	I	II	I	II	I	II	I	II	I	II	I	II	I	II	I	II	I	II
Collapsar [14]	●	●	○	○	○	○	●	◐	●	◐	◐	◐	●	●	●	●	○	●
Potemkin [30]	○	◐	○	○	○	○	●	◐	●	◐	◐	◐	●	●	●	●	○	●
Artail et al. [1]	○	◐	○	○	●	●	●	◐	●	◐	◐	◐	○	○	○	○	○	●
Hyhoneydv6 [24]	○	◐	●	●	○	○	●	◐	●	◐	◐	◐	○	○	○	○	○	●
Chovancová et al. [4]	○	◐	○	○	●	●	○	◐	○	◐	◐	◐	○	○	○	○	○	●
Sun et al. [28]	○	◐	●	●	●	●	○	◐	○	◐	○	◐	○	○	●	●	○	●
Jafarian et al. [13]	○	◐	○	○	○	○	○	◐	○	◐	○	◐	○	○	●	●	○	●
HoneyPortal	●	●	●	●	●	●	●	●	●	●	◐	◐	●	●	●	●	●	●

1. For each artifact, column I indicates an insider; II indicates a semi-insider.
2. Level of consistency: ● Consistent; ○ Inconsistent; ◐ Uncertain (depending on the network and firewall configuration).

observe all outbound traffic sent from the victim machine. Moreover, subnetworks may have different access control privileges in the intranet. For example, the semi-insider may access some external servers, while the hosts in the target subnetwork cannot do it. Also, the victim machine and the attacker's host machine may have different routes to the Internet. It is similar to the isolation mechanism of the honeypot system. Therefore, when detecting distributed honeypots, the semi-insider relies more on cross-checking the consistency of network address, OS information, access history, open ports, services, and link latency.

4.4 Attack Effectiveness

Based on our threat model, we examine whether existing distributed honeypot systems can provide a stateful environment to the attacker under NC3 attack. Among these systems, we only obtain the source code of Sun et al. [28] to test, while we analyze others based on their technique details described in the papers. The examination results are summarized in Table 1, which shows the usefulness of each type of artifact by three types of attackers in identifying each specific distributed honeypot system.

Insider. We first assume that all these distributed systems are deployed inside the subnetwork and suffered attacks from the insider.

Number of Hosts: Collapsar [14] allows network flow initiated by the back-end honeypot to return to the front-end network. As a result, the insider can continue to interact with the same network from the back-end honeypot during the post-exploitation stage. Its number of hosts doesn't change. Other distributed honeypot systems put the back-end honeypot in an isolated network environment from any legitimate hosts due to the containment requirements, and they don't duplicate the same number of decoy hosts in the back-end network. Thus, the numbers of hosts are different in two separated local networks when scanning from the attacker's host machine and the compromised victim machine respectively.

Network Address: Only Hyhoneydv6 [24] and Sun et al. [28] mentioned that they will use the same network address for both the front-end and back-end honeypot, while others assign different network addresses.

OS Information: Artail et al. [1], Chovancová et al. [4] and Sun et al. [28] mentioned that they use the same OS version in both the front-end and back-end honeypot. Others deploy different OSes in the back-end honeypot.

Open Ports & Services: For those combining the low-interaction honeypot and the high-interaction honeypot [4,13,28], the front-end honeypot may not provide the same open ports and services as the back-end honeypot. Particularly, when the attacker is able to create new open ports or services on the back-end honeypot, the front-end honeypot may not be well synchronized to conduct the same operations.

Access Route: Potemkin [30], Sun et al. [28] and Jafarian et al. [13] redirect the outbound traffic initiated by the back-end honeypot to other places for further analysis. They could have different routes to the Internet, particularly, with different default gateways. Others don't have this functionality so their access routes remain the same to the insider.

Access History: Only Collapsar [14] and Potemkin [30] allow the insider to interact with the back-end honeypot directly during the pre-exploitation stage. These interactions can be logged in the back-end honeypot. For others, the insider can detect the absence of previous interaction history easily.

Link Latency: Similar to the access history, the insider interacts with the back-end honeypot in Collapsar [14] and Potemkin [30] during the whole exploitation stage. Besides, Sun et al. [28] and Jafarian et al. [13] only redirect network flows of specific protocols to the back-end honeypot, while other requests are replied by the front-end honeypot. There is no latency change for them. Artail et al. [1], Hyhoneydv6 [24] and Chovancová et al. [4] redirect the attacker's connections from the front end to the back end after exploitation. The change of response speed and location can both cause the difference in link delay to the insider.

Network Flow: The network flows may deviate between the back-end honeypot and the attacker's machine. As honeypot systems [1,4,14,24] handle specific protocols (e.g., ARP, ICMP) in the front-end honeypot to speed up the response, the insider cannot receive them in the back-end honeypot. Since the containment policy prevents the insider from sending the packets from the back-end honeypot to other legitimate hosts, that traffic only exists in the back-end network [28,30].

Semi-insider. When these distributed honeypot solutions are deployed in isolated subnetworks and protected by internal firewalls, some outbound network flows of the victim host may be blocked from the semi-insiders. Therefore, the semi-insider cannot rely too much on the inconsistency in the network flow and routing information. Meanwhile, the compromised victim machine still can interact with more hosts in the Intranet and scan more open ports and services other than the attacker's host machine. As shown in Table 1, the semi-insider can still detect all these distributed honeypot solutions by checking the inconsistency from network address, OS information, access history, and link latency.

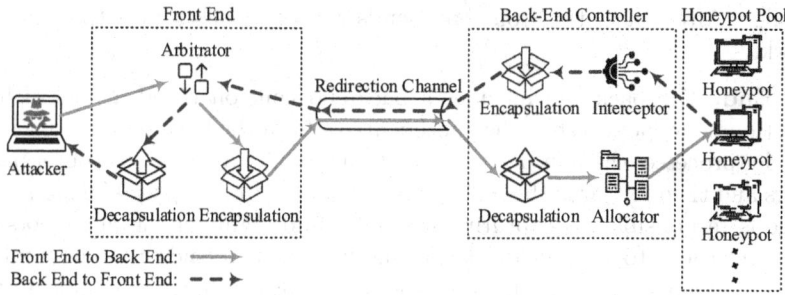

Fig. 2. The architecture of HoneyPortal system

5 HoneyPortal: The Countermeasure

Since it is difficult to simply rely on firewall configurations to defeat NC3 attacks, particularly, those conducted by the insiders, we develop a countermeasure called HoneyPortal.

5.1 System Design

Figure 2 shows the overall architecture of HoneyPortal, which consists of three main components: a *front end* residing in the protected local network, a *back end* in the honeypot service provider's local network, and a *redirection channel* connecting the front end and the back end. The front end is responsible for redirecting all network traffic to the back end. A controller on the back end forwards the packets between the front end and the corresponding back-end honeypot. A redirection channel is established to transparently connect the front end to the back end.

When the attacker sends a packet to the front end, the packet passes through the redirection channel and reaches the back-end honeypot. All the network interactions between the back-end honeypot and other hosts (e.g., an external server on the Internet or another legitimate host in the front end's local network) are redirected back to the front end, which conducts the network interactions on behalf of the back end and then sends the results to the back end.

Front End. The network admins can easily deploy the small-sized front end into the protected local network as the entrance of the honeypot system. When the front end receives any network packets from the front-end network, the arbitrator module in the front end forwards all those packets, including broadcast traffic (e.g., ARP requests), to the encapsulation module, which adds a new header to the packets and send them to the back-end network via the redirection channel. In other words, the front end does not directly respond to any network requests received from the front-end network. When the front end receives a packet from the back end via the redirection channel, the arbitrator forwards the packet to the decapsulation module to remove the outer header added by the back-end controller. After that, the front end sends out the packet into the front-end network.

Back End. The back end includes a back-end controller and a pool of high-interaction honeypots. When the packets arrive from the front end, the back-end controller processes them in the decapsulation module to remove the outer packet headers and then forwards them to the corresponding honeypot. The interceptor module is responsible for capturing the outbound traffic of the honeypots and forwarding them to the encapsulation module, which sends the encapsulated packets to the front end. In this way, the honeypot can only communicate with the outside via the front end.

To maintain the consistency of network context, the back-end honeypot needs to share the same IP and MAC addresses with its corresponding front end. The back-end controller maintains a configuration table inside the allocator module to establish a one-to-one mapping between the front end and the back-end honeypot. This table contains the IP and MAC addresses of the front-end host with the corresponding NIC or vNIC of the back-end controller. Honeypots can be deployed as virtual or physical machines, but they should be well isolated from each other.

Redirection Channel. A redirection channel is established to transparently bridge the front end and the back end. We have two options for HoneyPortal to redirect the traffic, namely, *server-based* approach and *router-based* approach. The server-based approach uses an intermediate server to forward the network packets between the front-end network and the back-end network. This approach is flexible in deployment. Honeypot operators can deploy the intermediate server in any place on the Internet, that is accessible to both the front end and the back end. The trade-off is that link latency will increase since the packets need to go through an extra device. The router-based approach needs to deploy or configure one edge router in both the front-end and back-end networks, and the GRE (Generic Routing Encapsulation) tunnel can be established between the two edge routers. If the operators can control and configure the edge routers, they can choose the router-based approach. End-to-end packet exchange can decrease transmission latency.

5.2   Implementation of HoneyPortal

We implement a prototype of HoneyPortal using the eXpress Data Path (XDP) [32] technique. The XDP program can attach a lower-level hook inside the kernel. The hook is implemented by the NIC driver, inside the ingress traffic processing function (NAPI Poll method) before an skb is allocated for the current packet. By processing the packets inside the XDP program, we can reduce the processing delay. Meanwhile, since the XDP program is not running inside the honeypot, we keep the processing stealthy to the constrained attackers. We implement the front end on a physical machine and the back end on a virtual machine.

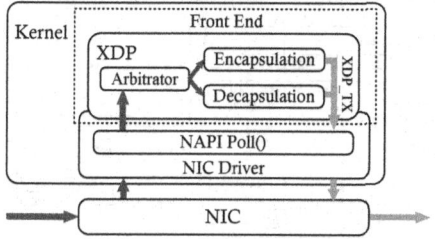

Fig. 3. The implementation of the front end

Front End. We implement the front end on the top of an XDP-enabled NIC (see Fig. 3), Intel X550-T2 network adapter with ixgbe 5.1.0-k driver. Specifically, we bind the XDP program to the XDP-enabled NIC within *Native* mode, since the native mode not only reduces the time of waiting for the memory allocation but also avoids extra packet duplication costs. By hooking the NAPI Poll method (i.e., `ixgbe_poll()`) of NIC driver after the DMA of the buffer descriptor, the intercepted packets can be processed directly before the skb allocation. After encapsulation/decapsulation in the kernel space, we leverage the XDP_TX action to send out the processed packets from the same NIC. Since the processed packets do not enter the network stack, we can accelerate the packet processing. The front end contains about 700 LOC in the C language.

Back End. We implement the back-end controller in the host OS and run multiple back-end honeypots in separate VMs, as shown in Fig. 4.

For the inbound traffic, the back-end controller leverages AF_XDP socket to process the packets intercepted by XDP in the user space through zero_copy. The XDP R module intercepts packets from the NAPI Poll method of the NIC driver and filters all UDP packets from the front end in the kernel space. Then, the receiver app decapsulates original front-end packets and looks up the configuration table to seek the entrance of the target virtual machine in the userspace. Next, we create AF_RAW socket S_i to inject front-end packets into vNIC $veth_i$ through the network stack. Finally, these packets are sent to the virtual machine via the veth pair.

For the current version XDP, all the devices must attach an XDP program using its default redirector module (`xdp_do_redirect()`) to receive packets redirected by other XDP programs. Though XDP supports XDP_REDIRECT action to deliver packets between NICs and vNICs, it will inevitably leave traces inside the honeypot. Particularly, the attacker can easily find out the existence of the XDP receiver module inside the honeypot. To solve this problem, we use the raw socket to inject packets into a veth pair in the userspace. The veth pair virtual NIC (vNIC) is the corresponding entry of the honeypot. The XDP program running on the veth pair vNIC with the skb model could intercept all packets from the virtual machine with no performance improvement. We create AF_RAW socket S_i to inject front-end packets into vNIC $veth_i$ through the network stack. Finally, these packets are sent to the virtual machine via the veth pair.

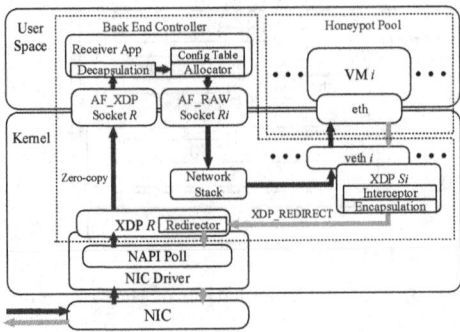

Fig. 4. The implementation of the back end

For outbound traffic, the XDP sender program S_i listens on $veth_i$ to intercept all network packets out of the honeypot before entering the virtual bridge. The XDP program running on the veth pair vNIC with the skb model can intercept all packets from the virtual machine with no performance improvement. In this way, each honeypot is well isolated to prevent the attacker from committing an ARP-spoofing attack in the back end. In practice, the VM doesn't calculate the checksum (IP, TCP, and UDP) of the packet. The checksum computation is done in the physical NIC, which is called Checksum Offloading [17]. Since the XDP program intercepts the packets in the vNIC, these packets haven't obtained the correct checksum. Hence, we re-implement the checksum computation functions in the XDP sender program to generate a correct checksum for them. Then, the module encapsulates these packets with new Ethernet, IP, and UDP headers. Finally, it leverages XDP_REDIRECT action to send these encapsulated UDP packets to the XDP program R, whose redirector module forwards them to the corresponding front-end hosts. The back-end controller based on AF_XDP contains about 1.6 K LOC in C language.

The VM-based honeypots can be easily extended to support container-based honeypots for better scalabilities [18]. The main configuration difference is that the veth pair is available for containers by default, but we need to set up a veth pair to act as the entrance for the VM-based honeypot.

Redirection Channel. For the server-based approach, we implement the intermediate server on one physical machine. The intermediate server uses a redirection module based on the NAPT (Network Address Port Translation) [27] technique to allocate specific ports (4000 and 5000) for the front end and back end to connect. When the traffic arrives at the pre-configured ports of the server, the intermediate server redirects it to the corresponding device. Since the packets from the back-end honeypot are encapsulated with outer headers, we inspect the internal headers of the packets to build the map between front-end hosts and back-end honeypots. In the router-based approach, we set up two Cisco C921-4P as edge routers connecting the front-end and back-end networks in GRE mode.

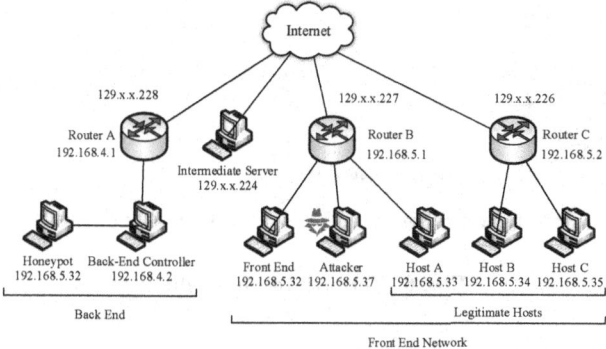

Fig. 5. Testbed for HoneyPortal

We configure the routing table of the routers to only allow the font-end hosts to connect the back-end controller, while other legitimate hosts cannot discover the back end.

6   Evaluation

We built a testbed to evaluate the effectiveness of HoneyPortal using the VM-based back end, as shown in Fig. 5. The protected local network consists of two subnetworks to simulate the scenarios that allow users to remotely connect to the local network. All host machines, including the intermediate server, use Ubuntu 18.04 LTS (kernel version 5.3.0) on Dell Precision 7810 desktops with Intel Xeon(R) E5-2620 CPU @ 2.40 GHz and 16 GB memory. Both the front end and the back-end controller are equipped with XDP-enabled Intel X550-T2 network adapters. In the back end, we use VMWare 15.5 to create VM-based honeypots with 2 CPU cores and 2 GB memory. We use Cisco C921-4P as edge routers A, B, and C to connect the front-end network and the back-end network to the Internet. These routers support the maximal 1 Gigabit Ethernet (GbE) link.

6.1   Defense Effectiveness

In the pre-exploitation stage, the attacker first scans the entire local network (192.168.5.0/24) to locate the potential victim machine. Via *Nmap* 7.60, the attacker can scan the front end to collect the information including network address (IP: 192.168.5.32, MAC: A0:36:9F:28:64:6E), OS information (Linux), open ports (22, 80, etc.), and services (FTP, SSH, Apache HTTP, MySQL, etc.), as shown in Fig. 6(a). Also, the attacker can obtain the access paths to outside servers (e.g., google.com, bing.com) via *traceroute* 2.1.0. Meanwhile, the attacker uses the *tcpdump* 4.9.3 to record the timestamp and protocol type of connections to the front end as the access history.

(a) Pre-exploitation Stage   (b) Post-exploitation Stage

Fig. 6. Network recon results

In the post-exploitation stage, after breaking into the back-end honeypot, the insider can redo the network reconnaissance from its host machine (192.168.5.37). On the back-end honeypot, the locally collected network information is shown in Fig. 6(b). Our experimental results show that HoneyPortal can ensure that the collected information is consistent with those collected in the pre-exploitation stage. The attacker can also obtain the application and network related logs (e.g., /var/log/apache2/access.log, /var/log/auth.log), which record the interaction between the attacker and victim, to check if the pre-exploitation recon actions are conducted on the back-end honeypot. Our experiments show that HoneyPortal can ensure the log records matching to the historical network activities in the pre-exploitation stage.

The front end, back-end controller, and redirection channel are well protected from attackers. First, since the front end redirects all traffic from the front-end network to the back end, it is transparent to the attacker. Meanwhile, as a redirector, the front end only includes a simple XDP application hooked to the NIC driver to process the receiving packets in the kernel space. The XDP application only uses simple processing logic to parse packet header instead of payload. Thus, the attack surface of the front end is minimized. Second, similar to the front end, the back-end controller only uses the XDP technique to process the packet headers and forward the packets, so it also has a small attack surface. Since HoneyPortal does not make any modifications to the back-end honeypot, the security of the back-end honeypot relies on the adopted honeypot productions themselves. Third, for the server-based redirection channel, the intermediate server could be a public server that only provides UDP redirection service. Besides applying mature security mechanisms on the intermediate server, we could enable a white list on its firewall to filter unauthorized connections. Fourth, traditional anti-honeypot techniques only focus on the fingerprinting of honeypot production. Thus, these techniques can only be used to identify the honeypot production itself, not the transparent redirection procedure of Honey-Portal.

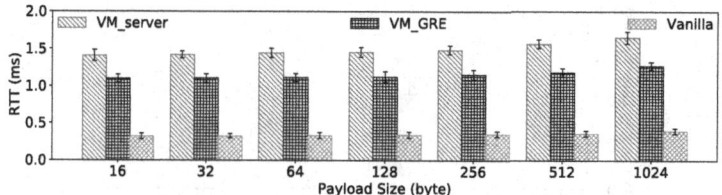

Fig. 7. Link latency (RTT) under different packet sizes

6.2 Processing Latency

Figure 7 shows that our redirection framework introduces additional latency when the payload sizes increase from 16 bytes to 1024 bytes. Comparing to the router-based approach (GRE), the server-based approach requires the packets to go through an extra device (a.k.a. the intermediate server), so the link latency of the server-based approach is a little higher than the router-based approach. Also, the link latency increases with the payload size.

To explore the dominant factor of increased latency, we measure the break-down processing latency of HoneyPortal, as shown in Fig. 8. The packet payload size is 64 bytes (default ICMP packet size in Linux). Since AF_XDP requires cooperation in both kernel space and user space, the back-end controller's processing latency is higher than the XDP-based front end. We can see the main contributor to the network delay is the link transmission delay, increasing along with the physical distance between the front end and the back end.

When deploying HoneyPortal in traditional local area networks that only consist of local computers and routers, the armored attacker may detect Honey-Portal by measuring the network latency differences if it can generate and observe the network flows between the target machine and the host machine. However, the deployment of virtual networks and the integration of cloud servers make it difficult for attackers to distinguish our honeypot systems from those legitimate remote host machines. First, large companies usually construct intercontinental virtual networks to connect remote locations with the help of MPLS [33] or SD-WAN [34], and the link latency varies significantly depending on the geographic distance. As a rule of thumb, 300 ms of network latency is technically accept-able to most business digital applications [31]. Second, an increasing number of companies have integrated public cloud services into their private networks [2]. Amazon has already provided a mature solution [16]. Therefore, when we deploy our intermediate server and the back end on the public cloud servers, the attacker cannot easily use the network latency to distinguish HoneyPortal, since other cloud-based servers may have the same amount of network latency.

6.3 System Overhead

We measure its CPU usage and memory consumption under the 700 kpps packet rates. For the front end, its loader in the user space costs lower than 0.1% CPU

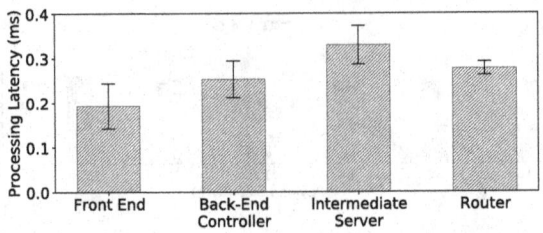

Fig. 8. Processing latency breakdown of HoneyPortal

usage and around 2 MB memory. The kernel module of the front end costs around 8 KB memory. For the back-end controller, it costs around 8% CPU usage and 105 MB memory in the user space, while it costs less than 1% CPU usage and around 12 KB memory in the kernel space. The experiment results show that HoneyPortal can be readily deployed in the real world without excessive performance overhead.

7   Discussion

Liability. HoneyPortal focuses on supporting distributed honeypot systems to defeat NC3 attacks, which enable insiders to detect the inconsistency of the network context before and after exploiting a victim machine. Although honeypot operators can deploy various isolation mechanisms (e.g., firewall, IPS system) in HoneyPortal based on their requirements, those constraints can be exploited by insiders to distinguish honeypots from real systems. Sophisticated insiders can always stay in the target network long enough to detect honeypots prior to launching an attack. In this case, a critical concern for the honeypot operator is to generate an alert as early as possible; even a compromised honeypot can be exploited to attack other legitimate hosts in the same local network. Hence, as a trade-off, the honeypot operator should not add any isolation mechanism between the front end and the back end. To minimize the impact of an attack on a network, the honeypot operator can configure the back-end honeypot to mirror network protections to that of other local (legitimate) hosts with an internal firewall. The internal firewall is responsible for detecting malicious activities and reduces the potential spread or propagation of a network attack to other networks in the environment thereby reducing the overall impact and risk of an attack. To defeat the semi-insider, the operator can deploy an isolation mechanism (e.g., firewall) between the front end and back end to detect and limit the spread of malicious payloads via the outbound traffic of the back-end honeypot. Section 4 indicated that semi-insiders may not be able to use the inconsistency in network flow to detect the distributed honeypot systems.

Scalability. In the stateless environment, the back-end honeypot only starts when the attack occurs. The sophisticated attacker (e.g., APT attacker) can easily detect the absence of previously regular interaction artifacts by continuously accessing the victim device over a long-term period. We intend to provide a stateful environment in HoneyPortal. Hence, we make a trade-off to keep the back-end honeypot running simultaneously with the front end.

Our prototype of HoneyPortal uses the XDP-enabled NIC and XDP techniques to reduce the packet processing overhead on both the front and back-end controller. However, the design of HoneyPortal framework supports the use of the NIC without XDP support. For example, the front end could be a software-based packet redirecting program instead of an XDP program to achieve the same goal. For the back end, the honeypot operators can deploy multiple honeypots on one physical machine. Therefore, HoneyPortal can smoothly integrate into existing honeypot solutions. The main performance bottleneck is the network bandwidth and available resources for the virtual machine in the back end.

8   Conclusion

In this paper, we first present a new anti-honeypot technique called network context cross-checking (NC3) against the distributed honeypot systems. We show that all existing distributed honeypot systems can be detected by attackers using NC3. As a countermeasure, we propose HoneyPortal, a transparent attack redirection framework to eliminate the inconsistency of network context in distributed honeypot systems while leveraging XDP as a method to improve network performance. We implement a prototype of HoneyPortal to demonstrate that HoneyPortal can effectively defeat an NC3 attack with a low performance overhead.

Acknowledgments. This work was supported in part by the Office of Naval Research grants N00014-16-1-3214, N00014-18-2893, and N00014-20-1-2407.

References

1. Artail, H., Safa, H., Sraj, M., Kuwatly, I., Al-Masri, Z.: A hybrid honeypot framework for improving intrusion detection systems in protecting organizational networks. Comput. Secur. **25**(4), 274–288 (2006)
2. Attaran, M., Woods, J.: Cloud computing technology: improving small business performance using the internet. J. Small Bus. Entrep. **31**(6), 495–519 (2019)
3. Bailey, M., Cooke, E., Watson, D., Jahanian, F., Provos, N.: A hybrid honeypot architecture for scalable network monitoring. University of Michigan, Ann Arbor, Michigan, USA, Technical report. CSE-TR-499-04 (2004)
4. Chovancová, E., et al.: Securing distributed computer systems using an advanced sophisticated hybrid honeypot technology. Comput. Inform. **36**(1), 113–139 (2017)
5. Cole, E.: Advanced Persistent Threat: Understanding the Danger and How to Protect Your Organization. Newnes, San Francisco (2012)
6. Dornseif, M., Holz, T., Klein, C.N.: Nosebreak-attacking honeynets. In: Proceedings from the Fifth Annual IEEE SMC Information Assurance Workshop, 2004, pp. 123–129. IEEE (2004)

7. Fan, W.: Contribution to the design of a flexible and adaptive solution for the management of heterogeneous honeypot systems. Ph.D. thesis, ETSI Telecomunicación (UPM) (2017)

8. Fan, W., Du, Z., Smith-Creasey, M., Fernández, D.: Honeydoc: an efficient honeypot architecture enabling all-round design. IEEE J. Sel. Areas Commun. **37**(3), 683–697 (2019)

9. Fan, W., Fernández, D.: A novel SDN based stealthy TCP connection handover mechanism for hybrid honeypot systems. In: 2017 IEEE Conference on Network Softwarization (NetSoft), pp. 1–9. IEEE (2017)

10. Fu, X., Yu, W., Cheng, D., Tan, X., Streff, K., Graham, S.: On recognizing virtual honeypots and countermeasures. In: 2006 2nd IEEE International Symposium on Dependable, Autonomic and Secure Computing, pp. 211–218. IEEE (2006)

11. Høiland-Jørgensen, T., et al.: The express data path: fast programmable packet processing in the operating system kernel. In: Proceedings of the 14th International Conference on Emerging Networking Experiments and Technologies, pp. 54–66 (2018)

12. Holz, T., Raynal, F.: Detecting honeypots and other suspicious environments. In: Proceedings from the Sixth Annual IEEE SMC Information Assurance Workshop, pp. 29–36. IEEE (2005)

13. Jafarian, J.H., Niakanlahiji, A.: Delivering honeypots as a service. In: Proceedings of the 53rd Hawaii International Conference on System Sciences (2020)

14. Jiang, X., Xu, D.: Collapsar: a VM-based architecture for network attack detention center. In: USENIX Security Symposium, pp. 15–28 (2004)

15. Kyung, S., et al.: HoneyProxy: design and implementation of next-generation honeynet via SDN. In: 2017 IEEE Conference on Communications and Network Security (CNS), pp. 1–9. IEEE (2017)

16. Larbi, S.: Options for extending layer 2 on-premises networks to VMware cloud on AWS (2020). https://aws.amazon.com/blogs/apn/options-for-extending-layer-2-on-premises-networks-to-vmware-cloud-on-aws/

17. Mantog, F.: System and method for checksum offloading, US Patent 7,181,675, 20 February 2007

18. Memari, N., Hashim, S.J.B., Samsudin, K.B.: Towards virtual honeynet based on LXC virtualization. In: 2014 IEEE REGION 10 SYMPOSIUM, pp. 496–501. IEEE (2014)

19. Miramirkhani, N., Appini, M.P., Nikiforakis, N., Polychronakis, M.: Spotless sandboxes: evading malware analysis systems using wear-and-tear artifacts. In: 2017 IEEE Symposium on Security and Privacy (SP), pp. 1009–1024. IEEE (2017)

20. Morishita, S., et al.: Detect me if you... oh wait. an internet-wide view of self-revealing honeypots. In: 2019 IFIP/IEEE Symposium on Integrated Network and Service Management (IM), pp. 134–143. IEEE (2019)

21. Mukkamala, S., Yendrapalli, K., Basnet, R., Shankarapani, M., Sung, A.: Detection of virtual environments and low interaction honeypots. In: 2007 IEEE SMC Information Assurance and Security Workshop, pp. 92–98. IEEE (2007)

22. Rrushi, J.: Honeypot evader: activity-guided propagation versus counter-evasion via decoy OS activity. In: Proceedings of the 14th IEEE International Conference on Malicious and Unwanted Software (2019)

23. Rytilahti, T., Holz, T.: On using application-layer middlebox protocols for peeking behind NAT gateways, January 2020. https://doi.org/10.14722/ndss.2020.24389

24. Schindler, S., Schnor, B., Scheffler, T.: Hyhoneydv6: a hybrid honeypot architecture for ipv6 networks. Int. J. Intell. Comput. Res. **6**, 562–570 (2015)

25. Shaikh, S.A., Chivers, H., Nobles, P., Clark, J.A., Chen, H.: Network reconnaissance. Netw. Secur. **2008**(11), 12–16 (2008)
26. Spitzner, L.: Honeypots: catching the insider threat. In: 19th Annual Computer Security Applications Conference, 2003. Proceedings, pp. 170–179. IEEE (2003)
27. Srisuresh, P., Egevang, K.: Traditional IP network address translator (traditional nat). Technical report, RFC 3022, January (2001)
28. Sun, J., Liu, S., Sun, K.: A scalable high fidelity decoy framework against sophisticated cyber attacks. In: Proceedings of the 6th ACM Workshop on Moving Target Defense, pp. 37–46 (2019)
29. Uitto, J., Rauti, S., Laurén, S., Leppänen, V.: A survey on anti-honeypot and anti-introspection methods. In: Rocha, Á., Correia, A.M., Adeli, H., Reis, L.P., Costanzo, S. (eds.) WorldCIST 2017. AISC, vol. 570, pp. 125–134. Springer, Cham (2017). https://doi.org/10.1007/978-3-319-56538-5_13
30. Vrable, M., et al.: Scalability, fidelity, and containment in the potemkin virtual honeyfarm. In: Proceedings of the Twentieth ACM Symposium on Operating Systems Principles, pp. 148–162 (2005)
31. Wang, D.W.: Software Defined-WAN for the Digital Age: A Bold Transition to Next Generation Networking. CRC Press, Boca Raton (2018)
32. XDP-project: The express data path (XDP) inside the Linux Kernel (2020). https://github.com/xdp-project. Accessed May 2020
33. Xiao, X., Hannan, A., Bailey, B., Ni, L.M.: Traffic engineering with MPLS in the internet. IEEE Netw. **14**(2), 28–33 (2000)
34. Yang, Z., Cui, Y., Li, B., Liu, Y., Xu, Y.: Software-defined wide area network (SD-WAN): architecture, advances and opportunities. In: 2019 28th International Conference on Computer Communication and Networks (ICCCN), pp. 1–9. IEEE (2019)
35. Zou, C.C., Cunningham, R.: Honeypot-aware advanced botnet construction and maintenance. In: International Conference on Dependable Systems and Networks (DSN 2006), pp. 199–208. IEEE (2006)

Author Index